Living with dyslexia

The social and emotional consequences of specific learning difficulties

Barbara Riddick

London and New York

First published 1996
by Routledge
11 New Fetter Lane, London EC4P 4EE

Simultaneously published in the USA and Canada
by Routledge
29 West 35th Street, New York, NY 10001

Reprinted 1998

© 1996 Barbara Riddick

Typeset in Times by
Datix International Ltd, Bungay, Suffolk
Printed and bound in Great Britain by
Mackays of Chatham PLC

British Library Cataloguing in Publication Data
A catalogue record for this book is available from the British
Library

Library of Congress Cataloging in Publication Data
A catalog record for this book is available from the Library of
Congress

ISBN 0–415–12501–4

This book is dedicated to Tom and all the other children who have struggled with dyslexia.

My Broter is Dyslexic.

Dyslexia means your born with something that means you do things slower But your not a slow learner a lot of people think my Brother is sthick But he is not

By Richard, aged 7 years, younger brother of Tom

Contents

Tables

Foreword

I welcome the publication of *Living with Dyslexia*. It should be very useful as an introduction, especially to teachers and student-teachers in the ordinary classroom, who under current legislation have a duty to identify and seek help for children with specific learning difficulties. The Government Code of Practice (1993) lays down that schools must publish their policy for children with special needs, and must be prepared to demonstrate that their policy is being implemented. Moreover a recent House of Lords judgment (1995) made it clear that Local Education Authorities have a positive duty to provide teaching for children with dyslexia. Practical advice on identification and on teaching methods is therefore needed at all levels. Parents of dyslexic children will also get help and encouragement from the positive and non-technical style of this study.

Mary Warnock
(*Baroness Warnock*)

Preface

Why a book on living with dyslexia? A simple answer is that this is still a relatively neglected area. At a more complicated level the reasons for this can be suggested. Much of the early work on dyslexia was carried out by interested clinicians such as Orton and Hinshelwood. Their approach had both the strengths and the weaknesses of the clinical approach. They made careful detailed observations of their clients' difficulties, but inevitably their primary focus was the clinical setting and not the day to day world that their clients lived in. More recently there has been an enormous expansion in experimental research trying to identify the cognitive (thinking) deficits underlying dyslexia. Whilst this research has greatly increased our knowledge of dyslexia its focus has been largely on looking at these deficits in the experimental setting and not on how these deficits are dealt with on an everyday basis. Turning to recent educational research much of this has focused on comparing different methods of remediation or teaching. These have generally been evaluated in terms of specific learning outcomes such as reading ages and not broader measures of educational and personal well being. This is not to deny that many vivid accounts of the personal difficulties encountered by both children and adults with dyslexia exist. These range from individual biographies to collections of case histories. The problem with these is that because of their piecemeal nature they are open to criticisms of bias, unrepresentativeness and lack of generalisability. One of the major aims of this book is to look at how information on living with dyslexia can be collected in a systematic manner and integrated with other forms of research to increase our overall understanding of dyslexia. Another aim has been to let children and their parents speak for themselves as far as possible so we can gain a clearer understanding of how living with dyslexia appears from their perspective. It is also hoped that in doing this the information presented will be of help to all those working with dyslexic children and will enable them to review or reflect on the nature of the support that they are offering both to dyslexic children and their families. Because the cognitive deficits underlying dyslexia are an integral and pervasive part of children's experience some understanding of these is necessary in order to appreciate what 'living with dyslexia' entails so a brief review of current thinking has been included. In a similar vein it was considered that as dyslexia is part of the wider construct of special needs, this wider perspective should also be reviewed. It is hoped that by doing this, the experiences of living with dyslexia can be placed within this wider context.

Despite the controversy in educational circles about the term 'dyslexia', this term was chosen because it was the one that the overwhelming majority of children and parents who were interviewed said that they found most helpful in understanding their specific difficulties. One of the aims of this book is to look at the advantages and disadvantages of using the label 'dyslexia' and to examine how it relates to other terms such as 'specific learning disability'. The intention is not to be dogmatic but to raise constructive debate about this and a number of other issues surrounding dyslexia. A major argument of this book is that we do need to take seriously the views of children and their parents on living with dyslexia if we are to have a comprehensive and properly informed understanding of the condition.

Acknowledgements

The research described in this book was supported by a grant from the Nuffield Foundation.

Many thanks must go to all the children who were interviewed as part of the study. A big thank you must also go to all the teachers and especially to Pat Evans at the Newcastle Branch of the Dyslexia Institute, who provided help and support and also agreed to be interviewed.

Thanks to the publishers John Wiley & Sons for allowing reproduction of three tables from a paper written by the author entitled 'Dyslexia and development: an interview study'. Thanks also to Carfax Publishing Company (PO Box 25, Abingdon, Oxfordshire OX14 3UE) for permission to reproduce material from a paper by the author published in *Disability and Society*.

Chapter 1

Defining dyslexia

An overview of dyslexia and specific learning difficulties

'When *I* use a word,' Humpty Dumpty said in a rather scornful tone, 'it means just what I choose it to mean – neither more nor less.'

'The question is,' said Alice, 'whether you *can* make words mean so many different things.'

'The question is,' said Humpty Dumpty, 'which is to be master – that's all.'
(Lewis Carroll *Through the Looking Glass*, 1865)

Both Pumfrey and Reason (1991) and Miles (1995) observe that the terms 'dyslexia' and 'specific learning difficulties' are often used synonymously although some authorities would see 'specific learning difficulties' as an umbrella term for a range of learning difficulties of which 'dyslexia' is one variant. At a very general level educationalists and particularly educational psychologists tend to prefer the term 'specific learning difficulties' and clinicians, voluntary organisations and concerned lay people the term 'dyslexia'. These differences of opinion can be seen as partly due to the different perspectives that educationalists and clinicians are likely to have. As the purpose of this book is to look at the views of people who have chosen to live with the term 'dyslexia', this is the term that has been used predominantly, although where quoted research or writing has used other terms such as 'specific learning difficulties' these terms have been included.

At a commonsense everyday level dyslexia is often defined as an unexpected difficulty in learning to read, write and spell. But like many definitions as soon as it is examined more closely it becomes more difficult to pin down and a number of problems and ambiguities arise. Who decides that the difficulty is unexpected, and on what basis? How behind does a child have to be for it to be counted as a difficulty and how is the difficulty judged or quantified? Do all children need to show the same sort of difficulty or can they show different types of difficulties and still be called dyslexic? In examining definitions of dyslexia it becomes apparent that different definitions highlight different aspects or levels of the problem. Frith (1992) has proposed that in looking at learning disabilities like autism and dyslexia it is important to look at the links between the different levels of explanation so that we can begin to see the links between biological causation, cognitive impairments, and behaviours such as poor reading and spelling. Although at present there isn't one agreed definition of dyslexia, the following, put forward by the World Federation of Neurology (1968) (cited in Critchley 1970), is one that is still widely used.

> Dyslexia is a disorder manifested by difficulty in learning to read despite conventional instruction, adequate intelligence and sociocultural opportunity. It is dependant upon fundamental cognitive disabilities which are frequently of constitutional origin.

It can be seen that a definition like this includes both behaviour, cognition and cause. Definitions like this are often referred to as exclusion definitions because it suggests that a child can only be defined as dyslexic if a number of factors are excluded. Critics would argue that this type of approach tends to favour the identification of middle class children and may have led to the fallacious assumption that dyslexia is a 'middle class disorder'. To look at the problem another way it suggests that socially disadvantaged children or mildly learning disabled children cannot be defined as dyslexic. But the evidence we have so far suggests that the cognitive impairments underlying dyslexia are evenly spread across the population and are as likely to occur in these groups as any other groups. What has not been researched to any extent yet is how the specific cognitive impairments underlying dyslexia interact with other impairments such as a hearing disability or with environmental factors such as lack of exposure to the printed word. It may for example be the case that whereas under optimal conditions children can compensate for a certain degree of specific cognitive impairment that these same impairments coupled with an unfavourable environment may lead to considerable difficulties in learning to read and write. Jordan and Powell (1995) point out that recent research suggests that there may be a link between Aspergers syndrome (high functioning autism) and dyslexia and suggest that dyslexia-type difficulties should not be overlooked simply because a child has already been identified as having autism.

Similar problems exist with what are known as discrepancy definitions of dyslexia. In this case it is the child's poor performance in learning to read and write in relation to their age and level of intelligence that is stressed. Critics would again argue that this tends to favour more intelligent and more middle class children where it is supposed that the gap between their expected performance and their actual performance is more apparent. Another difficulty is that obvious discrepancies between reading and spelling scores tend to diminish as children get older so that by adolescence this approach will exclude many children who do have the specific cognitive impairments underlying dyslexia such as poor short-term memory. Korhonen (1995) found for example in a longitudinal study that children who had reading difficulties at 9 years of age had a significantly worse digit span at 18 years of age, were significantly worse on a word fluency task and were slower and more error prone on a spelling task in comparison with a control group. Research like this underlines that older dyslexic children and adults still have difficulties which put them at a disadvantage especially in situations such as written examinations. So whilst discrepancy definitions may be good at identifying some children with dyslexia they may well lead to bias in who is identified and the under identification of some groups of children. Part of the reason for the reluctance of some educationalists to recognise dyslexia in the past may have been connected to their underlying disquiet about the way it was defined and the implications that this had for the identification of children and allocation of resources.

CASE STUDY

Lucy was in care until she was 5 years old. She lived in several foster homes and children's homes and at one point was classified as emotionally disturbed and delayed in her development. At 5 years of age when she was adopted it was noted that her language was still difficult to understand. She also suffered from a number of middle ear infections. At school Lucy was quiet, shy and well behaved. Her family who were skilled working class did their best to support her but did comment on her inability to keep up in learning to read and write compared with a cousin of the same age. At the age of 7 when Lucy was moved to the junior school she was put in a remedial class. This class had a mixture of children in it ranging from one child with severe learning disabilities to another with severe emotional and behavioural difficulties. Lucy sat quietly at the back with her best friend and generally went unnoticed. She learnt to read but was embarrassed about reading aloud to the rest of the class because she often had difficulty in knowing how to say words out loud. When Lucy was 9 years of age the school happened to be involved in some research examining children's hearing levels. Both Lucy and her best friend failed the initial screening test and were given more extensive audiometric testing. They were both found to have an educationally significant hearing loss which in both cases was remedied by the removal of their tonsils and adenoids. Lucy's best friend moved away at this point and Lucy was put up three classes to the top class in her year. She missed a considerable amount of schooling in the following year because of some major operations on her legs. Lucy felt lonely and demoralised in her new class. The teacher rarely praised her and seemed to have a negative view of her. She was placed on the bottom table for most subjects and near to bottom in the end of year report. By 10 years of age Lucy's reading had improved considerably, her comprehension was generally good, but she sometimes got the wrong end of the stick because of inaccuracies in her reading. Her spelling was still relatively weak and she had considerable problems with the timed mental arithmetic test which took place in the class every day.

Lucy failed her 11 plus examination and went to the local secondary modern school. Here her very low self-esteem began to improve although there were still occasional humiliations. For example when she was 14 the class were asked to write an essay on the peasants' revolt. The teacher before handing the essays back described how there was some idiot who had written about the pheasants' revolt. Lucy laughed along with everybody else until she got her essay back and realised with great embarrassment that it was her. Lucy went on to gain three A levels, a degree and a professional qualification. It was only as an adult when her own daughter was diagnosed as dyslexic that she realised that she might have been dyslexic herself. Testing confirmed that she had many residual signs of dyslexia and her spelling was still in fact relatively weak. At work for example she misspelt Malcolm as Malcom and Sheila as Shelia and business as buisnes until these errors were pointed out to her.

This case study describes someone who went to school during the 1950s and 1960s. Although it can be argued that educational practice is rather different now it does highlight the problems of having an exclusion definition. It would be easy to assume that Lucy's learning difficulties were a result of her early deprivation, her hearing impairment and her prolonged absence from school. All factors which would have excluded her from being defined as dyslexic. This is not to say that these factors didn't have an important influence on her learning but to illustrate how specific learning difficulties can co-exist with other problems or be exacerbated by other problems.

Another problem with some of the earlier definitions of dyslexia is that they defined dyslexia largely or exclusively in terms of a reading problem. Although learning to read is invariably a problem, the majority of dyslexic children do eventually learn to read. In the case of Lucy, by 10 years of age it is doubtful that she would have been identified as dyslexic on the basis of her reading age. But like the majority of dyslexics Lucy was still having considerable problems with her spelling. In order to deal with these kinds of criticisms modern definitions of dyslexia have tried to specify the cognitive impairments underlying dyslexia and the range of skills affected by such impairments. The following definition is given by the British Dyslexia Association (Peer 1994).

> Organising or learning difficulties affecting fine co-ordination skills and working memory skills. It is independent of overall ability and conventional teaching. When untreated there are significant limitations in the development of specific aspects of speech, reading, spelling, writing and sometimes numeracy – which may lead to secondary behavioural problems – although other areas of ability are unaffected.

Although critics might disagree with the specific details of this definition few would disagree with the need to have a definition that draws on the considerable body of cognitive research. One point that emerges more clearly from this type of definition is that dyslexia should be regarded as a complex syndrome with different individuals showing different aspects of the syndrome. Another point is that it is the underlying problems in short-term memory and speech sound recognition that should be emphasised. Along with these more positive definitions of dyslexia some researchers have also tried to list positive signs or indicators of dyslexia. Miles and Miles (1990) suggest the following as possible indicators of dyslexia in primary age children.

1 confuses left and right
2 difficulty in saying long words
3 difficulty in subtracting
4 difficulty in learning tables
5 difficulty in saying months of the year
6 confuses b and d for longer than most children
7 difficulty in recalling digits
8 family history of similar difficulties.

Miles emphasises that a dyslexic child won't necessarily show all these difficulties and that a non-dyslexic child may well have problems with some of the items. What he claims is important is the overall clinical picture which is obtained. So a dyslexic child for example may have difficulty with several of these items and show a marked delay in their reading and/or spelling age compared with their chronological age and be struggling at school. Miles has incorporated all these items into the Bangor Dyslexia Test. In order to select items that do consistently distinguish between dyslexic and non-dyslexic children Miles (1983) has compared children from both groups across age ranges on 7 out of 12 items in the test. He found that although no item on its own distinguished dyslexic from non-dyslexic children, dyslexic children did consistently receive a higher overall score on this test.

In devising the Bangor Dyslexia Test Miles addressed two important issues. The first was the need to check out whether signs picked out by clinicians really were reliable indicators of dyslexia. The second was to have a test that was based on theoretical assumptions about the cognitive deficits underlying dyslexia. In this case it was argued that problems with naming were brought about by deficits in short term memory and difficulties in accessing long term memory. Items like digit span and subtraction test short term memory and items like naming months and saying multiplication tables test long term memory. Although critics have pointed out the test's lack of comprehensiveness it does have the strong advantage of being quick (average 10 minutes) and easy to administer so that it can be used by classroom teachers. The disadvantage is that some items do involve clinical judgement. Miles acknowledges that the Bangor Dyslexia Test only samples a limited range of items and that some of these items need modification if it is to be used with children under 7 years of age. It is also the case that in the 10 years since its development cognitive research has considerably added to our understanding of dyslexia. Stanovich (1991) for example has suggested that testing of phonological awareness should play an essential role in the identification of specific learning difficulties.

EARLY IDENTIFICATION

One area in which there has been particular progress has been the identification of cognitive deficits in infant and preschool children (Bryant and Bradley 1985, Jorm *et al.* 1986). Bryant and Bradley, for example, found that children of 3 and 4 years of age who did relatively badly on a rhyming task were at higher risk of having subsequent difficulty in learning to read. Case studies also confirm that by 7 many dyslexic children feel they have failed in the classroom setting. Until recently the received wisdom was that a child couldn't be diagnosed as dyslexic until about 7 years of age. This seemed to be based on the notion that a diagnosis could not be made until a measurable discrepancy between their reading age and their chronological age could be demonstrated or in other words until they had failed at learning to read. This fits with the older discrepancy and exclusion approaches to defining dyslexia and illustrates the importance of having an approach to the condition that identifies positive signs and the cognitive deficits underlying it. This more recent approach suggests that as the cognitive deficits that lead to difficulty in learning to read and spell are identifiable at a pre-reading stage, it should be possible to identify early on children who are at increased risk of having difficulty in learning to read. Singleton (1993) and Fawcett and Nicolson (1994) have put forward this point of view and both are currently working on the development of screening tests for 4–5 year old children.

INCIDENCE OF DYSLEXIA

Given the difficulties in defining and identifying dyslexia, it is hard to come up with a precise estimate of the number of individuals with this impairment. The consensus among many researchers (Miles and Miles, 1990, Singleton and Thomas 1994) and organisations such as the British Dyslexia Association (Peer 1994) is that at a conservative estimate 4 per cent of the population are severely dyslexic and another 6 per cent have mild to moderate dyslexia. It is often pointed out that on average this indicates that there will be one severely dyslexic child in each class. Until recently most researchers also reported a ratio of about three boys to every one girl with dyslexia. Shaywitz *et al.* (1990) have questioned this ratio and present evidence that in the USA girls with reading disabilities are under identified. At present more evidence is needed before anything clear cut can be said. But it does relate back to an earlier point about the dangers of setting up expectations that tend to preclude certain children from being defined as dyslexic for whatever reason. Ellis (1993) points out that the percentage of children who are defined as dyslexic is in some sense fairly arbitrary in that it depends on the particular criteria that are used. So for example the percentage of children with dyslexia will vary if a spelling age of 18 months below the norm is chosen as opposed to a spelling age of 24 months below the norm.

A classic study by Hallgren in 1950 found that 88 per cent of individuals with dyslexia also had at least one close family member with the same condition. More recent studies like the one by Finucci *et al.* (1976) have come up with a similar figure of 81 per cent. Critics could argue that these figures can be explained away by environmental factors, but closer examination of the figures suggests that this is unlikely. Children with an affected relative not living with them are just as likely to have difficulties and other siblings living at home may have no difficulties at all. Twin studies have also confirmed that there is a genetic component to dyslexia. The Colorado Twin Study (DeFries 1992) is one of the largest and best designed of these studies. This study involved 101 identical twins and 114 non-identical twins. For identical twins the concordance rate for reading problems was 70 per cent and for the non-identical twins it was 43 per cent. Given that much recent research has focused on the cognitive impairments underlying dyslexia this suggests that what is inherited is not a reading disability *per se* but a defect or deficit in one or more of the cognitive skills underlying language and reading. Olson *et al.* (1990) found that the phonological skills for breaking words down into syllables and for reading nonsense words were highly heritable whereas reading comprehension was not. This suggests that some children inherit specific phonological disabilities that can have a serious affect on their ability to learn to read. So far information on the heritability of dyslexia has largely been considered in relation to biological and cognitive research. One area that has not been explored is the possible personal implications for the child of having a parent or close relative with the same disability. This will be discussed in more detail in chapter 9 of this book.

DELAYED OR DIFFERENT?

One of the key debates on dyslexia is whether it is a clearly identifiable separate cognitive condition or whether it is merely a term for those individuals who fall at the bottom end of the continuum between good and poor readers. Leading researchers such as Snowling (1987) and Miles (1983) have argued that it is a clearly identifiable condition whereas Ellis (1993) argues that we still don't have sufficient evidence to be sure about this point. Again the issue of definition seems crucial in considering the available evidence. Siegal (1989) claims to find no difference between dyslexic and non dyslexic poor readers in their cognitive disabilities. But dyslexia is defined in this study, in terms of a discrepancy between IQ and performance, so that lower IQ children are automatically excluded from being defined as dyslexic.

THE HISTORY OF DYSLEXIA

It is only since literacy on a universal scale has become the norm that dyslexia has become a significant issue. The early literature on dyslexia was nearly all medical in origin and mainly focused on the clinical case study approach. In Britain in 1917 an opthalmologist named James Hinshelwood published a book entitled *'Congenital Word-blindness'*. As the title implies this book focused on the visual problems that were thought to underlie dyslexia. This early preoccupation with visual problems was hardly surprising given Hinshelwood's background and the fact that several of the striking characteristics of dyslexia appeared superficially to have a visual basis. The reversing of letters such as b and d, and words such as 'no' and 'on' and frequent omission of suffixes such as 'ing' all seemed to imply that a visual deficit underlay dyslexia. Orton (1937) in the USA published an influential book entitled *'Reading, Writing and Speech'*. Orton also thought that visual problems underlay dyslexia. Perhaps because of his background as a psychiatrist Orton was very concerned with the emotional consequences of the repeated failure that dyslexic children encountered. It is sometimes suggested (Snowling 1987) that this early dominance by the medical model has led to some of the reservations expressed by educationalists. Whilst this may be the case it doesn't fully explain the degree of difficulty encountered in considering dyslexia in relation to other special needs. Until the mid 1970s school medical officers were involved in the identification of all children with special needs but, for example, in the case of sensory and physical impairments the transition to an educational model appears to have been relatively smooth. The difference with dyslexia appears to be that there are no clear physical markers, so that until recently dyslexia was defined almost entirely in terms of behaviour, i.e., difficulty in learning to read and spell. The difficulty with this approach was that all sorts of assumptions were made as to why a child was failing to learn to read. These included lack of parental interest, too much parental interest, emotional or behavioural problems, poor attention or motivation or that the child was immature and/or a slow learner. It was less often considered that the primary cause of the child's reading difficulties might be specific cognitive impairments and that if any of these other behaviours were observed that these might be a secondary outcome of the child's difficulty in learning to read. This is not to deny that environmental factors may play an important part in the process and that for some children the way that reading is taught may be of critical importance. But research by Croll and Moses (1985) found that when 428 junior school teachers were surveyed about children with learning difficulties including those with reading problems, in only 2.5 per cent of the cases were school factors thought to play a part. In 55 per cent of poor readers, low ability or IQ was implicated and in over 40 per cent of cases environmental factors outside of the school, such as lack of parental interest were given as the reason for children's poor performance. Alessi (1988) in a similar study in North America asked 50 school psychologists to comment on over 5,000 referrals. It was found that general within-child factors or home environmental factors were always seen as the cause of failure and failure was never attributed to the curriculum. Thus until recently it appears that reading failure was most commonly attributed at the within-child level to generalised slow learning and at the environmental level to adverse factors outside of the school. This is the direct opposite to what is proposed produces dyslexia/specific learning difficulties, which at the within-child level is specific as opposed to general impairments and at the environmental level is adverse factors within the school. Given these very different perspectives it's perhaps not surprising that specific learning difficulties including dyslexia have been under identified in the past and have led to some controversy and disagreement among educationalists.

Although far severer in outcome the condition probably closest to dyslexia in terms of its lack of 'visibility' is autism. Frith (1992) argues that in both cases looking at behaviour alone is not sufficient in defining these disorders because behaviour is influenced by factors like experience and motivation and is therefore constantly changing and varying. She argues that we need to identify the cognitive deficits underlying the behaviour in order to come up with a clearer definition. The advantage of doing this is that behaviours that look very similar on the surface may be found to have very different roots. A child for example who doesn't say nursery rhymes might not do so because of simple lack of exposure to them or because they lack the phonological (sound) awareness. It's interesting to compare development in the awareness of autism and dyslexia. In 1907 when Kanner first described autism he suggested that one of the criteria for diagnosing a child as autistic was normal or near normal intelligence. This idea was quite prevalent until clear evidence of organic brain damage became available in the 1970s. By then it became clear that around 70 per cent of autistic children had moderate to severe learning disabilities. So autism like dyslexia started with an exclusion criteria which it later dropped. This doesn't mean to say that all children with severe learning disabilities are autistic but that the two conditions can co-exist. Kanner also thought that autism was more common among highly educated middle-class parents who he claimed caused the condition by their cold, rejecting style of parenting. This claim has been completely refuted by later research and autism has been found to be evenly distributed across social classes. But it does make the point that it's easy to assume that any differences in parenting style are the cause of the difficulty rather than the consequences of it. With dyslexia some educationalists (Portsmouth and Caswell 1988) have argued that it is largely in the imagination of middle-class parents and others have argued that parents produce or exacerbate difficulties because of their own concerns and anxieties.These kinds of views appear to be based solely on professional opinions and have no empirical research to back them up.

RESEARCHING DYSLEXIA

As already indicated the first research on dyslexia was of a clinical case study approach. Three major criticisms are made of this type of research. One is that clinicians see a biased often self-selected sample of the population, secondly it can be misleading to generalise from a single case, and thirdly this type of research doesn't distinguish cause from effect. So for example in the case of letter reversals like b/d which are often noted by clinicians it still doesn't indicate whether the reversals are simply the result of inexperience at reading or whether reversals hold reading up and therefore contribute to lack of reading experience. Despite the criticisms of the case study approach authorities as diverse as Cronbach (1984), Snowling (1987) and Miles (1990) have emphasised the important contribution that case studies can make. Case studies can suggest any commonalties, issues or hypotheses that need systematic testing. In turn findings from experimental research can be checked against case studies to see that they have real world or ecological validity. Finally case studies can flesh out and breathe life into experimental data and give more understanding of the complexities and wider context surrounding the data.

One particular issue that arises in looking at any learning disability is whether a child's development is simply delayed or whether it is basically different in some way. So in the case of dyslexia the question would be one of whether, for example, dyslexic children learn to read in the same way as other children, albeit more slowly, or whether there is something different about the way they learn to read. Case studies may well provide some hunches or clues to a question like this. For example, the frequently reported difficulties that dyslexic children had in learning things like days of the week and nursery rhymes suggested that they might have an auditory sequencing problem that was affecting their ability to learn to read. But experimental research was needed to check out these hunches and to obtain a more specific picture of what might be going on. Much of the early research on dyslexia used control groups of non-dyslexic children of the same age. On the face of it this would seem a reasonable thing to do, but it does lead to difficulties in drawing interpretations from the data. If, for example, you do find a difference between the reading of dyslexic and non-dyslexic children how can you be sure that this is because of some fundamental difference between them and not simply because the dyslexic children are performing like children who are 2 years younger in their reading age? In order to get round this problem the more recent good quality research has also used where possible control groups of younger children matched in reading age to the dyslexic children. In this case it is argued that if any differences in reading performance are found these can't simply be put down to differences in reading experience. Despite changes in methodology, views still differ on how results should be interpreted. Bryant and Impey (1986), for example, argue that children's difficulties are better viewed as developmental delays rather than permanent impairments, whereas Frith (1992) argues that there are permanent impairments underlying dyslexia. Snowling (1987) hypothesised that there were two major sub-groups within dyslexia. One group she postulated were developmentally delayed for a variety of reasons and were therefore not ready to learn to read at the normal time. She suggested that these children had only mild phonological impairments but that the balance between their phonological skills and other skills had to be maintained if their development was to proceed along normal lines and not become atypical. Snowling described a second group of children who had specific severe phonological impairments probably due to underlying language deficits whose development would be different rather than delayed. Snowling stressed that in all cases the way in which children's impairments interacted with compensatory strategies and the environment would have a bearing on the outcome. An important point that both Snowling and Frith made is that dyslexia is a developmental disorder and the way in which any underlying impairments were expressed would change with age and experience.

Because in case studies reversal and orientation errors were often observed in children's reading and writing (e.g. was/saw, on/no) it was hypothesised that visual perceptual problems might underlie the difficulties that many dyslexic children have. Experimental research in the 1970s seemed to suggest that dyslexic children were slower at processing visual information (Stanley 1975). But more recent research (Swanson 1984) suggests that dyslexic children don't have problems with visual information *per se* but that what they do have difficulty with is naming or labelling visual information. Ellis (1981) in a classic experiment tested dyslexic and non-dyslexic children on a letter comparison task. Children were shown letters that were physically alike: (AA), or physically unalike: (aA or AB). They had to indicate as quickly as possible if the letters in a pair were alike. For all children their reaction time was quicker when the letters were physically alike but dyslexic children were relatively slower when the letters were semantically alike but physically dissimilar. It was postulated that this was because they had greater difficulty when they had to retrieve letters from their memory rather that make a simple physical comparison. Because research like this indicated that dyslexic children's problems were more likely to be related to impairments in working memory (short term memory) and phonology, these are the areas where researchers have concentrated especially over the last 10 years.

Phonological difficulties

There is a growing consensus that phonological processing skills are directly related to children's ability to learn to read (Torgesen *et al.* 1994, Snowling 1995). Phonological processing skills involve listening to the sounds made in oral language and using knowledge of these in learning to decode written words. There have been three major areas of research on phonological skills, these have been on phonological awareness, phonological memory and accessing phonological information from long term memory. Phonemes are the smallest sound elements that a word can be divided up into and much of the earlier work on phonological awareness focused on the relationship between single phonemes and single letters. Goswami and Bryant (1990) pointed out that children's knowledge of syllables and sensitivity to rhyme and alliteration are also an important part of phonological awareness. Several researchers had shown that before children can read they can pick out words that rhyme (Bradley and Bryant 1985, Gates 1992). So if for example a child was presented with the word 'sky' and asked which of 'rat', 'fly' and 'log' ended with the same sound they would successfully pick out 'fly'. The significance of this finding is that children who display good phonological awareness before they learn to read typically go on to learn to read more easily than children who have difficulty with this task. It has also been found that children who have significant difficulty learning to read often have poor phonological awareness (Alexander *et al.* 1991). Snowling (1980) found that dyslexic children had poor non-word naming skills. This is one of the most reliable and consistent findings to emerge from this field of research. In these types of investigations children are asked to read out one by one a list of pronounceable made up words such as 'pret' and 'mub' and 'clube'. What is found is that dyslexic children as a group do worse on this task than non-dyslexic children. This suggests that dyslexic children lack the necessary phonological skills to work out how to say the words correctly.

Longitudinal studies

An important point that emerges from this research is the value of longitudinal studies. Cross sectional studies which have looked at a group of children at a particular point in time have made a significant contribution but there are certain questions they cannot answer. Are, for example, the children who are identified as having reading difficulties at 6 years of age the same children who are identified as having reading difficulties at 5 years or 7 years of age? If a cross sectional study finds that 7 year olds with poor reading also have poor phonological skills are we to assume that the poor phonological skills have contributed to the poor reading or that the poor reading has contributed to the poor phonological skills? In Bradley and Bryant's (1985) study mentioned above on pre-reading children's detection of rhyme they followed the progress of these children in learning to read over a three year period and by doing so were able to show the links between phonological awareness and the development of reading. Torgesen, Wagner and Rashotte (1994) in the USA also followed children from kindergarten through to second grade. They tested all children on phonological tasks and reading tasks at all three intervention points. They found that reading difficulties were associated with difficulties not only in phonological awareness but also in phonological working memory, and access to phonological information in long term memory.

Long-term difficulties

Evidence is also mounting that in severer cases these early deficits in phonological processing skills persist over a number of years and in some cases into adulthood (Bruck 1992). Single case studies which have followed individuals over time and consistently tested their phonological skills, wider cognitive skills and literacy skills have also confirmed that for many individuals phonological processing deficits play an important role in their poor literacy development (Hulme and Snowling 1992, Funnell and Davison 1989). Hulme and Snowling describe the case of JM a boy of 16 years of age who had been followed for the previous 8 years. When first seen at the age of 8 years despite his superior intelligence he was only beginning to learn to read and write. At this stage he could not read unfamiliar words or made up words and his spelling was often unphonetic, for example, 'CAP' was spelt 'GAD'.

Over the next 4 years JM learnt to read but it was thought he did this largely by visual strategies as his non-word reading and spelling still showed poor phonological skills. At 13 years he was asked to repeat 40 non-words and got 25 of these correct. This was well below the average of 35.5 correct answers given by reading age matched controls. On the basis of this and other similar findings it was suggested that the key problem that JM had was in output phonology. Lundberg (1994) compared 15 year old dyslexic students with matched non-dyslexic controls and found that they performed far worse on a variety of tasks such as reading non-words and syllable reversal. Korhonen (1995) in a longitudinal study followed nine dyslexic children from 9 years of age to 18 years of age. It was found that many of the difficulties that the children had such as poor rapid naming and poor reading and spelling persisted over time. Although this is still an area for debate Korhonen argues that these results favour the idea that there are permanent underlying deficits in dyslexia which don't appreciably improve with age. This doesn't mean that children with dyslexia can't develop compensatory strategies to deal with their problems but that their primary cognitive deficits are likely to persist over time.

Are all dyslexics the same?

There are several reasons for considering this question. The first and most obvious is that it has implications for teaching and intervention. If there were distinct sub-types within dyslexia different types of teaching and intervention might be required to meet the needs of these different groups. Allied to this it might have implications for the kind of criteria by which dyslexics are identified. There are also implications for the kind of methodology used to research dyslexia. If group comparisons are made between dyslexic and non-dyslexic subjects with results averaged out over the group, individual differences will be lost and may distort the way in which the results are interpreted.

The reader might be forgiven for thinking that on the evidence produced so far all dyslexics have pretty much the same underlying cognitive impairments. But many leading researchers over a long period of time (Johnson and Myklebust 1967, Boder 1973, Coltheart *et al.* 1983), have argued that there are sub-types within dyslexia. Johnson and Myklebust (1967) first proposed a distinction between auditory and visual dyslexics. They were actually referring to relative strengths and weaknesses in relating sounds to words and not to visual perceptual difficulties as such. But their work was often taken to support a simplistic division between visual and auditory difficulties. Allied to this the fallacious assumption was sometimes made that if a child performed badly on a so-called visual item that this implied a visual processing problem. But critics like Lieberman (1983) have pointed out that children may well use verbal strategies in solving so called visual problems.

Before going any further with this discussion there are some general issues to consider. If we talk about sub-types in dyslexia are we talking about differences in fundamental impairments or differences in the compensatory strategies that children use? We also need to know if different sub-types reflect genuine differences in the underlying impairments or differing degrees of the same impairment. Both Goswami and Bryant (1990) and Ellis (1993) have argued that we also need to look at the pattern of reading differences in ordinary readers. It may be that any differences found between dyslexic readers simply reflect the normal range of differences found between ordinary readers. According to Ellis ordinary readers can be placed on a continuum between those that rely heavily on visual whole word strategies and those that rely heavily on phonic strategies. The former rely on visual whole word recognition because they have poor phonic skills, whereas the latter rely on phonic skills because of their difficulty in accessing the visual lexicon and subsequent poor sight vocabulary. Ellis claims that the majority of children fall somewhere between the extremes of this continuum with a reasonable level of skill in both visual and phonic strategies. He goes on to conclude that if this is the case that we should expect the same distribution of difficulties among dyslexic children with some at either extreme with severe phonic or visual difficulties but the majority showing a mixture of visual and phonic impairments. Seymour (1986) carried out cognitive tests on 21 dyslexics using an individual case study approach, with the express intention of looking to see if they could be divided into sub-types on the basis of their impairments. He found that although a few could be classified as phonological or visual dyslexics the majority showed great variability in the type of processing deficits that they displayed and that it was not possible to classify dyslexics in terms of neat sub-types. The problem with this study is that only a small sample was involved and the variability in their age, IQ, and reading performance may have masked any consistent cognitive differences. Other researchers like Snowling (1995) and Stanovich (1985) argue that a fundamental impairment in phonological processing underlies the difficulties encountered by all dyslexics. Snowling maintains that the differences seen in performance between different dyslexics are due to the severity of their phonological impairment and the way in which this interacts with other cognitive capacities.

The possible role of visual processing deficits

Stanovich (1993) although a strong supporter of the phonological impairment hypothesis acknowledges that cognitive researchers have tended to neglect research on visual perception and that visual processing deficits may occur alongside phonological deficits in some children. Willows and Terepocki (1993) observe that much of the research that has dismissed the role of visual deficits has been of a short term laboratory based nature and that unlike clinicians and teachers the researchers have not been able to follow children for long periods of time, in some cases over several years. They go on to argue that by combining evidence from a large number of case studies (e.g. Boder 1973, Farnham-Diggory 1978, Rawson 1982) it is possible to outline the developmental difficulties often displayed by a child with visual processing deficits. These include:

1 Difficulty in recognising letters and numbers with frequent misidentification especially of visually similar letters.
2 Poor recall of letters and numbers. Even when the child has learnt to recognise letters and numbers accurately they still show poor ability in recalling what they look like. This is reflected in poor letter and number formation and frequent reversals.
3 Poor word recognition even for high frequency words such as 'the', 'is' or 'said'. Refusals, omissions, hesitations and substitutions are all common although the child strives hard to keep the text meaningful but in some cases the high number of substitutions can significantly alter the meaning of the text. Will often not recognise a word when it has appeared several times in the text even when they have got it correct on some previous occasions.

RT at 8 years, despite an IQ in the very superior range, frequently couldn't recognise common words such as 'the', 'then, 'she', 'here' and 'said' and frequently reversed 'was' and 'saw'. He reversed almost any letter it was possible to reverse including j, r, c, a and s as well as more common ones like b, d, and p. He also reversed most numbers. His handwriting was appalling and individual letter formation was highly idiosyncratic.

4 Poor recall of words. As with word recognition the child shows difficulties even with high frequency words. Spelling and written work is of a poor standard with many misspellings.

   RT at 11 years spells first 'fist', despite often being asked to spell this word and often being corrected.

One criticism that can be levelled at all this evidence is that many children, not just dyslexic children, make these kinds of errors. Clinicians and educators would argue that it is the nature and frequency of these errors which distinguish dyslexic children. This can only be reliably established by comparing children, for example on standardised spelling tests or tests of letter identification. The problem with spelling in particular is that it is often in free writing that spelling errors are most prominent Again practitioners would argue that context and past experience are important in judging a child's performance. RT at 11 years made the following spelling errors. To judge their significance it is useful to know that RT had written a key to a map of a national park centre he had visited that day. He had seen all these words written earlier in the day and spelt 8 out of 14 words incorrectly. This was an average performance for him despite the fact that he had had two and a half years' specialist tuition in addition to his normal schooling.

hostel – hotsle
broad leaf – boad leve
walk – wark
mountain – moutin
information – Ifomsion
visitor centre– vister center

Whereas some of these errors such as 'vister center' might not surprise many teachers, others such as 'hotsle' are more unusual. This seems to show an insensitivity to orthographic patterns as the letter combination 'tsl' is unknown in English. Willows and Terepocki argue that not all these developmental errors can be explained by phonological impairments. As Orton (1937) pointed out children don't just reverse letters that can easily be confused with other letters such as m and w they also reverse letters such as j or r where no confusion with another symbol appears to be involved. It is hard in a case like this to argue that some form of labelling or linguistic difficulty has led to the reversal. Willows and Terepocki, after reviewing all the research evidence currently available on reversal errors, state that:

> At this point, it seems about equally probable that reversal errors are a fascinating key to understanding the problems that some individuals have in processing symbolic information as they are a 'red herring' leading researchers and clinicians astray.

Another possibility is that for some children reversal errors are only of significance if combined with other cognitive impairments. RT's older brother CT had shown similar reversal errors and poor handwriting in infant school. These had been commented on by all his teachers as being in excess of what they normally saw. Although he made a slow start with reading, at the age of 6 his reading suddenly 'took off' and by 7 years his reading age was 2 to 3 years ahead of his chronological age. He was also considered by top infants to be a good speller and this was confirmed by his SATs results. The difference appeared to be that CT had very good phonological skills whereas RT had always displayed poor phonological skills and auditory sequencing skills. He had for example had difficulty learning to count to ten, saying the days of the week and months of the year whereas these tasks gave his brother no difficulty. It seems likely as Ellis (1993) has suggested that many dyslexic children like RT have a mixture of phonological and visual impairments and that some non-dyslexic children like CT rely heavily on one form of processing to perform competently.

Visual perceptual difficulties

Another area where there needs to be more research is that of reported visual perceptual problems. Research in this area is controversial but does suggest that a small percentage of dyslexic children do report problems such as print going fuzzy, blurring and moving round despite them having seemingly normal vision (Garzia 1993). One issue is whether this occurs in a percentage of non-dyslexic children and is therefore not of major significance or whether again it interacts with other factors or is a major source of difficulty in its own right. Garzia (1993) gives a useful and balanced overview of the possible relationship between vision and reading. He concludes that optical difficulties do play a part in delayed reading in a small number of children. These difficulties are not related to simple short sightedness but to a variety of conditions such as poor binocular vision or poor eye movement control. He suggests on this basis that comprehensive visual screening which looks at a variety of factors should be given to all reading delayed children especially if they have been complaining of any visual discomfort when reading.

Two mothers out of the 22 interviewed in the main study to be described in this book said that their children had often commented on these kinds of visual problems. JA for example had commented several times to his mother that words seemed to jump out of the page at him and that sometimes they seemed to disappear off the page. Interestingly JA when tested with the WISC (Wechsler Intelligence Scale for Children) showed no unevenness in his profile as is often found in dyslexic children and no signs of specific auditory or visual processing problems, but his mother reported that he had been treated for several years for a severe squint. This may just be coincidence but it does stress the need to be aware that there may be multiple and complex causes for the difficulties displayed by individuals with dyslexia. Rayner (1993) argues that we are wrong to assume that there is only one 'cause' underlying dyslexia and although in the short run it makes research and remediation more difficult, in the long run we will get better results if we appreciate that dyslexia can have many causes and will in turn require remediation geared to these different causes. Whatever the final outcome of this debate, most researchers would agree that at a behavioural level there are considerable individual differences between individuals with dyslexia despite the striking commonalties. Even if only one specific cognitive impairment was found to underlie dyslexia this is hardly a surprising finding when the number of potential factors interacting with the primary deficit are taken into account. These can include:

1 other cognitive skills
2 early language experience
3 learning style
4 personality
5 formal teaching of reading
6 developmental stage
7 compensatory strategies
8 social experiences.

At present there is little research looking at how a primary deficit might interact with factors like the ones named above. What this does suggest is that at present we need to remain open minded about the likely causes of dyslexia and that we mustn't prematurely advocate blanket approaches to remediation.

DYSLEXIA: MORE THAN A READING PROBLEM

One of the dangers of discussing dyslexia is that it is easy to slip into discussing it largely as a reading problem. One reason for this is that the term 'dyslexia' has often been used in conjunction with other terms such as 'reading disabled', 'reading delayed' and 'specific learning disability (reading)'. Another reason is that research on dyslexia often compares dyslexic children to both ordinary readers and children considered to have other forms of reading delay. Allied to this there is a large body of research on the reading process that research on dyslexia can draw on and relate to. Given that reading difficulties are for most dyslexic children the first obvious educational problem that they present with, the focus on reading is understandable. But whereas most dyslexic children do eventually learn to read the majority have long term spelling difficulties (Miles 1983). Ellis (1993) says that: 'The difficulties that developmental dyslexics experience in writing and spelling are often at least as severe, if not worse than their difficulties at reading.'

In addition to writing and spelling difficulties Miles and Miles (1990) claim that many dyslexics also have difficulties with some specific aspects of numeracy such as learning multiplication tables. Riddick (1995b) found that by 10 years of age the majority of dyslexic children were far more concerned with their writing and spelling difficulties than their reading and that as they progressed into secondary school concerns over the speed and accuracy of their work increased. The problem with characterising dyslexia at the behavioural level (e.g. difficulty copying off the board, poor spelling, problems learning tables) is that you can end up with a list of seemingly unrelated difficulties. Cognitive psychologists would argue that by identifying the processing deficits underlying dyslexia it is possible to get a more coherent picture of the types of learning problems that may be encountered. In the above case it could be argued that poor working memory skills could account for all three types of difficulty. McLoughlin *et al.* (1994) in considering adults with dyslexia argue that their fundamental difficulty should be seen as one of poor working or short-term memory. The advantage of this approach is that it is then possible to understand and anticipate the kind of tasks that will give them difficulties and to plan effective ways of compensating for these difficulties.

Because of concern over the performance of children with dyslexia in the educational setting most of the research so far has focused on the academic difficulties in reading, writing, spelling and to a lesser extent maths. But people with dyslexia and their families talk of a wide range of situations in which their underlying cognitive impairments can put them at a disadvantage or make the situation more difficult for them to cope with. Fawcett and Nicolson (1994) suggest that there needs to be more research based on the everyday difficulties that people with dyslexia report that they have. They reported that in a series of studies not only were young children with dyslexia worse on short term memory tasks and phonological skills but they were also worse on motor tasks such as bead threading and putting pegs in a board. Rudel (1985) reported that there were difficulties in newly acquired motor skills although these were usually outgrown by the age of 9 or 10. Clinicians, educationalists and parents of children with dyslexia have consistently pointed to motor difficulties especially in sequenced activities such as tying shoe laces. Augur (1985) suggests that difficulties in dressing, doing up buttons, kicking or throwing a ball, hopping, and skipping are all commonly observed in young dyslexic children. What is not clear at present is what proportion of children with dyslexia have these kinds of difficulties and what the range and extent of them might be. Miles (1993) reports that dyslexic children (76 per cent) are almost twice as likely to show confusion over left and right as non-dyslexic children (36 per cent). As he points out we should take this kind of information as indication of a tendency and not over generalise this as something all dyslexic children will have problems with or something that is exclusive to dyslexic children. As Pollock and

Waller (1994) point out for many children these kinds of difficulties may be put down to confusions in verbal labelling and such children do in fact seem to have quite a good sense of direction whereas there does appear to be a smaller group of children who do have real difficulties with space and time. The area where there is least research at present is on the day to day implications of living with cognitive impairments such as a poor short term memory. At a commonsense level it's not difficult to imagine that a child who doesn't know the days of the week and cannot remember messages from school is likely to be more confused and disorganised in their daily life than a child who does have these skills. In the study to be described in this book a mother spoke about an instance where her son couldn't remember the name of his new teacher or the number of his class. On returning from the dentist's he needed to ask where he would find her, but was too afraid to do so because of not knowing her name. He was eventually found sitting in the cloakroom and received a telling off for not having joined his class. A student who was recently assessed for dyslexia spoke about the constant difficulties she got into because she couldn't remember people's names. She talked about a recent incident where she couldn't remember the names of some of her fellow course students after the summer vacation and they had taken offence at this. The difficulty in researching these kinds of experiences is in sorting out which of them are specifically related to dyslexia and which of them are common to people in general. It may well be the case that many of these experiences are not exclusive to individuals with dyslexia but that they are far more common.

SUMMARY

1 Different definitions of dyslexia fulfil different purposes and reflect different perspectives.
2 We need to know about the cognitive deficits underlying dyslexia in order to have a proper understanding of how it affects individuals.
3 The cognitive deficits underlying dyslexia can be identified at an early age.
4 In the majority of cases there is a genetic component to dyslexia.
5 The cognitive deficits underlying dyslexia are likely to remain.
6 Cognition as well as behaviour needs to be considered if children with dyslexia/specific learning difficulties are to be accurately assessed.

Chapter 2

The educational perspective

'Dyslexia is a professional battlefield. Nothing is more likely to induce apoplexy among the combatants, and confusion among the spectators.'

(Swann 1985)

At a very general level research and writing on dyslexia can be put under three major headings. First, there is the large body of cognitive research some of which was briefly summarised in the first chapter of this book. Second, there is a broad band of educational research and writing, and finally there is a surprisingly small amount of research on the social and personal consequences of dyslexia. Inevitably there is considerable overlap between these areas and, for example, some of the studies on intervention have been derived directly from cognitive research but have clear educational implications. Despite the overlaps there is a case to be made for suggesting there is still a lack of engagement between these various areas of research. The major concern thus far of cognitive psychologists has been to identify the processing deficits underlying dyslexia. They have been less concerned in looking at how these deficits might interact with broader everyday influences such as a child's view of herself as a learner. In contrast much mainstream educational research and writing has ignored or denied the existence of dyslexia as a concept and it has therefore not been directly researched or written about. Many educationalists would argue that they have included many so-called dyslexic children within a different conceptual framework which sees them as part of the continuum of children with specific learning disabilities within the broader category of children with special needs. From this perspective there has been a considerable amount of research especially on children who have had difficulties learning to read. The problem is that because some cognitive and educational researchers have started from different perspectives with different approaches to defining and identifying children with a difficulty it is hard to compare and draw meaningful conclusions from their relative research. As stated before there is less research at present on the social and personal consequences of dyslexia. Much of what exists comes from outside the mainstream of academic research and consists of personal accounts in the form of autobiographies or collections of case studies. At this informal level there are also the opinions of clinicians and specialist teachers on the personal consequences of dyslexia. At a more general level there is research on children's self-concept as learners (Burns 1982) and the personal development of a range of children with special needs.

In Britain the steady stream of research and writing by Professor Tim Miles (1982,1987,1990,1993) at Bangor University has consistently drawn on and integrated research and writing from all three areas. At the request of the British Psychological Society Pumfrey and Reason (1991) conducted a national inquiry called *Specific Learning Difficulties (Dyslexia): Challenges, Responses and Recommendations*. This gathered information from a wide variety of sources and covered research and writing from all the three areas mentioned previously in this chapter. Some of the major conclusions to arise from this report will be discussed later in this chapter. In the USA Stanovich (1988,1991,1993) has commented particularly on the interface between cognitive and educational research and thinking.

SPECIAL NEEDS HISTORY AND CURRENT PRACTICE

From the educational perspective the problems of defining and identifying dyslexia are inextricably bound up with more general issues about defining and identifying special needs. Prior to the Warnock Report in 1978 children were categorised according to handicaps such as 'severe educational subnormality', 'moderate educational subnormality', 'blind and partially sighted', 'maladjusted' and so on. Although the degree to which the Warnock Report either influenced or reflected current educational thought can be debated most would agree that it encapsulated some important changes in thought and has had a profound influence on the future development of special education. The Warnock Report was critical of the principle of categorisation for a number of reasons and therefore recommended the abolition of statutory categories of handicap. One of the Warnock Report's major objections to categories was that as many of them derived from a medical basis they said little about a child's educational needs. So for example the category of 'physical impairment' could include children with normal learning abilities but some or no problems of curriculum access as well as children with specific learning disabilities or moderate or severe learning disabilities. It also highlighted that for some children the degree of disability that they encountered was directly related to the educational environment. So a child with spina-bifida who needed a wheelchair to get around might encounter relatively little educational disability in a school with good wheelchair access and considerable disability in a school with poor access. The report thus stated that 'Whether a disability or significant difficulty constitutes an educational handicap for an individual child, and if so to what extent, will depend upon a variety of factors.'

In making this statement it pointed out that schools varied considerably in their expertise, organisation, outlook and resources and that even within a single school the impact of a severe disability could vary depending on the child's personality, the degree of support and encouragement that they received from their family and the interests that they had outside school. This has clear relevance to dyslexia and suggests that the degree to which a child has difficulties will depend on the degree of support available to them. The report suggested that the concept of 'special educational need' should replace the categories of handicap and that each child should be looked at individually to ascertain all the factors affecting their educational performance. Allied to this the Warnock Report wanted to get away from the rigid division of children into handicapped and non-handicapped and to suggest that children were viewed on a continuum of special educational need. The Warnock Report estimated that in the course of their school career nearly one child in five would at some point require special educational provision. It emphasised that the majority of these children would be in mainstream schools, and would not be handicapped in the traditional sense of the word and would not require long term special educational provision. 'Their learning problems, which may last for varying periods of time, will stem from a variety of causes. But unless suitable help is forthcoming, their problems will be reinforced by long experience of failure' (Warnock Report, DES 1978).

So Warnock was emphasising that dyslexic children if viewed as part of the continuum of children with special needs were in danger of having their difficulties exacerbated by repeated failure unless appropriate support was available. The point about not having a rigid division between handicapped and non-handicapped does highlight some of the problems inherent in a concept such as dyslexia. At what point do we call a child dyslexic rather than a poor speller? But this is not a problem peculiar to dyslexia: labels as diverse as 'autism', 'clumsiness' and even seemingly more quantifiable ones such as 'visual' and 'hearing impairments' all raise the same issue of where the cut off point is drawn. This is an issue of how a label is applied and it does not necessarily invalidate the label itself.

Another criticism of categories particularly pertinent to dyslexia is that they draw resources away from children who don't fit a particular category. But this criticism is actually about the way in which the allocation of resources is linked to categories and not about categories in themselves. Critics of the use of the label dyslexia would argue that this label is used to distance dyslexics from common or garden backward readers and by doing so imply that a special and different level of support is required. Supporters of the term 'dyslexia' would argue that this criticism is based on an outdated discrepancy and exclusion definition of dyslexia and that if a process based definition of dyslexia is used (as described in the first chapter) then many children formally classified as backward readers might in fact be classified as dyslexic. They would also argue that identifying the underlying processing problems that an individual child has is very much in line with Warnock's recommendation that 'remedial' children should not all be lumped together and that skilled assessment should discriminate between children and inform the type of specialist support they required. This approach does not suggest that dyslexic children should receive proportionally more support than other children it suggests that all children should receive support specific to their learning needs.

A final and strong criticism that the Warnock Report had of categories was that they led to stigma and negative labelling sometimes of a long-term nature. The Warnock Report was expressing a view widely held in the 1970s and 1980s (Szasz 1961, Goffman 1968) about the problems of labelling. Few would disagree about the negative connotations attached to certain labels and the harmful consequences that can ensue. But the danger is that this can lead to oversimplification and over generalisation of the argument. It can be argued that the nature, purpose and context in which a label is used all influence the degree of positive and negative outcomes associated in using it. A child with a visual impairment for example may not want to be publicly labelled as such within school, but may want teachers to know enough about the impairment so they can adapt teaching appropriately. The child may also want at a personal level to understand the visual difficulties that they have and be given some idea of whether any improvement or deterioration can be expected in their sight. Norwich (1990) in a comprehensive critique of the objections given to categorisation in the Warnock Report states that 'The relation between any general category and its use for individuals is a complex one.'

This issue of categorisation or labelling in relation to dyslexia will be looked at in more detail in chapter 6. As a general point it can be suggested that the concept of dyslexia was being debated during the 1970s and 1980s within a cultural context which was doubtful or sceptical of the value of labels. But it can be argued that in order to have a full and accurate picture of a child's learning difficulties we need to know how all the environmental factors which are in operation interact with the within-child factors to produce a particular outcome. Some special educationalists, in extending the thinking of the Warnock Report, were highly critical of explanations of learning disability which focused on within-child factors. Whilst they were correct to criticise the exclusive use of within-child factors the danger was that in some cases by denying the role of these factors they were adopting what could be called the 'without-child' approach.

The Warnock Report specifically mentions the needs of dyslexic children as part of a wider group of children with reading, writing and spelling difficulties. It comments that it hopes that its new recommendations on assessment leading to the formulation of individual need will be of particular help to this group of children. The report goes on to say

Although there are no agreed criteria for distinguishing those children with severe and long-term difficulties in reading, writing and spelling from others that may require remedial teaching in these areas, there are nevertheless children whose disabilities are marked but whose general ability is at least average and for whom distinctive arrangements are necessary.

Following on from this statement the report stresses that there needs to be a more discriminating approach in the assessment of children with reading, writing and spelling difficulties and that teachers and others involved should be better informed of what is already known. One of the outcomes of the Warnock Report was that it recommended that any child who was having educational difficulty could if necessary and with family agreement be statemented. This statement was to involve a detailed assessment of a child's needs with a clear specification of the kind of special provision that was required. The Warnock Report did not envisage all children with a special need being statemented, but that a statement should be made when the child's needs could not be met by the level of provision generally available in school. This meant that a dyslexic child could be statemented and special provision obtained in cases where the school was not able to provide sufficient support. In theory this seemed a reasonable plan but in practice there were a number of difficulties.

1 Ascertaining the level of provision generally available in school is not a simple matter. In the area of reading for example the different ethos, organisation, priorities and resources available in different schools means that the needs of a range of children with reading difficulties including those with dyslexia, would be met to differing degrees.
2 Local Education Authorities varied considerably in the proportion of children with specific learning disabilities that they were willing to statement (Pumfrey and Reason 1991).
3 A crucial part of the statement (SE4) has to be filled in by an educational psychologist or special needs adviser. During the late 1970s and 1980s many educationalists were critical of the concept of dyslexia (Miles and Miles 1990), so getting a sympathetic assessment could be difficult.
4 In some cases professionals such as educational psychologists felt under pressure to tailor their statement of need to what they knew was available in other words to what a child could have rather than what a child should have.

These recommendations by the Warnock Report for the provision of special education linked to a statement of need were made into a legal requirement for LEAs by the passing of the 1981 Education Act. This meant that LEAs were legally obliged to statement and provide for any child who would require extra resources in ordinary school or a place in a special school. In practice this meant that LEAs were to protect children with severe and complex difficulties with a statement, but that specialist reading provision even when delivered offsite was seen as part of the school's normal provision. At present the impact of the 1988 Education Reform Act and Local Management of Schools is still being assessed. The 1988 Act promoted the philosophy of parental choice based on the ideology of parents as consumers. Choice of school was to be facilitated by the publication of school league tables based on school and public forms of assessment. Concerns were expressed that this may lead to some schools being reluctant to accept children with special needs because they might depress the school's overall results. Concerns were also expressed over Local Management of Schools, because in this case schools would manage their own finances and could make their own decisions on what proportion of their budget should be allocated to children with special needs. This was of particular importance to non-statemented children with special educational needs whose special provision would no longer be funded by the LEA. Wider issues about the diminished role of the LEAs in providing co-ordinated and balanced provision for differing groups of individuals with special needs were also raised. This is especially important at a time when parents are being encouraged to take a more active role in the decision making processes within school. A particular concern is that as parents of children with special needs are a minority group, the needs of their children might not be given the attention that they deserve. Because of increasing disquiet (Warnock 1994) about the level and equity of special provision for non-statemented children, in September 1994 it was made a legal requirement that all state schools,

Have regard for the Code of Practice on the Identification and Assessment of Special Educational Needs.

Publish information about the policies for children with special educational needs.

(DFE 1994)

The Code of Practice does not lay down specific practices for schools but aims to provide step by step guidelines of which schools should take note when considering the needs of a particular child. They suggest three steps or stages that a school might go through but qualify this by saying that a specific school might organise itself in such a way that it utilises only two stages or as many as four stages, the emphasis is on the professional judgement of the school to do what is most appropriate given local factors and ongoing organisation. It is recommended that close consultation with parents should take place throughout this process. Where a three stage model is adopted, the first stage involves the child's teacher recording any observed learning difficulties and discussing these with the child's parents, and in collaboration with the parents offering the child support and encouragement. Where it is felt that more support and advice is needed stage two can be set in motion.

This involves a meeting between the child's parents, the child's teacher and the school's special needs co-ordinator so that an individual education plan can be drawn up. This should then be reviewed after a fixed period of time to see if the targets that have been set for the child have been met. If progress has still not been made then stage three of the process can be put into action. This involves calling in outside specialists such as educational psychologists or special needs advisors to give a more detailed assessment of a child's needs so that a new individual education plan can be drawn up. If progress is still not being made the head teacher can, in consultation with all those involved with the child, ask the LEA for a statutory assessment to be made. This Code of Practice was drawn up as a practical guide to the 1993 Education Act, part 3 of which was specifically on children with special educational needs. Under this arrangement, as in the past, the major responsibility for identifying special needs rests with classroom teachers. Mary Warnock (1994) comments that,

> It is therefore of the greatest importance that teachers, even when quite young and inexperienced, should know what to look for as signs that a child has a specific learning difficulty or dyslexia, which may well not manifest itself until school work begins.

It is interesting that Mary Warnock who signalled the change to a more relative and less categorical approach to conceptualising special needs back in 1978 is in 1994 arguing that teachers should be aware of the signs that may indicate a specific learning disability or dyslexia. She also gave the introductory address to the third International Dyslexia conference in 1994 and is currently president of the British Dyslexia Association. But as shown earlier in this chapter the Warnock Report expressed considerable concern over the needs of children with specific learning disabilities so Mary Warnock is showing consistency in still voicing these concerns. She says that what has changed is that we now have considerably more knowledge on the occurrence of such difficulties and the devastating effect that they can have on children's lives. She argues that on this basis it is essential that all teachers are presented with this information as part of their initial teacher training.

The Code of Practice also emphasises that supporting individual children with special needs will only work if there is a whole school policy on special needs backed up by appropriate resources. The school governors, staff and parents and LEA should be involved in the formulation of the policy. Under the 1993 Education Act the school governors have a legal responsibility to show what funds have been spent on special needs. This all sounds impressive on paper but as usual much will depend on how it works out in practice, as no additional resources are being made available. It can be argued that in the context of the school league tables, the testing of pupils, the national curriculum and Local Management of Schools, the Code of Practice at least reasserts the importance of meeting special needs and refocuses schools' attention on them. Whether schools, after all the changes and pressures they have encountered in the past few years, feel willing or able to refocus remains to be seen. Some may feel that an effective special needs policy will in the long run enhance a school's performance as measured by school league tables whereas others may feel that the ethos and priorities underlying these differing demands are difficult to reconcile. The director of education for the London borough of Hillingdon (Andrews 1994) has argued that rather than labelling children as having special needs we should be emphasising that it is schools that have special needs in terms of resources, training and support. From the point of view of dyslexic children the worry is that initial identification is up to the classroom teacher who in some cases may not have the training to spot the specific learning disabilities that a child has or may misinterpret their significance. Under these circumstances there is no legal action that parents can take to ensure that the school meets their child's special needs. Although individual parents can complain to the school governing body much depends on the assertiveness and articulateness of the parents and the receptiveness of the school governing body as to what the likely outcome will be. Many would argue that this would be an undesirable position for schools to get into anyway, as an equitable special needs policy requires them to be proactive and not end up with a policy dictated by the vagaries of individual demands. A recent survey by Baskind and Thomson (1994) found that the majority of special needs governors were well intended but under informed and only three out of the group of twenty that they looked at had received any training in special needs.

MODELS OF GOOD PRACTICE

One of the observations that is often made is on the enormous variability in schools' approaches to meeting special needs. Some schools, especially where there is good LEA support, already have a comprehensive approach to meeting the needs of children with specific learning disabilities. Cleveland LEA for example has a policy of not statementing children with specific learning disabilities where possible, and instead providing them with a package of support (Stansfield 1994). This support includes placement in an intensive reading class, access to a learning support service, microelectronic equipment, and advice on this equipment for parents and schools. The intensive reading classes for primary school children involve both withdrawal and within class support from a team of ten specialist teachers. At secondary level there are four learning support teachers whose aim is to move away from support to specific children to supporting and training teachers within the secondary schools to meet the needs of their own pupils. Information technology (IT) support is overseen by an IT special education needs (SEN) co-ordinator who is responsible for inservice training and for assessing and administering the loan of microelectronic equipment. There is also an examinations concessions group who have drawn up a set of procedures to ensure that children with special needs get the best possible concessions during public examinations.

In 1987 Hertfordshire LEA decided to review its provision for pupils with specific learning disabilities. At that time some children were given support in school, others were given additional remedial reading support and in a few severe cases where access to the curriculum was limited an out of county placement to a special independent school was made. It was felt that this service didn't allow for advice and support to teachers in mainstream schools, nor did it allow for children to be supported across a number of curriculum areas. It also ran counter to the prevailing ethos of supporting all children with special needs where possible within the mainstream school. In response to this review in 1990 the first base school was set up with the specific brief of providing a three-tier support service for children with specific learning disabilities. Stott (1993) a teacher at the base school has outlined the nature of this service.

> The base provides a three-tier service to the first and primary schools in the immediate locality. The first phase offers advice to mainstream class teachers who have identified individual pupils with specific difficulties in reading, writing, spelling and, in some instances, mathematics. The second phase supports individual pupils within their own mainstream schools, either on a withdrawal basis or within the classroom, often both. The two base specialist teachers offer this peripatetic support once the school's educational psychologist has assessed pupils that have needs that can best be served by base support. The third phase offers a place at the base school to those pupils whose difficulties are so great that access to the whole curriculum is denied. This third phase necessitates a full LEA Statement of Educational Need as prescribed by the Education Act 1981.

As can be seen from this description some interesting parallels can be drawn between this three stage model and the stage model of support outlined in the Code of Practice. In both cases initial identification is the responsibility of classroom teachers, but in the Hertfordshire model it can be argued that the LEA plays a major role in formulating and resourcing the kind of support deemed necessary to meet the needs of children with specific learning difficulties. Whilst it can be argued that it is important for individual schools to develop their own special needs policy and take full responsibility for children with special needs the question has to be asked as to how comprehensive a service schools can provide without the wider support and resourcing of their LEA. Stott (1993) in order to evaluate the effectiveness of the base school model sent questionnaires to all classroom teachers in three base schools, three schools supported by the base schools and three schools not currently receiving support. Teachers in the mainstream schools all emphasised the importance of inservice training and support to improve their understanding of specific learning difficulties and their specific teaching strategies. Teachers in supported schools showed greater knowledge and understanding of specific learning disabilities than teachers in the unsupported schools. Stott suggests that this shows that the base school model is not only effective in supporting individual children but is also effective in providing support and training to teaching staff.

Lewis (1995) describes the setting up of a specialist unit for dyslexic children in a comprehensive school. The school has 40 places for students with statements of educational needs of a dyslexic or specific learning disability nature. He talks about the conflicting demands of the national curriculum and the need for these pupils to have individualised structured teaching sessions within the school day and explains how this has been achieved within these constraints. He like Stott emphasises the importance of all the teachers in the school being informed and responsible for children with specific learning difficulties and argues that the approach taken by the school has benefited many other children in the school. He also talks about the need to discuss with each pupil the nature of their support and the goals that they want to achieve. Dyson and Skidmore (1994) carried out a survey of 27 Scottish secondary schools and 14 English secondary schools which were nominated as having developed good practice in relation to specific learning difficulties. As they point out this survey relied on self reporting by schools so it can only tell us what schools believed they were doing. Dyson and Skidmore report that although there was great variability in how schools organised their support some strong underlying factors were in evidence. These included the targeting of support for children in individualised packages which they term as 'eclectic, pragmatic, responsive and customised'. They found that all such schools had a clear conceptualisation of specific learning difficulties embedded in a strong whole school special needs policy. Within this framework four major aims or areas of support were identified, these included:

1 direct help with specific difficulties to improve basic skills;
2 improving curriculum access;
3 encouraging coping strategies and independent learning;
4 building up confidence or self-esteem.

There are also examples in both London and Scotland of LEAs who have set up contracts with local dyslexia associations to provide their expertise and structured teaching methods to the education system.

SUMMARY

1 There are diverse models of good practice for supporting children with dyslexia/specific learning dificulties in the mainstream school.

2 All teachers need to be trained to be aware of the signs of dyslexia/specific learning difficulties.
3 The best combination is where there is good whole school policy combined with a high level of individual teacher awareness.
4 There is no blueprint for providing support for children with dyslexia/specific learning difficulties, each school needs to formulate its own plans based on its own circumstances.

Chapter 3

Researching the social and emotional consequences of dyslexia

'It was traumatic for him, incredibly traumatic, every morning I had to pull him up screaming "I don't want to go to school" and then I had to pull him all the way down to the school.'

As was mentioned in the introductory chapter of this book there is little research on the social and emotional consequences of dyslexia. Pumfrey and Reason (1991) in their comprehensive report *Specific Learning Difficulties (Dyslexia)* state that more research on this area is essential. Despite the paucity of research, concerned clinicians and educationalists have consistently pointed to the devastating effects that dyslexia or specific learning disabilities can have on some children's lives. Concern can be traced from Orton's early clinical work through both the Bullock (1975) and Warnock (DES 1978) Reports to the recent report by Pumfrey and Reason. It appears that whatever the debate about terminology and identification, at a global level there is agreement that such difficulties can have a detrimental effect on both the lives of children and their families. Despite this agreement this is a difficult and complex area to research. To start with both dyslexia and social and emotional difficulties have to be clearly defined and identified before the relationship between them can be examined. To date much of the research has looked at children with reading disabilities or more generally at children with learning disabilities. This research has generally used a group comparison design so that, for example, the self-esteem of a group of reading-delayed and non-reading-delayed children would be compared. The problem with this approach is that individual differences between children can be masked and it doesn't relate the individual's specific experiences to their level of self-esteem. We might expect for example that a dyslexic child who has been well supported at home and at school would be more likely to have a reasonable level of esteem than a child who has not been supported well at either home or school. Another difficulty in researching this area, is that dyslexia is a developmental disorder which changes in its manifestations over time. It may be that social and emotional experiences change or fluctuate considerably over time and that circumstances, cumulative experiences and maturation all affect the likely outcome at a given point in time. If for example a study looked at 10 year old dyslexics who had learnt to read and were well supported in the classroom and compared their self-esteem to that of their classmates no significant difference might be found. If this were the case this would be an interesting and valid finding in its own right. The danger would be in over generalizing this finding and saying that dyslexic children don't have lower self-esteem than other children or even that 10 year old dyslexic children don't have lower self-esteem than other children. These same children at 7 years of age before they were identified as dyslexic and offered support may have had very low self-esteem compared with their classmates. So as with all cross sectional research the age and stage at which a child is studied is of key importance. Yet another difficulty is in selecting the right measures to tap into any difficulties or differences that dyslexic children display compared with their peers. A study by (Porter and Rourke 1985) found that 10 per cent of a sample of a 100 learning disabled children had somatic problems such as migraines or stomach upsets despite scoring normally on an inventory of social and emotional functioning. These kinds of difficulties may account for some of the mixed findings to emerge from this area. Porter and Rourke found for example that 50 per cent of the children in their sample did not show social or emotional difficulties and in a study by Speece *et al.* (1985) one third of the learning disabled children showed no social or emotional difficulties. The problem with these studies is that they are not specific to children with dyslexia, but they do underline the point that it is important not to assume that all children with dyslexia will automatically have social or emotional difficulties.

Because of the difficulties involved in following the ups and downs of children's lives and understanding the complexities of them, interest has more recently focused on different more qualitative methods of research such as ethnography, case studies, interviews and grounded theory. Whilst case studies and interviews are scarcely new to the scene, the more recent focus on trying to see things from the individual's perspective has probably informed and influenced how they are likely to be carried out. Quantitative and qualitative methods are sometimes seen as being in opposition to each other, whereas Mittler (1985) in reviewing research methods in special education states that, 'it would be dangerously misleading to polarize or stereo-type these methods as lying at opposite ends of a continuum'. He goes on to point out that these methods are often used in combination by researchers and that a study might, for example, start with a broad quantitative survey and then move into detailed qualitative case studies of individuals. At present the main body of evidence on the social and emotional concomitants of dyslexia comes from personal accounts and life histories. Probably the best known personal account in Britain is recounted by Susan Hampshire the actress in her book entitled *Susan's Story* (1981). As well as detailed individual accounts, several collections of interviews with parents of dyslexic children, and adults with dyslexia have been published (Osmond 1993, Van der Stoel 1990, Melck 1986). Although these books have included some comments by dyslexic children, the views of parents have predominated. Kavanaugh (1978) in the USA published a book entitled *Listen to Us!* which was based entirely on the views of dyslexic children, which were first aired during discussions between them. Much of this work has been produced by lay people often with first hand experience of dyslexia. The aim has been 'to tell it how it is' and not to answer theoretical questions or provide highly systematic accounts. But in their own right they have provided an important level of description about how individuals live with dyslexia and they have raised numerous questions for further research. In particular it can be argued that they have challenged some of the more dogmatic ideology surrounding dyslexia and have provided compelling accounts of how dogmatism and ignorance can combine to provide poor and in some cases atrocious educational practice. In addition to this single case studies have occasionally appeared in books and journals, but these have often focused on reading failure rather than dyslexia. Edwards (1994) provides detailed personal case studies on eight boys attending a residential school for children with dyslexia. Despite the enormous diversity of these various accounts, consistent themes, issues and experiences can be identified and these will be discussed in more detail later in the chapter and will also be linked to findings from the study described in this book. Because of the limited amount of research on the social and emotional consequences of dyslexia a number of overlapping areas of research relevant to this issue will be briefly reviewed.

SELF-ESTEEM/SELF-CONCEPT

Although the terms self-esteem, self-concept and self-image are sometimes used interchangeably they do have different but interrelated meanings. Self-concept is defined as an umbrella term that encompasses an individual's evaluation of themselves at a cognitive (thinking), affective (feelings) and behavioural level. Self-esteem is taken as a measure of how far an individual's perceived self (self-image) matches up to their ideal self. Burns (1982) in an extensive review of the literature relating to self-concept and education argued that there are clear links between an individual's self-concept and school performance. He suggests that where an individual has poor academic performance and low motivation in school this is often linked to a poor self-concept. Lawrence (1987) and Huntington and Bender (1993) make similar claims for the link between poor school performance and low self-esteem. Drawing on the work of Rogers (1951) many writers have suggested that in order to develop a positive self-concept an individual needs a sense of acceptance, competence and worth. It is postulated that these are learnt through social interaction firstly within the family, then school and the wider environment. This is seen as an interactional process with the child influencing the environment and the environment influencing the child. Both Burns and Lawrence in their overviews of the area stress that although families have an important role in the fostering of good self-concept or self-esteem, teachers also have a vital role in this process. Lawrence states that, 'whenever the teacher enters into a relationship with a student a process is set into motion which results either in the enhancement of self-esteem or in the reduction of self-esteem.' Lawrence goes on to suggest that many good teachers intuitively enhance the self-esteem of their pupils, but even so they might benefit from more explicit knowledge of the factors that help to enhance self-esteem.

One of the problems in reviewing the literature on self-concept and self-esteem in relation to academic performance is that it is unclear if poor self-esteem leads to poor performance or if poor performance leads to poor self-esteem. A third possibility is that some kind of interactional process takes place. Lawrence (1985) in reviewing research in this area favours an inter-actional explanation and argues that on this basis it is important to work on a child's self-esteem and skills in tandem. Most researchers agree (Battle 1990, Coopersmith 1967) that self-esteem and self-concept are developmental in nature and move from a global, relatively undifferentiated state in young children to a more complex hierarchical state with a number of clearly dif-ferentiated components feeding into global self-esteem as a child gets older. There is still much debate as to the precise nature of any hierarchical model and the developmental history underpinning it. Marsh (1992) has carried out extensive research in this area and gives a simplified outline of how such a model might look.

What is also uncertain is the degree of individual differences in the way

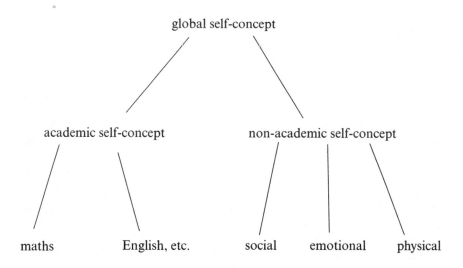

that the self-concept is structured and operates. It may be that some individuals operate more heavily on the basis of a global self-concept whereas others operate more heavily on the basis of differentiated aspects of self-concept. Battle (1990) claims that once an individual's level of self-esteem is well established it becomes difficult to alter and remains relatively stable over time. Studies that attempt to measure self-esteem run into a number of methodological difficulties. The first is in selecting a valid and reliable means of assessing self-esteem: this is usually done by means of a self-esteem inventory which relies on the subject responding to a set of specific questions. This raises questions about how honestly and accurately the subject responds to the questions. More recent well designed self-esteem inventories try to get round this problem: the *Culture-Free Self-Esteem Inventories* (Battle 1992) for example include a lie scale. Given that we know that a number of variables such as the gender, colour and role of the tester can affect children's performance differentially on various tests of ability it might also be the case that the role of the self-esteem tester and the context in which the test is carried out might affect the children's responses differentially. It has been suggested that some children with learning disabilities might defend themselves by denial and that this might in turn influence how they respond to a self-esteem inventory. Self-esteem inventories vary in accordance with the model of self-esteem that they are based on. The major difference is between those that simply give a global self-esteem score (Coopersmith 1967, Lawrence 1982) and those that in addition to a global score divide self-esteem up into a number of contributing areas (Battle 1992, Marsh *et al.* 1991) such as academic, physical and social self-esteem. Children's self-esteem scores may therefore vary depending on the sensitivity and appropriateness of the instrument used. Another difficulty in assessing self-esteem is that little is known about the way in which day to day events may influence children's self-perceptions. A study by Callison (1974) found that children's self-concept could be altered by a single incidence of feedback. In this study he first gave 8-year-old children half of the Piers-Harris Self-Concept Scale followed by a maths test. Half of the group of 28 were told that they had performed badly on the test and half were told that they had performed well. They were then given the second half of the self-concept scale to complete. It was found that children who had been given negative feedback scored significantly lower in their self-concept scores on the second part of the test. This suggests that events immediately prior to a self-esteem or self-concept inventory or scale could significantly influence the results. Despite these methodological difficulties there is general agreement that a number of behaviours are characteristic of children with high self-esteem and a number of other behaviours are characteristic of children with low self-esteem. Children with high self-esteem are said to display more confidence in their own ability, to be more willing to volunteer answers and try out new learning situations, whereas children with low self-esteem show little confidence in their own ability, give up easily and are often fearful of or avoid new learning situations. A crucial difference appears to be that whereas children with high self-esteem generally expect to succeed, children with low self-esteem generally expect to fail. Butkowsky and Willows (1980) in a study comparing children with reading difficulties with children of average or good reading ability found many of these characteristics. The poor readers in their study had lower expectations of success not only on a reading task but also on a drawing task. They responded more negatively to failure and were more likely to give up thus increasing the likelihood of future failure. They also differed in their attribution style to good readers. Poor readers tended to 'blame themselves' by attributing failure to their own incompetence and success to environmental factors such as luck, whereas good readers attributed success to their own ability. Again the question can be raised as to whether attribution style is a cause or an effect of poor reading or both. Pumfrey and Reason (1991) suggest that this style of thinking fits well with Seligman's notion of learned helplessness. Seligman claims that individuals who have been put in a negative situation from which they cannot escape and feel that they have no control over will become apathetic and demoralised. More importantly when these individuals are put in a more positive situation they persist in their apathetic behaviour and thus display learned helplessness. In a similar vein Bannister and Fransella (1971) in extending Kelly's (1955) work on personal construct theory argue that in order to change an individual's behaviour you need to change their personal constructs (self-beliefs). Although some empirical evidence has been presented to support this point of view, behaviourists can equally present evidence that changing behaviour can lead to a change in self-concept. Recent theorising (Beck *et al.* 1979) attempts to reconcile these positions by arguing for a cognitive behavioural approach that recognises the interrelated nature of cognition (thinking) and behaviour. This gets back to Lawrence's point that in the absence of more convincing evidence it's safest to assume that we need to work on both children's self-beliefs and their learning skills. Lawrence (1971, 1973, 1985) found that an individual counselling approach focused on children's self-beliefs was consistently more successful than a traditional remedial reading approach alone in improving the performance of poor readers. Lawrence found that counsellors did not need to be highly trained professionals and that anyone with a warm sympathetic approach could with limited training fulfill the role. Pumfrey and Reason (1991) argue that at a commonsense level working on individual skills in combination with personal support would seem the best option. They suggest that this support doesn't need to be in the form of formal counselling sessions and that what is required is an interested adult who gives the child support and encouragement. This issue will be further explored in chapter 10 where children's and adults' views on the teachers they find most helpful will be examined.

Self-esteem in children with dyslexia or specific learning difficulties

The studies mentioned so far focus on backward or reading-delayed children and not on children defined as having dyslexia or specific learning difficulties. Whilst the groups are likely to have included such children they were not differentiated from other children and it is therefore impossible to say if these children responded in the same way as other children to specific interventions. A longitudinal study (Gjessing and Karlsen 1989) of 3,000 children in Norway did distinguish a sub-group of children with specific learning disabilities from the cohort. It was found that these children all responded differently to the same instruction with some making very good progress and others making poor progress. This suggests that it is important not to over-generalise in talking about children's responses to intervention and to be alert to individual differences. Nonetheless it was found in this study that dyslexic children along with reading-retarded children in general had a poor self-concept which was reflected in their lack of self-confidence and poor peer relationships. Several earlier studies (e.g. Rosenthal 1973, Thomson and Hartley 1980), have found that dyslexic children have low self-esteem compared to non-dyslexic children. Thomson (1990) used the Battle (1981) *Culture-Free Self-Esteem Inventories* to test the self-esteem of three groups of children with dyslexia. The first group were tested when they were first interviewed for a place at a specialist school for dyslexia, the second group had already attended the school for 6 months and the third group had attended the school for 18 months. Thomson found there was a significant increase in self-esteem over this period of time which he attributed to the benefits of specialist schooling. The results from this study would have been stronger if the same group of children had been followed and tested at each of these time intervals but despite this, several interesting points emerged from the study when the 4 subscales for general, social, academic and parental self-esteem were compared. On the first test children's lowest area of self-esteem was for social (32 per cent) followed by academic (45 per cent) and their highest was parental (87 per cent). By the third test their social esteem was 84 per cent and their academic was 77 per cent and their parental remained at 87 per cent. This would suggest that the major source of low self-esteem for these children was the mainstream school environment and especially children's sense of failure in comparison to their peers. Studies by Chapman *et al.* (1984) and Fairhurst and Pumfrey (1992) have found that reading-disabled children score lower on their perception of academic ability compared to non reading disabled children. Chapman *et al.* found that children's perception of ability was closely related to success in school and was relatively independent of intelligence as measured by the WISC–R, a standard IQ test. They suggest that although it can be argued that children are being realistic about their level of ability in terms of school performance that these kind of beliefs may set up a self-fulfilling prophecy of expecting to fail. Whereas Chapman *et al.* were looking at 9 year olds, Fairhurst and Pumfrey were looking at third year pupils in three secondary schools. They found that in addition to the lower self-concepts as learners that the poor readers had a significantly higher rate of absence than the competent readers. They suggest that this high rate of absenteeism combined with their low self-concept and poor performance in school can all combine in a negative downward spiral for some of these children. Another factor that they found contributing to this overall picture was that the poor readers also scored lower on a sub-scale designed to look at their perceptions of their role in the classroom, it showed that they felt less valued and less important than the better readers. Casey, Levy, Brown and Brooks-Gunn (1992) studied a group of middle class pre-adolescent children with reading disabilities. They found that these children had low self-esteem and were more anxious and less happy with school than a control group of non reading disabled children. The problem with cross sectional studies like these is that they only give us a snapshot of the child's self-concept at a given point in time, they say nothing directly about how the child came to acquire their particular self-concept or what sort of developmental history it might have followed. This is a more difficult area to research as a number of complex and interacting variables are likely to be involved. These include the child's temperament, cognitive abilities, and social and educational experiences. Burns (1982) argues that despite these complexities there is clear evidence that children's self-concepts as learners are strongly influenced by their teachers. One particularly important question that arises is what the long term effects of such negative attributions might be. Kosmos and Kidd (1991) carried out a study on the personality characteristics of adult dyslexics. They found that dyslexic women scored high on the pleasing others scale and dyslexic men showed a lack of self-confidence, a tendency to self-defeating thoughts and questioning of their own ability to reach goals. These findings, it could be argued, fit with a poor self-concept or low self-esteem. Even if these results are replicated it still doesn't demonstrate that poor self-concept in adulthood is a result of earlier schooling, as it could be an outcome of difficulties that the adults are still facing especially in the work situation. Susan Hampshire, the actress, recounts what happened when she was asked at the height of her fame and success to read a story on children's television. She had spent four days trying to learn this story word for word as she knew she would not be able to read it directly from the book whilst on camera. Despite her strong reservations because of her dyslexia her protests were waved aside and she started to be filmed reading from the book with the following consequences:

> I was now not only sweating, blind, uncoordinated and laughing inanely, but started to shake as well. . . . In the pit of my stomach lay the pain of frustration and humiliation.

But methodologically these kinds of experiences are difficult to disentangle in terms of causation and Susan Hampshire herself relates these feeling in part to her childhood:

> Once inside the studio, the feeling of emptiness in my head that I had as a child returned. I looked at the book and I couldn't see it. The more I panicked the less I could see.

A danger of case studies is that as with astrology just the bits that fit the story might be picked out. But as argued in Chapter 1 if they are used judiciously in conjunction with more empirical research they can add life and insight to bare figures. In the Kosmos and Kidd study for example it was claimed that dyslexic women scored higher than non-dyslexic women on the 'pleasing others' scale. More research would be needed to verify this but it does fit with Susan Hampshire's claim that as a child and to a lesser degree as an adult she desperately wanted to please others. The following three quotations on this issue are all from her autobiography.

> I desperately wanted to be liked and I assumed that no one could like someone as stupid as me.
>
> I wanted to please.
>
> If you are inventive, loving, always smiling and laughing, people will forget that you are stupid.

Another methodological problem is that because the majority of studies have focused on reading delay and not dyslexia they have only examined self-esteem in relation to reading competence. As was demonstrated in chapter 1, there is increasing evidence that the cognitive deficits underlying dyslexia are long term for more severely affected individuals and that spelling and writing are equally if not more difficult areas for them to master. This being the case, studies that look at the self-concept or self-esteem of dyslexics over the time period when they are struggling with these skills would add to our understanding of the relationship between self-concept and academic performance.

Although there is a large literature on parenting styles and the development of self-esteem in children within the context of the home environment there is almost no research on how parents respond to the kind of low self-concept or esteem which appears to be related to learning difficulties at school. In the study to be described in this book concern over low self-esteem and how to improve it was a major preoccupation of the majority of mothers in the study. This will be discussed in detail in chapter 8 of this book.

TEACHER EXPECTATIONS

In looking at the relationship between teachers and their pupils and the way that this might affect pupil's self-concept, a body of research on how teachers' expectations of individual pupils can affect their performance has grown up. Although it's been heavily criticised on methodological grounds probably the best known study is the one carried out by Rosenthal and Jacoboson (1968). In this study teachers were told that certain children were going to 'bloom' over the following year on the basis of their IQ scores. These children were in fact picked at random and the teachers were given false information on their IQ scores. It was claimed by the researchers that these selected children did increase significantly in IQ compared to non selected children. Rosenthal and Jacobson suggest that this might have been brought about by the teachers treating these children differently to other children and for example giving them more positive attention. Because of the wide amount of interest that this study attracted and the serious doubts over its validity several better designed studies were carried out. These came up with conflicting results. In (1974) Brophy and Good reviewed nearly all the work on teachers' expectations. They suggested that whereas it was difficult to demonstrate this effect in experimental studies there was clear evidence from more naturalistic studies that teachers' inaccurate expectations of pupils could have an effect on their performance commensurate with the teachers' beliefs. Hargreaves (1972) has suggested that one reason for the mixed results obtained in this area is that for teacher expectations to have an effect on the child, the teacher must be seen by the child as a significant other, and the teacher's and the child's perceptions of ability must be congruent. So where a child has a poor academic self-concept, the teacher views the child's ability as poor and the child regards the teacher as a significant other the child is most likely to be affected by the teacher's negative expectations. Both Rogers (1982) and Good and Brophy (1987) in reviewing this area conclude that although the potential is always there for the influence of teacher expectations they only influence children sometimes and to a relatively small degree. But on the other hand the effect of this in interaction with other factors especially if it is compounded by more than one teacher may have a significant influence on a child's performance and self-concept as a learner. Good and Brophy (1987) in their review also looked at all the research on how teachers' expectations were transmitted. They concluded that there tended to be consistent differences in the way that some teachers responded to low and high achieving pupils. The low achieving students were less often chosen to answer questions even when they volunteered to answer. When it came to giving verbal feedback some teachers praised everything that low achieving children contributed whereas others were overly harsh and critical of their contributions. It was also found that in comparison to high achievers that low achievers were given less time to answer questions and were seated further away from the teacher. All the studies mentioned so far are aimed at children in general and say nothing specific about children with specific learning disabilities or dyslexia. But if it is assumed that these children are often viewed as low achievers then presumably the kind of expectancy effects described so far may well take place. More empirical research is needed to see if this is the case and if so, how the particular nature of the learning difficulties affects teachers' expectancies. One particular issue for dyslexic children is the extent to which their slow and poor written work influences teachers' expectations of them. This issue will be discussed further in chapter 9 because both children and parents in the research study to be described mentioned the problem of low expectations on the behalf of some teachers.

Burns (1982) suggests that there are four areas that teachers should concentrate on if they want to ensure that they aren't unwittingly transmitting different expectations to high and low achieving students. These include:

Interacting evenly with all pupils

Give all pupils the same amount of attention and the same degree of positive feedback. Burns suggests that because this is difficult to keep track of it helps to be systematic and keep records of seating plans, assembly contributions, project supervision and so on. The important point is that all children get an equal amount of attention and are equally invited to participate in the life of the classroom and for that matter the school in general. Evidence from personal accounts suggest that a significant proportion of dyslexic children become quiet and withdrawn in school and try not to draw attention to themselves. They may therefore be easier for the teacher to overlook. In the interviews carried out for the study reported in this book many of the secondary school pupils in particular felt that they were ignored and overlooked by teachers. Younger children as well sometimes felt overlooked partly because the poor standard of their work meant that it was less often displayed in prominent places and they were less often picked to carry out special tasks and their work was less likely to be read out in class.

Talking to all pupils

Although it can be very difficult, especially in large classes it is important to ensure that all children are spoken to on a personal basis however briefly and that teachers should whenever possible be receptive to any contact that the child makes. As most teachers are only too aware it is particularly important that quiet and unforthcoming children do not miss out. Given what is already known about the risks of poor self-concept in children with a range of learning disabilities it would seem particularly important that they get this kind of personal contact. Several children in the study to be described said that they tried to make themselves as invisible and unnoticed as possible in the classroom.

Realistic praise

Getting the balance right between being over critical or indiscriminately lavish in praise can be difficult and the ideal balance will vary from child to child. It can be argued that whereas the effects of harsh criticism are easy to identify and understand the effects of overpraising are less obvious especially as it is often done with the best of intentions. What seems important (Rowe 1974) is that praise is linked systematically to the child's performance so it provides an effective form of feedback and is valued by the child. What also seems important is that any negative feedback is given in a positive context and the child is given constructive advice on how to improve their performance. This is basic good practice that many teachers already follow, but keeping the right balance when faced with a piece of written work where the handwriting is almost indecipherable and the spelling atrocious can be more difficult. One experienced and sympathetic classroom teacher recounted to a dyslexic boy's mother her bewilderment when faced with his first piece of free writing of the year. There were so many errors in letter formation, sentence construction and spelling for a child of 10 years that she felt unsure about where on earth to begin. She decided after some thought to praise various aspects of the content and to pick up on a few of his most consistent and basic errors. Several classroom teachers in informal interviews recounted similar problems. Some of them felt that because of their own lack of knowledge about dyslexia and the fact that they were not following a specific intervention plan with the child their feedback tended to be rather random and idiosyncratic and they were dubious about its long term effectiveness. This suggests that praise will be most effective in enhancing learning when a teacher has a clear understanding of the underlying difficulties and how they can be helped. Gross (1993) suggests that because of the tendency of children with learning difficulties to 'blame' themselves for failure and to attribute success to 'luck' it is important that negative feedback is aimed only at specific external and changeable aspects of their performance (for example, 'I think you were so involved in writing this really exciting story that you forgot your capital letters today.') and that when giving positive praise for performance this is linked to general attributes of the child ('you've done really well to remember capital letters, it shows what a hard worker you are and how much you are helping yourself to improve.').

Matching tasks to individuals

Much has been written about the need to individualise learning and match tasks to individuals and many would argue that this has become a basic tenet of good practice. Even so many would also point out that environmental factors such as class size, amount of extra support for special needs and possibly the requirements of the national curriculum can all impinge on a teacher's ability to individualise learning. Burns emphasises that what is important is that children are set realistic rather than arbitrary goals and that being successful at tasks they find challenging but not overwhelming will help to improve their self-esteem. Again the problem arises that if teachers have little understanding of the learning problems involved in dyslexia it will make it difficult for them to set appropriate goals. Under the Code of Practice they should be able to get advice from the special needs co-ordinator and, if required, outside agencies. Given the wide range of responsibilities and tasks already required of classroom teachers they should feel entitled to receive adequate training and support on individualising learning for children with specific learning difficulties.

BEHAVIOURAL AND EMOTIONAL DIFFICULTIES

Along with low self-esteem there is a general consensus from a mixed body of research that children with reading disabilities are more likely to have behavioural or emotional difficulties (Tansley and Panckhurst 1981, Gentile and Macmillan 1987, Hinshaw 1992, Huntington and Bender 1993). Evidence would suggest that overlap exists between these areas and that many of the methodological problems encountered in researching self-esteem are also evident in researching behavioural and emotional difficulties. Again much of the research has focused on children with a range of reading disabilities and not on children with specific reading difficulties. This is not to imply that the experiences of all reading-delayed children are not of concern but without looking at different sub-types we cannot tell if the commonalties in their reactions outweigh any specific differences. Differences in the criteria for identification, the sensitivity and appropriateness of the measuring instruments and the sampling strategy used probably account for the variability found in estimates of the prevalence of behavioural and emotional difficulties in children with reading difficulties. Some of the available data has come from samples of children referred for special educational or clinical intervention and the reliability of prevalence estimates based on these samples is open to question. Maughan (1994) provides a useful review of much of the research in this area in terms of both methodology and data. She suggests that the most reliable estimates of prevalence rates generally come from epidemiological (whole population) studies although these are still open to problems of measurement and definition. The large scale Isle of Wight epidemiological study found that a quarter of 10-year-old children with specific reading retardation also displayed antisocial behaviour (Rutter, Tizard and Whitmore 1970). This immediately raised the question of whether poor reading led to antisocial behaviour or antisocial behaviour led to poor reading or if some common underlying factor such as social deprivation or cognitive deficits was related to both sets of difficulties. They found that the reading retarded children with antisocial behaviour were similar in many respects to the reading retarded children without behavioural difficulties and bore less resemblance to the children who just displayed antisocial behaviour. This was taken as evidence that behavioural difficulties were generally secondary to reading difficulties. This kind of study says little about the processes that lead from reading to behavioural difficulties so more recent studies of a prospective longitudinal design have been used to look at the development over time of behavioural and emotional difficulties as well as providing further evidence on prevalence rates. These studies have followed children from before they enter school or on entry to school over a number of years (Jorm et al., 1986, McGee et al., 1988, Pianta and Caldwell 1990). Overall these studies have found an increasing correlation between reading difficulties and behavioural problems over the primary school period. They also found that in the early and middle primary school years that these difficulties mainly took the form of inattentiveness and restlessness and that overt behavioural difficulties in the form of conduct disorders were less frequent at this age although they increased somewhat by late primary. These findings fit well with accounts by dyslexic children and their parents of their experiences at school.

'I want to be like invisible, I just cut myself off.'

(Riddick study, 1995b)

'Eventually I'd sort of turn off and dream my way through the day. Actually that's quite easy to do if you're undisturbed for long enough. You get almost catatonic. I don't think that it helped that I was always very well behaved, very quiet. So no one took any notice.'

(Osmond 1993)

'So I just used to sit there and sort of dream and look out of the window ... Nothing was interesting to me. I became withdrawn and bored and sort of put my mind on hold. I felt very isolated and alone.'

(Osmond 1993)

'She told me he sometimes deliberately broke the point of his pencil 10 times a day.'

(Van der Stoel 1990)

'I was for ever being told off and was the laughing stock of the class. Turns at reading aloud were a disaster. Well then I really threw in the towel! I'm quite a spitfire and my self control went completely.'

(Van der Stoel 1990)

In the Bruck (1985) inner London study which looked at a clinical sample of learning disabled children from socially disadvantaged backgrounds, it was found that 85 per cent were rated as having poor adjustment during the school years when compared to a control group of non learning disabled children. Spreen's 1987 study reported similar findings. In both cases it was found that adjustment problems had significantly decreased by adulthood suggesting that they were closely related to children's experiences in school. It was found in these studies that learning disabled girls were particularly vulnerable to adjustment problems and that especially in adolescence problems of withdrawal were common. In adulthood it was found that the reading disabled women tended to score higher on measures of anxiety and depression. Hales (1994) also found that by young adulthood levels of anxiety were particularly high in dyslexic women. As yet no clear cut explanation is available for these differences and more research is needed to look at a wide range of factors such as possible differences in amount of self blame, sensitivity to criticism or expectations of others which might lead to these findings.

Another finding from the longitudinal studies is that some reading disabled children show behavioural difficulties before they enter formal schooling. Whether these behavioural difficulties are a concomitant of the pre-reading linguistic difficulties that a proportion of reading delayed children have or whether they are due to other factors such as adverse social environment is as yet not clear. What is apparent is that the linkage between reading and behavioural difficulties is a complex one, which will probably reveal multiple causation and interactional effects. Nonetheless the evidence in general, corroborated by personal accounts, suggests that some primary age children will present with overt behaviour problems but that more are likely to present as well behaved, quiet and compliant although they have detached themselves from much of the learning process. It is these unengaged children, many would claim, who are easier to overlook especially in large or demanding classes.

Hales (1994) suggests that in the past the social and emotional consequences of dyslexia have been underestimated and that research that has treated dyslexics as 'broken learning machines' has only given us a partial understanding of what dyslexia entails. Hales administered a personality questionnaire (16 PF, Cattell *et al.* (1970)) to a group of 300 people with dyslexia aged from 6 years to 18 plus years with the majority being of school age.

He cautions that it would be naive to expect there to be a specific dylexic personality but he argues that this research can give us some indications of how individuals with dyslexia develop over time. He found that infant age children had scores which indicated that they were tense and frustrated, in the middle school years scores indicated low motivation and high anxiety and at secondary school a desire to keep in the background. Hales also found that during the middle school years there was a noticeable drop in confidence and optimism especially among girls. One of the most striking findings overall was the inverse relationship between anxiety and IQ with low IQ children from middle school years onwards tending to have higher levels of anxiety. This counters the myth that is sometimes subscribed to that 'intelligent' children suffer more and underlines the importance of not having assumptions about how particular groups of children will respond to dyslexia. Hales speculates that more intelligent children may be more sympathetically treated by the world or they may be able to develop better coping strategies. Further research is needed to corroborate these findings but they do show that we need to know more about how children with dyslexia develop over time.

The effect of emotion and mood on thinking

Given the low self-esteem and high anxiety in literacy tasks that is often reported for individuals with dyslexia, it is surprising that cognitive psychologists researching in this area haven't looked at this issue more closely. Research by Zatz and Chassin (1985) for example found that high test anxiety impaired the performance of children and Darke (1988) found that working memory was particularly affected by anxiety. As poor working memory is already considered to be a key part of the processing difficulties that dyslexic children encounter it seems likely that anxiety will further impair their performance. Yasutake and Bryan (1995) give a useful review of some of the research in this area and conclude that positive affect (emotion) can enhance children's performance on tasks like learning new vocabulary and doing maths and that negative affect can detract from their performance. They claim that for learning disabled (US term closest to specific learning difficulties) children, the benefits of positive affect are particularly large and suggest that simple strategies to increase postive affect could be used in the classroom. In two studies by Bryan and Bryan (1991a) it was claimed that simply getting children to close their eyes and think of something 'wonderful' for 45 seconds improved their performance on 50 maths sums compared to children who were asked to count to fifty. It may well be that some teachers already use similar strategies in the classroom. One particularly good and positive teacher of top infants explained how she attempted to make spelling tests less stressful by trying to convince all the children in her class that they really enjoyed them!

LOOKING IN DETAIL AT LIFE HISTORIES, CASE STUDIES AND INTERVIEWS

The great strength of these approaches is that they can give a holistic and long-term account of an individual's life. A criticism can be that they emphasise a within-person perspective, but examination of these accounts reveals that much of the focus is on how individuals see environmental factors impinging on them. Cognitive deficits are usually only raised in relation to various environmental demands such as learning to read and spell. Miles and Miles (1990) have warned against the danger of confusing primary and secondary difficulties. If a child with a primary cognitive impairment has difficulty learning to read and in response to this goes on to develop behavioural difficulties, it is important that the behavioural difficulties are not then seen as the primary cause of the child's reading difficulties, although by now they may well be a strong contributory factor. On the uncluttered world of the page this might seem an insultingly obvious point but in the messier world of the classroom such issues can become more confused. One mother in the study to be described recounted a clear example of this. She was a primary school teacher herself and was aware that her son was having immense difficulty learning to read and write, although at that point he had not been identified as dyslexic. At 7 years of age he had a new teacher who was not sympathetic to his problems, he became very distressed and his behaviour at school deteriorated.

'It got to the stage where I heard myself saying as my little boy cried himself to sleep at night, "It's not long now" (to the end of term).'

He started wetting the bed, and came home shaking if he had a spelling test to revise for the following day. His bad behaviour at school was frequently reported to his mother.

'The problem was by then you couldn't see the wood for the trees because the behaviour problems had become paramount.'

Harry's mother suggested to the teacher that Harry's behaviour might partly be a response to a learning difficulty of some kind and was told

'Rubbish he's just very immature, when he learns to behave properly and knuckles down to the work he'll be OK.'

The following year when Harry was 8 years old he had a teacher who was more sympathetic in her outlook. She realised in conjunction with Harry's mother that something underlay the bad behaviour that he was displaying in class. By half-term she had identified him as dyslexic and appropriate support was set in place. From this point Harry's behaviour started to improve again.

Although a life history approach cannot be used in an empirical sense to 'prove' cause and effect it can suggest what might be happening and guide teachers and parents in checking out their suspicions or hunches. It can be argued that a life history approach is a useful adjunct to a curriculum based approach that focuses on the learning difficulties that a child is having at a specific point in time. Children bring to a learning situation their past experiences and expectations and by understanding these it is easier to get a wider picture of what might be happening. The problem for many teachers is that they don't automatically have access to a child's life history and what they do know may be second hand and filtered through the school's perceptions of the child's past experiences. Harry, for example, had an August birthday and therefore was a little immature for his year group. In addition some of the cognitive deficits underlying dyslexia such as problems with sequencing led to difficulties with tasks like tying up shoe laces which added to the picture of a somewhat immature child. The problem was that this was then used exclusively to account for his disruptive behaviour whereas a fuller picture which showed that he was reasonably well behaved in the infants and responded well to supportive and encouraging teaching would have suggested that immaturity alone was not a sufficient explanation for his behaviour. In addition his mother's reports of his specific difficulty with reading tasks and the distress that they were causing him would suggest that this area needed investigating.

Life history inevitably involves bias and self selection of what is presented and this can cause problems of validity and believing for both teachers and parents. This is made more difficult because they are observing children in totally different environments to which children may respond in different ways. Many of the parents in the study reported in this book and in other case studies said that their dyslexic child became quiet and withdrawn when they entered school. But this was often not noticed by the school because they had not seen the child before school or in the home environment so from the school's point of view the child's behaviour was normal and not a cause for concern. Again many parents reported that their child was showing distress at home as a direct consequence of going to school but it was difficult for the school to take this on board as the child was not showing this distress to a noticeable degree at school. The old adage 'seeing is believing' seems to apply and can perhaps explain some of the difficulty parents and especially teachers have in believing one another. The following is a typical account given by many parents on the difference in their child at school and at home.

> 'He became a withdrawn, frightened, timid child at school. But once he was at home he was completely different. He'd be full of confidence and happy once he was outside, playing with his motorbike.'
>
> (Osmond 1993)

Edwards (1994) documents in detail the lives of eight teenage boys attending a boarding school for children with dyslexia. In a sense it can be argued that these boys ended up in boarding school because they were extreme cases in terms of their reactions to mainsteam school, with all eight displaying behaviour problems and seven out of the eight truanting. Edwards points out that she originally chose these boys as examples of 'successful dyslexics' who'd developed well in their special school and was shocked herself when she started interviewing them to find the degree of pain and humiliation these boys still felt over their past experiences. They all felt they had been neglected, humiliated and teased in their mainstream schools and five of them felt they had been treated unfairly or punitively by teachers. In all eight cases this had led to lack of confidence, self doubt, and sensitivity to criticism and in five cases boys reported that at the worst points in their school career they had felt extremely isolated and despairing often wanting to hide or die. These same themes of distress and humiliation run through the interviews reported by Osmond and Van de Stoel and these sorts of experiences were not uncommon in the study to be described in this book. Whilst the degree and the range of such difficulties can be debated it is clear that how dyslexic children and their families cope with dyslexia is closely related to how such children are treated in school.

SUMMARY

1 Both quantitative and qualitative methods have a role to play in researching the social and emotional consequences of dyslexia.
2 For dyslexic children reading, writing and spelling are their primary problems but these can lead to secondary problems such as inattentiveness, low motivation, restlessness or disruptive behaviour.
3 Reading-disabled children do as a group have lower self-esteem than non reading-disabled children.
4 Teachers have a strong influence on a child's self-concept as a learner.
5 Systematic strategies can be employed to improve a child's self-esteem and self-concept as a learner.
6 Dyslexic children need specific help for their literacy difficulties allied to general help for their social and emotional well being.

Chapter 4

Introducing the study

'Phenomenology as a research approach attempts to study human experience as it is lived.'

(Layder 1989)

As has already been pointed out in this book there appears to be little systematic research on the social and emotional consequences of dyslexia despite the indications from personal accounts that some children and adults with dyslexia do experience such difficulties. One reason for this may be that social and emotional difficulties are more difficult to quantify and much might depend on the sensitivity of the measures used. Another reason which applies to many areas of special needs is that the majority of research is carried out by academics and educationalists. It can be argued that inevitably their own role and perspective influences the kinds of questions they choose to ask and the kind of research they carry out. From the perspective of school and cognitive psychology it is the difficulty in learning to read, write and spell that is probably most striking. In contrast children and parents are not generally in a position to carry out or inform academic research so issues of particular concern to them may not be adequately researched. Oliver (1981) has criticised much academic research on disability on these grounds and has argued for the need for the voices of disabled people to be heard so that they can set their own agenda in terms of the research that needs to be carried out. Having said this there has been a steady output of research which has looked at the day to day lives of individuals with special needs or disabilities. Burton (1975) for example investigated the family life of children with cystic fibrosis, Anderson, Clarke and Spain (1982) interviewed and assessed teenagers with cerebral palsy and spina bifida and Madge and Fassam (1982) in a book entitled *Ask the Children* interviewed children with a variety of physical disabilities about their lives both at home and at school and in both special and mainstream schools. Radical critics would argue that however sensitively done the researchers are still setting the agenda and deciding the kinds of questions that should be asked. In response to this sort of criticism case studies have been gathered where individuals have been allowed to speak for themselves and no set questions have been imposed upon them (Campling 1981). Whereas the studies by Burton, Anderson *et al.*, and Madge and Fassam all used a carefully selected representative sample more informal case studies such as those on dyslexia by Osmond (1993) and Van der Stoel (1990) have not employed a systematic sampling policy. These more informal studies are thus open to the criticism that the views of an un-representative sample are being heard. In the case of dyslexia it is often suggested that the views of middle class parents and their children predominate. Similarly the welter of evidence from clinical case studies, parents' letters and so on, on the social and emotional consequences of dyslexia are all open to the charge of unrepresentativeness. Another difficulty is that because many LEA's don't recognise dyslexia, it is only by parents taking the initiative to have their children assessed outside of the formal educational system that their children are identified. But again critics would claim that such parents are 'pushy, neurotic and over ambitious' and their views are not representative of parents as a whole. The problem has been that in quite rightly criticising the lack of representativeness, some critics have dismissed the evidence completely rather than seeing it as a starting point for more systematic research. As Riddell, Brown and Duffield (1994) found in their Scottish based survey of special needs obtaining a representative sample of children with dyslexia was easier said than done. They found that because many LEA's were critical of the term 'dyslexia', children had not been identified on this basis and it was therefore difficult to obtain a representative sample of such children. Only in a case where an LEA has a clear and comprehensive policy for identifying and supporting children with dyslexia is it possible to obtain a representative sample of children. The purpose of the present study was to investigate the currently more commonplace situation of children who are identified and supported either partly or entirely outside of the LEA system.

Although many opinions are offered by professionals (Riddick 1995a) as to why parents choose to call their children dyslexic, there appears to be no empirical research to back up their suppositions. One of the major aims of the present study was thus *to look closely at the process by which children are identified and labelled as having dyslexia.* Another related aim was *to gain a clear understanding of how living with dyslexia appears from the individual perspectives of children and their parents.* And a final aim was *to explore the possible social and emotional consequences of having dyslexia.*

The study involved interviewing 22 children and separately interviewing their mothers. In both cases a standardised semi-structured interview schedule was used. Madge and Fassam (1982) used a similar methodology to learn about the lives of physically disabled children and made the following comment on their use of a direct interview technique: 'First of all we found that valuable information on the attitudes, experiences and needs of physically disabled children can be gained from asking direct questions.'

Both Greenspan (1981) and Hodges (1993) consider that structured interviews can be used as a way of assessing the well being of children and adolescents. Greenspan argues that parents' and children's reports should not be looked upon as interchangeable and that ideally separate information should be obtained from both sources. Greenspan also asserts that children and adolescents can reliably self report and that the accuracy of this has been verified by checking children's accounts with information from someone who knows the child well. In the current study children ranged in age from 8 to 14 years. They all had a discrepancy of at least 2 years between their reading and/or spelling age and their chronological age or scored below the 5th percentile on the Wide Range Achievement Test (WRAT) reading and/or spelling test. All the children were assessed either by LEA educational psychologists or by chartered clinical psychologists. They all attended either the Newcastle or the Durham branch of the Dyslexia Institute for 1 or 2 hours of specialist tuition a week, usually out of school time. All the children attended mainstream school for their full time education. Ten were at junior school, one was at middle school and eleven were at lower secondary school. Children attended 20 different schools located in 6 different Local Education Authorities. The children were all white and of British origin which reflected the intake of the Dyslexia Institute and the predominantly white population of the north east. The high ratio of boys to girls again reflected the intake of the Dyslexia Institute and the ratio that is usually reported for individuals with dyslexia. Although research by Shaywitz *et al.* (1990) in the USA suggests that reading disabled girls are under identified. Of the 22 families 12 were classified as middle class and 10 were classified as working class. Three of the families were headed by a single parent mother and the children had no contact with their fathers. Children ranged in IQ on the Wechsler Intelligence Scale for Children from 92 to 128 with a mean of 110.

This sample was chosen to be as representative as possible of the children attending the Dyslexia Institute and was not intentionally biased in favour of any particular sub-group. Twenty-two out of the 23 families approached for the main part of the study agreed to take part. One mother refused, because although she was keen to be interviewed herself she felt that her son had been so distressed in the past by the difficulties he had associated with his dyslexia that he disliked talking about the subject and it was never directly discussed at home. As well as the three fatherless families, several fathers worked away from home for long periods of time (for example, in the navy or on oil rigs) and several more worked away from home for shorter periods of time (for example, on business). It was also the case that it was almost entirely mothers in this sample who brought their children to the Dyslexia Institute for sessions and they stated that their husbands, although generally concerned, had little day to day involvement in the issues surrounding their child's dyslexia. For these reasons mothers alone were interviewed although fathers were not specifically excluded, and their views were discussed during the interviews.

Table 4.1 Basic information on the main study sample of children with dyslexia at the time of their interview

Child	M/F	Age on interview	Age on assessment	Reading age	Spelling age	IQ WISC	School	Affected relative
DG	M	12.6	11.10	6.10	8	113	J	?
JK	M	9.11	10.7	WRAT 12%	WRAT 1%	92	J	YES
SH	M	8.5	7.7	5.9	5.7	105	J	YES
SW	F	13.9	13.5	10.0	WRAT 4%	100	S	?
RS	M	11.8	11.1	8.3	8.3	106	S	YES
HW	M	8.6	8.3	WRAT 1%	WRAT 7%	123	J	YES
								YES
AR	M	10.6	7.6	6.0	>5	128	J	YES
DSt	M	13.3	9.11	8.5	7.11	123	S	YES
DSl	M	11.11	9.9	6.6	6.5	95	J	YES
GS	M	11.3	10.6	9.2	8.4	120	J	YES
LS	M	13.11	12.5	10.0	8.9	avg*	S	YES
EB	M	13.2	11.10	6.9	>5	avg*	S	YES
EC	F	11.8	11.1	8.3	8.3	106	J	YES
MK	M	10.6	8.0	6.0	5.11	avg*	J	YES
MC	M	9.11	8.2	<5	5.10	92	J	YES
RT	M	11.5	10.6	8.11	8.6	avg*	S	NO
JA	M	13.1	10.0	7.0	7.0	119	S	NO
SH	M	11.9	9.9	7.9	7.0	106	S	YES
KP	M	12.4	10.5	7.9	–	126	S	YES
MF	F	11.9	11.1	6.8	8.2	107	S	YES
LA	F	12.0	11.2	9.1	9.0	105	S	YES
SS	M	14.3	11.2	8.9	7.8	113	S	YES

Notes: * Some psychologists preferred to give the band an IQ score fell into rather than a specific figure.
? under *Affected relatives* refers to two cases where there had been no contact with the child's father or family so this information was not known.

The information in table 4.1 is basic information that was collected on all the children. Detailed psychological reports itemising children's cognitive difficulties in more detail were available, but lack of space and confidentiality mean that only occasional points from these are included. The WISC–R (Wechsler Intelligence Scale for Children–Revised) is a popular assessment tool because as well as giving an overall IQ score it also gives separate Verbal and Performance IQ scores. These two areas in turn are made up of a number of sub-tests.

Peer (1994) claims that what is striking on tests like the WISC, the Binet and the BAS (British Ability Scales) is that children with dyslexia often show an uneven or 'spiky' profile. With the WISC each sub-test is given a

Table 4.2 Sub-tests of the WISC–R

Verbal		Performance	
Information	14	Picture completion	13
Comprehension	19	Picture arrangement	13
Arithmetic	10	Block design	17
Similarities	19	Object assembly	15
Vocabulary	13	Coding	10
Digit span	16	Mazes	17

scaled score out of 20, with 10 being an average score. A variety of profiles are found with the ACID profile being considered one of the most typical. In the ACID profile poor arithmetical, digit span, coding and information skills are found. These are attributed to the child's poor working memory and poor visuo-motor skills. High scores in other areas such as comprehension, similarities and block design suggest good abstract reasoning. RT, a child not included in the main sample, achieved the scores given with the sub-tests when tested at 7 years 2 days on the WISC–R. Interestingly he commented spontaneously that he had remembered the numbers in the digit span test by saying them in twos to himself. A strategy which is known to improve digit span performance! His mother also noted that at 5 years he still couldn't count to ten and at 7 he still didn't know his telephone number or his two times table which had been taught at school. This raises the question of whether RT used a compensatory strategy to improve his performance on the digit span test. It also illustrates the importance of pooling information from a number of sources and not making decisions on the basis of single test scores which can be influenced by a wide range of factors. Although RT ended up with a score on the border of the superior/very superior range, he was still unable to read and was seen by his teacher as rather slow. The question of different profiles is still an area for some debate but the general point is that uneven profiles like RT's do indicate marked areas of strength and weakness which may lead to puzzling school performance.

THE INTERVIEW SCHEDULE

Children, parents and teachers were talked to on an informal basis to ascertain major issues before the interview schedules were devised. Both specialist teachers and parents were consulted about the suitability of the content and arrangement of questions for the children's schedule. Greenspan (1981) on the basis of ten years' research claims that children can be interviewed about personal and emotive topics without any negative effects as long as the interviews are well conducted and take place within a supportive environment. The schedules were then piloted on five mother–children pairs before being used in the main part of the study. As one of the purposes of the study was to look at both the differences and similarities in the perspectives of children and mothers, questions were designed with this in mind. So, for example, both children and their mothers were asked a number of identical questions such as how would they explain dyslexia to someone else. In addition both children and mothers were asked questions that were specific to their role and perspective. Mothers, for example, were asked how they had first heard about dyslexia and what sort of personal support they tried to offer their children, whereas children were asked questions about whether they thought other children noticed their difficulties and, if so, did they try to explain them. A mixture of open ended, fixed alternative, factual and scaled questions were asked. The purpose was to obtain qualitative data, backed up by some simple descriptive and quantitative information. So, for example, mothers were asked, 'In general how do you feel at the moment about (child's name) having dyslexia?' They were also asked fixed alternative questions such as, 'What influence, if any, do you think being dyslexic has had on (child's name)?' 'None/some/a lot.' Probes were also added so that qualitative information could also be obtained from questions like these, but these were rarely needed as most respondents spontaneously explained their choice of category. By having a mixture of questions simple cross checking of information was possible. Miles and Huberman (1984) suggest that simple forms of counting are a useful way of checking that qualitative data is being represented and interpreted as accurately as possible. Validity was also checked by triangulation between teachers, parents and children's responses and by comparing information with that available from reports and documents. Mothers were asked a total of 36 questions, covering early development, identification, support at home and at school, specialist support, effects on the child and family, and expectations for the future. Children were asked 28 major questions covering home life, difficulties related to dyslexia, support at home, school and Dyslexia Institute, views on dyslexia and how they thought other children viewed their problems. (See appendix for the full parent and children's interview schedule). Whenever data is presented giving the number or proportion of children or mothers who reported a certain thing this is always from this main study. Most of the quotes used to illustrate these figures are also from this main study.

Parents gave their permission for access to educational and psychological reports and assessments. Because these were of a confidential nature they have not been directly quoted from but have been used to provide background information. The names of all the children and parents have been changed to protect their identity. Several mothers said that they were quite happy to be named and to stand by the views they had expressed but it was thought best to have an overall policy of anonymity for all those who participated. For similar reasons schools, LEAs and teachers have not been named and where necessary names have been changed.

Table 4.3 Interviewees

	Semi-structured interviews
Children (aged 8 to 16 years)	24
Mothers	24
Specialist teachers	5

In addition to information from this main study qualitative information from other interviews is also included. All five teachers at the Dyslexia Institute the children attended were interviewed and some of their views are reported where they are relevant to general issues about 'living with dyslexia'. Two children in their mid-teens and their mothers were interviewed in a later study. The same basic interview schedule was used but an additional section on subjects such as exams and technology was added. These two children had also attended the Dyslexia Institute and had been identified and assessed in a similar manner to the main study. In total data from 53 semi-structured interviews is included.

A small amount of information from informal interviews with class teachers and educational psychologists has been included when it has been of particular relevance to a specific child or issue. In an ongoing study at the University of Northumbria students with dyslexia have been interviewed and assessed on a number of measures including self-esteem, anxiety, writing performance and educational performance. This data will be published at a later date but occasional points of relevance have been included. Similarly qualitative information from students and adults during assessment for dyslexia has been included. Data on another child, RT, who has been followed for a number of years and for this reason was not included in the main study is also occasionally given.

Chapter 5

Early indicators

'I just knew something was wrong but I didn't know what it was.'
(Mother of 5-year-old boy with dyslexia)

Given the controversy over dyslexia and the many informal explanations given by professionals as to why parents call their children dyslexic (Riddick 1995a) an important part of the study was to look in detail at how and why parents came to identify their children as dyslexic. As with many disabilities that do not have easily identifiable physical markers it appears that the process by which parents do this is often a gradual one that takes place over a period of time. In order to try and follow this process a roughly chronological perspective was followed in asking questions (see appendix for the full parental questionnaire) and in presenting the information a roughly chronological framework has been used. In order to give a coherent explanation to some questions mothers would shift between the past, present and future and in presenting the evidence maintaining this has sometimes been necessary. Where possible the information has also been placed within the context of other research on identifying both dyslexia and special needs in general.

RELATIVES WITH DYSLEXIA

As a prelude to asking about early indicators, parents were asked if any close family members had dyslexia or similar problems. As has already been discussed in chapter 1 there is strong evidence that a predisposition to phonological difficulties and subsequent dyslexia is inherited in something like 80 per cent of cases (De Fries 1991). This is an active area of research, so these figures are best viewed as provisional and open to future revision, but the principle of high heritability does raise some important questions about its significance in identifying dyslexia. If, for example, a parent has been identified as dyslexic does this mean that the family are more likely to identify any of their children who have similar problems at an early age? In a similar vein does this information on heritability alert professionals to the increased risk of reading and spelling disorders that some children run.

Table 5.1 A close relative with dyslexia or similar problem (n = 22)

Yes	18
No	2
Not known	2*

* Two mothers were single parents who had had no contact with their child's biological father or family since the child's birth.

Finally what is the personal significance for children with dyslexia of having an adult relative and especially a parent who is dyslexic? This last issue will be examined in more detail in chapter 11 on personal support. In response to the general question about family members with dyslexia or similar problems the following information was given.

In six cases a father and in five cases a mother of a dyslexic child were claimed to be dyslexic or to have had similar difficulties. Thus 50 per cent of children were being brought up in families where one parent was thought to have had similar problems as a child. In some cases several members of a family were identified as having reading and spelling difficulties. Uncles, aunts, cousins and siblings of the dyslexic child were all mentioned several times. This evidence is not being offered in a strictly empirical sense as most of it is inferential, but it does offer some insight into the way that lay people characterise and identify difficulties. In seventeen out of the eighteen cases the adult was only identified as possibly dyslexic after the related child was formally identified as dyslexic. In two cases mothers had been formally assessed after their children were identified and in both cases they were confirmed as dyslexic. In the rest of the cases more informal evidence was offered. Where mothers thought that their husbands had had similar difficulties they would often recount that their husband had hated school, had not learnt to read until late and was still an appalling speller.

'His dad can't spell and he had a lot of problems in school. He hated school from day one, you know, and he can understand how he really feels. Sarah, his sister, had extra reading in junior school and her spelling is still very poor.'

'My younger brother had severe spelling and writing difficulties at Harry's age (8 years) and became a truant.'

'His dad really. His spelling is dreadful. He didn't get any exams at school.'

'I think my brother had a problem. But obviously it was never detected. He had difficulty with reading, but basically it's his spelling. It's atrocious.'

'My husband has terrible spelling. He was ten before he learnt to read. He hated school and he left the moment he could.'

Two wives mentioned that their husbands had changed jobs specifically because of their literacy difficulties and another wife said she did her husband's paperwork because of his literacy difficulties. In some cases the husband's difficulties were openly discussed and acknowledged at home but in other cases although wives had strong suspicions, their husbands did not openly acknowledge their problems. Mothers with dyslexia spoke quite openly about their own difficulties and recalled specific examples of the kinds of difficulties they encountered in school.

'I had great problems from that (copying off the board) at school. I can remember everybody else going out to play and I was still sitting there copying it down and I think that's something they don't realise.'

Mrs Harding also recalled similar difficulties with copying off the board.

'Oh it was horrific. I'd get the wrong line down, then I'd score it out.'

She recounted her own difficulties in writing letters to her husband in the forces and her determination to improve her spelling and writing. At school she had acted the class clown and tried to cover up her difficulties with reading and writing as much as possible.

'I bluffed my way through school cos you couldn't dare admit you couldn't do it. I'd love to get myself assessed. It's not because you've got nothing upstairs. If I've got a form to fill in I always take it home and do it. But I find I'm getting a bit better. I build on what I've got.'

So for half the families in this sample, although the term 'dyslexia' had not been used in the past, at least one parent had experienced similar difficulties and in all these cases spelling was still considered to be a problem. In many cases mothers spoke of dyslexia in a way that implied that they saw it as on a continuum. Mrs Street who had a dyslexic son and had been identified as dyslexic herself also commented on her daughter's difficulties.

'My daughter has difficulty with spelling. I'd say she's slightly dyslexic.'

'Her middle sister has slight reading and spelling problems but the other two are OK.'

'Well, I'm a weak speller and Emily, that's his younger sister, has weak spelling compared to her other abilities.'

Mothers thus appeared to distinguish between siblings who had no problems, siblings with slight problems and siblings with severe problems. There was also some concern over whether younger siblings were going to have the same difficulties especially if they appeared to be following a similar developmental pattern. In considering identification it would therefore seem important to recognise that in a substantial proportion of families this doesn't take place on a 'blank canvas' but against a background of experience of similar difficulties. None of the parents knew about the heritability of such difficulties before their child was identified as dyslexic so this experience was not explicitly used by families to help identify their child as dyslexic.

EARLY SPEECH DELAY AND DIFFICULTIES

Orton (1937) claimed that speech delay and stuttering were more common than usual in a sample of dyslexic individuals examined by him. Clark (1970) carried out an extensive 3 stage survey of 1554 primary age children born within a 5 month period in Dumbarton in Scotland. At 9 years of age 19 children were identified as being two or more years behind in their reading despite having average or above average intelligence. In this group of severely reading disabled children language difficulties were common with articulatory and auditory discrimination difficulties being the most typical. The Isle of Wight study (Rutter *et al.* 1976) found that speech milestones were more commonly delayed in children with specific reading retardation. Snowling (1987) and Stackhouse (1990) both present evidence to support the claim that dyslexia should be viewed as a type of speech and language disorder. They both consider that whereas some dyslexic children present with obvious and specific language difficulties in their earlier years, for others the difficulties are more subtle and difficult to identify. At present the degree of overlap between children with speech and language disorders and children with reading and spelling problems is not clear. Stackhouse (1991) says

> It would be wrong to suggest that all children with reading and spelling problems have a speech and language disorder and it would be equally wrong to give the impression that all children with speech and language problems will also have a specific learning difficulty.

She goes on to suggest that the children who are most at risk of having reading and spelling problems are either those with developmental vocal dyspraxia (difficulty in saying words despite no obvious physical impairment) or those with phonological disorders who have difficulties contrasting sounds in order to distinguish between spoken words. This was of relevance to the present study because 7 out of the 22 mothers said that their child had some form of early language difficulty.

Mothers were asked two major questions about early identification. One question centred on when they first became aware there was a problem and what the nature of the problem was, the other on their child's development prior to them being aware there was a problem. So the second question (2a) specifically asked,

> Looking back were there any earlier signs that (child's name) might have difficulties?

Table 5.2 Mothers' recall of early developmental problems which with hindsight they think relate to dyslexia

Developmental problem	n = 22
Difficulties learning days of week/months of year	13
Clumsy	9
Late learning to ride a bike or swim	8
Difficulties learning nursery rhymes	7
Difficulties learning the alphabet	7
Late talker	7
Poor at remembering instructions	4

This question was basically asking mothers with the benefit of hindsight if they could identify any earlier difficulties that they thought had a bearing on the specific reading difficulties that they all identified as the first real problem that their child encountered at school.

As can be seen from table 5.2 a simple head count was made of the different difficulties mentioned by mothers. Most of these mothers were being asked to recall their child's development from several years previously and it therefore seems likely that these figures might be an underestimate rather than an overestimate. Alternatively it could be the case that people unconsciously add information that fits a certain picture. But evidence such as early reports and the fact that 4 out of the 7 children claimed to have early language delay and did in fact receive speech therapy, would suggest some degree of accuracy in mothers' recall.

> 'Well first of all he didn't start talking until he was two and a half, and then he went to speech therapy for six years. Because he had problems with his pronunciation and his fluency.'

> 'He was very late talking. He must have been two and three quarters before he was putting a sentence together.'

> 'She wasn't talking at two, apart from a few simple words like "mum" and "dad". We put it down to all the ear infections she'd had.'

> 'He only had a few single words by two and his speech was never very clear, so then he had speech therapy.'

This evidence is not being presented as strict empirical evidence but simply to suggest that parents can identify a range of impairments before they formally recognise that their child is having difficulty learning to read and write. This evidence also fits well with more empirical evidence on a range of early difficulties. Clark (1970) in the previously mentioned study found that as well as many of the 19 severely reading disabled children having specific language difficulties a number of them also had difficulties in the visual motor sphere. Clark also pointed out that the configuration of difficulties varied from child to child and that no set pattern could be identified. Fawcett and Nicolson (1994), whilst acknowledging the importance of the relationship between phonological deficits and dyslexia, argue that we might be premature in simply identifying one specific deficit and that this in turn may be the outcome of more general processing deficits that affect a number of skills, or may be only one of a number of deficits. They go on to suggest that a more 'ethological' approach which looks at the kind of difficulties that children display on a day to day basis is an important adjunct to more empirical research. 'Those who have round the clock experience of living with dyslexic children often form a very different view of their skills than do researchers who see them only for a brief testing period.'

They also point out that in Augur's (1985) summary of the kinds of difficulties mentioned by parents as well as language difficulties, motor difficulties were common. In the present study it can be seen that although language difficulties are the most frequently mentioned a significant number of children are also thought to have had motor difficulties in their early years.

> 'He was clumsy, very clumsy. He used to fall off chairs and things. We used to laugh about it, but looking back at it, it was probably symptomatic somehow. It was just one of those things, he was a clumsy child, couldn't learn to ride a bike and things like that . . . Couldn't clap in time or remember his nursery rhymes.'

Whereas some children were described as having a whole range of difficulties in other cases mothers were quite emphatic about the kinds of difficulties their child did not have.

> 'He couldn't learn the alphabet, couldn't learn days of the week, his tables he still doesn't know (age 12) and just very poor short-term memory, but he's always been very well co-ordinated.'

> 'He had a good memory for some things, but nursery rhymes and things like that he couldn't do.'

> 'It took a long time for him to learn to ride a bike. He spoke pretty quickly, everything like that. The main thing I found with David, if you asked him to do something, to go and fetch something, he'd come back and say, "What did you want?" I could never train him to do that . . . He would get mixed up with the days of the week and say, "Thursday, Wednesday," but he was able to tell the time very quickly.'

> 'He was laid back in everything. He was late walking, late talking. He'd choose the shortest way to say anything.'

Apart from those children who had severe language difficulties, parents didn't appear to view their children's pre-school impairments as a major problem or an indicator of future difficulty. Within the context of the family it appears that most of these impairments were easily accommodated and were not in themselves generally a cause for serious concern. Two mothers for example in recalling that their children had never learnt nursery rhymes said that at the time they had simply attributed this to their children not being interested in nursery rhymes. In general these early impairments were accommodated by parents in terms of individual differences in development both in terms of age and range. Only two mothers out of the 22 thought that even with hindsight there were no pre-reading indicators that their child might have a problem.

'Really he didn't have any problems, he was fine. It was really the actual reading he got so frustrated on.'

Again this evidence is not being offered in a strictly empirical sense because mothers will vary in their recall of difficulties and also in what is perceived as a difficulty. Even with easily quantifiable behaviours such as the number of times a baby wakes up at night (Scott and Richards 1988) mothers vary in their perception of whether this is a problem or not. What is important is that as well as being in line with other parental accounts and the more empirical evidence, it suggests that mothers can with hindsight identify a range of early impairments but they did not treat these at the time as serious long term indicators of future problems. In the cases of the children who were described as having the more severe and widespread impairments mothers saw them as immature and hoped they would catch up. Parents whose children had speech delay felt that far from alerting them that their child might have future difficulties with literacy, this tended to confuse the issue and hold up their realisation. So speech delay or problems were often seen as an explanation by mothers for their children's slow progress in learning to read and write. Mrs Thompson described this process clearly:

'And it was while he was attending speech therapy. I was becoming aware that there were problems with what he was doing at school. But of course he was in the Junior school when I started doing something about it, and really it was because he had speech problems I had put a lot of it down to his speech problems, and I thought if he matures and his speech gets better, he'll grow out of it.'

It was not suggested to any of these mothers by either clinical or educational professionals that their child might be at increased risk of having a specific reading or writing difficulty. As these children were identified no sooner than the other children in the sample it appears that their speech difficulty was not alerting professionals to the increased risk of a reading difficulty.

Mothers whose children had other kinds of early difficulties, most commonly intermittent hearing problems, also said that this tended to delay their realisation that their child had a long term reading and writing problem and not just a temporary delay caused by the difficulty. Mrs Slatter, for example, fell into this group. Her son Dean had been diagnosed as having a hearing problem at the age of 6 years and had also missed quite a lot of schooling during the Infants because of two operations. Mrs Slatter also felt that others used this as an explanation for Dean's literacy problems.

'A lot of people reckon it's the operations he had in a short space of time.'

It may well be that these factors contributed to Dean's difficulties, but his mother felt that the problem was that these were used as a total explanation and it was assumed that Dean would catch up, without the need for any specific help.

Many of the mothers in this sample stressed that their child was basically happy and well adjusted before they went to school. None of the mothers in this sample thought that their child was particularly difficult or anxious before they went to school, nor did any of the mothers describe themselves as particularly anxious about how their child would cope with school. A few of the mothers whose children had the most extensive difficulties seemed to have some inkling that all might not be well but the majority were surprised by the difficulties their children encountered in school. An issue relating to identification that several mothers brought up was the birth order of their child. In this study there were 10 first-born children, 11 second-born and one third-born. Several mothers of first-born children felt that this held up their realisation that there was a problem because there was nothing to compare their child with.

'But the trouble is when it is your first child, there's nothing to judge it against.'

Whereas mothers of second- or later-born children were aware of the differences many stressed that they held back or avoided making negative comparisons if they could on the grounds that each child was different and they didn't want to prejudice their later child's development by having a negative view of them.

'I was very aware I had a daughter first. I didn't want to compare him . . . not to put pressure on him because she had done it.'

Despite this, mothers of second- or later-born children did feel that the differences they could see did help to alert them to the difficulties that their younger child was having.

'He didn't recognise words in books that his older brothers had.'

'At two, three and four he didn't do any of the things that Emma (older sister) did.'

MOTHERS' ASSESSMENT OF CHILDREN'S INTELLECT

An important question that arises from this evidence is that if mothers are aware of these various impairments how did they relate these to their child's overall level of intellectual functioning? To examine this issue mothers were asked to answer 'yes' or 'no' to the question:

Did you always feel that (child's name) was as intelligent as other children?

If they answered 'yes' to this question they were also asked:

Can you give me some examples of what convinced you of (child's name) intelligence?

Out of the 22 mothers 18 said that they had always thought that their child was as intelligent as other children and 4 said that they had had their doubts. The results were a little more complex than they first appear. Mothers for example who said they had their doubts varied considerably in the expressed degree of these. One mother for example said:

'I had fleeting doubts when he was a toddler.'

whereas another commented:

'You do begin to doubt, maybe he isn't very bright. You think, well, we've both got degrees, maybe your expectations of the child are quite high, maybe it isn't fair.'

Several of the mothers who said 'yes' to this question felt that although they had no doubts about their child's intelligence during the pre-school period they did later begin to wonder if they were right because of their child's lack of progress in learning to read and write and the lack of a satisfactory alternative explanation for their child's difficulties, combined with their perception that the school saw their child as a slow learner.

'You do tend to believe the professionals. You think, perhaps I'm wrong. Perhaps he is thick.'

Out of the 22 mothers 18 gave specific examples of the sort of qualities that convinced them that their child was as intelligent as other children.

'He was quite logical. He would ask logical questions and he would reason things out. We would give him a box of Lego, and, I mean, the constructions! They used to be absolutely magnificent. So there was no reason why he shouldn't be able to read and write. Up till then, till he was four and a half, he was just the same, you know, as the other children, because I was working with children of that age.'

Mrs Kerslake in the above quote was typical of the many mothers who were surprised when their child had difficulty learning to read and write. Mark had walked and talked at the normal time, although looking back, with hindsight, he did have difficulty learning the alphabet and days of the week. Mrs Kerslake reported that her husband, who was now a mechanic, had not learnt to read until he was 10 and still had very poor spelling.

Mrs Philips said that her daughter Katy had been 'a bit clumsy' and was not talking at two, but they had put this down to her having a lot of ear infections.

'But she was very perceptive. We had this plan for this new sink, none of us could work it out she was the one who spotted the mistake. That's typical of her. She's good at hypothetical thinking.'

Katy was one of four children, so her mother could compare her development with her brothers and sisters. Mrs Falkner also commented on her daughter's thinking skills.

'Just that she took things in quite easily. She was quick on the uptake. Any games that you played, she seemed to be there, as long as it didn't involve any reading or that sort of thing.'

As well as stressing children's good thinking skills several mothers also commented on their children's good language skills. This may seem more surprising given the evidence on dyslexic children's poor phonological and word finding skills. It could be that these are the children who are least affected by these kinds of deficits or that because of the specific nature of these deficits, children can still have strengths in other aspects of language use. One mother, for example, whose son was very late talking commented on how her son used words in the right context.

'He had a good vocabulary and he used words in context. If we went anywhere he was a sponge for information and he could remember it well.'

'He could talk non stop. He had very good language skills. His vocabulary was good. He was just a bright normal child.'

Two mothers said that in confidence they thought that if anything their dyslexic child was brighter than their non-dyslexic sibling.

'Oh it was just his use of vocabulary, it was more advanced than his brother. In fact I'd go as far as to say, I know you shouldn't compare brothers, but he always seemed to be that bit further on than Michael.'

Mrs Roberts' son received an IQ score in the superior range on the WISC which would add support to her observations.

A simple count was made of the qualities mentioned by mothers and for convenience these qualities have been listed under three main headings, although these headings are somewhat arbitrary and some items could be placed under more than one heading.

Good abstract reasoning

good at reasoning things out	2
picks things up easily	2
good hypothetical thinker	1
very perceptive	1
asks logical questions	1
comes out with intelligent things	1
intelligent answers to questions	1
understands explanations	1
understands games easily	1

Good memory and language skills

good vocabulary	4
uses words well in context	2
oral skills ahead	2
good at discussion	1
good long term memory	3

Intelligent practical skills and interest in learning

good at lego	2
very sensible	1
keen for information	2
keen to do things	1

The nature of intelligence and how it should be defined and assessed is still an area open to debate. There isn't sufficient space in this book to go into this in any detail. Good contemporary reviews are provided by Richardson (1991) in Britain and Sternberg (1990) in the USA. Richardson picks up on Binet's view that intelligence is about 'good judgement' which is based on good high order reasoning skills. Sternberg takes a more pragmatic view of intelligence and defines it as the ability to cope effectively with one's environment although he again would see good reasoning skills as an important part of this. Traditional standardised IQ tests for children such as the Binet and the Wechsler Intelligence Scale for children include a number of items intended to test reasoning skills and language and memory skills. Sternberg et al. (1981) has researched and reviewed both lay people's and experts' views of intelligence. He found that there was basically good agreement between lay people and experts on what constituted intelligence. The evidence here would suggest that mothers are using the kinds of categories that most professionals would consider appropriate in judging a child's intelligence. It could be argued that although they are using appropriate categories they are wrong in their judgements of how well their child is performing relative to other children within these various categories. There is no way, as this is retrospective evidence, of directly testing this. But the fact that all the children in this sample had average to above average intelligence would suggest that these mothers were making reasonable judgements. In summary, it appears that mothers generally felt quite strongly that their child was basically as intelligent as other children. None of these mothers were suggesting that their child was exceptionally intelligent, they were simply saying that their child was as intelligent as other children and that lack of intelligence did not seem to be a viable explanation in their view for their child's subsequent difficulty in learning to read and write. The majority of mothers recognised at the time or with hindsight that their child had certain specific difficulties or impairments but they felt that there was sufficient evidence to believe that their child was fundamentally intelligent.

WHEN WERE PROBLEMS FIRST SPOTTED, AND BY WHOM?

Mothers were asked how old their child was when they first became aware that their child might have problems. They were also asked if they or someone else was the first person to spot the problem and what kind of problems their child displayed. As has been suggested before recognising that your child has a problem is often a gradual process. Children ranged in age from 4 to 7 years when their mothers first thought there was a problem. The average age was five and a quarter, although this included one child whose aunt was head of a teacher training college and had two dyslexic sons of her own, so he was identified particularly early through this connection. If this child is excluded the average age for first suspecting there was a problem was around five and a half years. One mother thought that her four-year-old son was going to have problems because he didn't display any of the pre-reading skills that his two older brothers had displayed. Apart from these two cases the other twenty mothers all felt that their awareness that there was a problem was closely tied to their child's formal education and particularly the introduction of pre-reading or reading activities at school. Even so most of these mothers said there was a gradual building up of suspicion, with them trying where possible to give their child the benefit of the doubt. One mother said, for example, that her suspicions gradually built up over a two year period from when her child was 4 to 6 years old, but that she had made excuses for him not beginning to learn to read because he had an August birthday and she had therefore put his lack of progress down to immaturity.

'I just knew he didn't fit into any normal category. He had a lot of the characteristics of a slow learner, but he certainly wasn't a slow learner. He broke every Frank Smith* rule in the book, he couldn't remember from one day to the next, and in the end I did what a lot of other mothers of dyslexic children have done, I threw the reading book across the room.' [* Smith is a psycholinguist who has a strong influence on many teachers' approach to reading.]

These difficulties were accompanied by her son showing severe distress at home and considerable behaviour problems at school. This mother was an experienced primary school teacher, but she was mystified by her son's difficulties.

'I kept saying to my husband, "I wish someone could tell me what is wrong with this child."'

Several mothers said that initially, although they knew something was wrong, they couldn't put their finger on what it was.

'I just knew something was wrong, but I didn't know what it was.'

'I mean as soon as he started school I knew something was wrong because from being a bright little boy he started getting quieter and quieter and I knew there was something wrong at school. And I would go in and say, "How's Josh doing", and it was just a bit slow, you know. He's young for his age and so on. And I just couldn't get through to anyone that he'd changed, that he'd got a problem, that he wasn't dim.'

In response to the question about what kind of indicator first alerted them to their child's difficulties, 80 per cent of mothers said it was their child failing to learn to read and the remaining 20 per cent said it was the fact that their child was failing to keep up or was making slow or no progress.

'She had been at school two years and she could only string about four words together and even then she had difficulty . . . she couldn't read at all, basically.'

'I noticed he would never read, they bring this book home and he never wanted to read it. I mentioned it at school. The teacher said, "Oh, he's very bright it'll come." That sort of put it off.'

'Well he didn't seem to have any problem before he went to school, it was when he got to school he had these problems. Definitely by the second year I knew there was a problem. He obviously looked under so much pressure, his body language and that, he looked pale and agitated and he couldn't tell what it was. I could tell he wasn't learning to read and things very quickly, but then again I didn't want to be too pushy. Because I knew too many people who were always going up, and you think, "Hold on he'll do it, he'll learn and then he didn't."'

'She became withdrawn and quiet at school; at home she was babyish and clinging, she seemed miserable a lot of the time. She brought her troubles home with her. She dreaded going to school.'

Another mother whose son had to be dragged screaming to the infants every day commented,

'I thought there was no hope when he was in the infants.'

What emerged was that for many mothers their concern was largely contingent upon their child's response to not learning to read. Out of the 22 mothers, 17 said that their children became stressed and unhappy during their time at infant school because of the problems they were having with their academic work. Mothers saw this as a problem that arose specifically from the demands and expectations of school and not one that emerged from their own expectations. Others, such as educationalists, may argue with the validity of parents' views, but there was no evidence at a qualitative level that these parents were any different in their range of views and expectations to other parents. It was also the case that 18 of these parents had other non-dyslexic children who were progressing through school without any dispute or difficulty. One mother, for example, said that she fully accepted that her older non-dyslexic son was not at all academic and she had taken his relatively poor performance at school quite philosophically. Only two mothers in this sample reported that disruptive behaviour at school was an early indicator of their child's problems. The majority of mothers reported that their children became quiet and withdrawn at school and expressed much of their unhappiness at home. Many mothers reported an increase in temper tantrums, nervous habits such as stuttering, insomnia and bed wetting and increased crying and reluctance to go to school.

'He used to burst into tears for the least little thing, and he used to have these temper tantrums in sheer frustration. In fact he often said, "Do I have to go to school?" '

This was not a particularly extreme example and Mrs Roberts and her son Adam were seen by others as calm sensible people and Adam behaved well in school. Despite this, Mrs Roberts said she had difficulty when she broached the subject of Adam's problems with his teacher.

'Well, she said I was being a bit neurotic, and it was a question of he wouldn't do any reading and he wouldn't do any writing, and I said, "Do you not think the word is 'can't' " and she says, "No, I don't!" '

What seemed to be happening was one of two things, either children displayed different behaviour at school and at home and this therefore gave parents and teachers different perspectives or children displayed troubled behaviour at school which was interpreted differently by teachers and parents. In both cases it can be argued that the validity of parents' views was being denied or disputed.

The specialist teachers at the Dyslexia Institute were also interviewed about their perception of parents, among other issues. They had all previously been classroom teachers in mainstream schools, and felt that since working in a situation where they had a lot more individual contact with parents they had become much more likely to believe in the validity of what parents told them. One teacher, for example, said that her father had also been a teacher and that she felt she was brought up in a teaching culture where blaming parents was the norm.

LEARNING TO READ

These concerns of mothers were heavily reinforced by their experiences of helping to teach their children to read. Out of the 22 schools 19 had a school reading scheme which involved children bringing home books to read to their parents. The most common word used to describe this experience by mothers was 'traumatic'.

'Over the years it was terrible, it was traumatic. They just don't want to read books.'

Mrs Thompson similarly mentioned that the main difficulty was in getting her son to even start reading a book.

'And if there was a problem, it was just to get Ryan to read a book. You see, you try all the different approaches, the calm laid back approach, the forceful approach, you try everything and nothing works.'

Mrs Andrews when asked about teaching her son to read simply said

'I tried, and tried and tried and tried.'

Mrs Falkner experienced similar problems with her daughter Mandy.

'Oh, hated it. Mention reading a book and there where tears and all sorts. And I mean, even though the teachers kept saying you must get her to read, I'd say you try and get her to read, because she's not interested.'

Mrs Hansen's rueful comment on the school's paired reading scheme was

'I've read lots of books he hasn't.'

Other mothers found that their children became over dependent on the pictures that accompany the words.

'He didn't even use to bother to look at the words. He knew he hadn't got a hope in hell of getting them right. He just used to look at the picture and work out the best thing to say. He was quite good at that! He often didn't say anything like the number of words on the page and he didn't even use to start words with the right letter. That went on for years.'

All these mothers had other children who had learnt to read quite easily using these methods so it seems highly unlikely that failure could be attributed to the particular approach taken by mothers. Several mothers mentioned the frustration of finding that their child frequently couldn't remember a simple word that they had read only a line or two before or that they persistently muddled up words like 'was' and 'saw' and often omitted simple words like 'and' and 'the' or constantly failed to put endings like '-ed' and '-ing' on words. Whilst many early readers make these kinds of errors it was the frequency and persistence with which errors were made that mothers noticed combined with their child's obvious dislike of reading.

'It took her about three years to learn to recognise the word "said". I thought she was never going to do it!'

Osmond (1993) in his interviews came across similar experiences,

'He'd bring reading work home from school and we'd try and read it with him. But it was an impossible excercise. One word he'd read correctly on one line, but it would be wrong on the next. They'd be simple words like "and" and "the". It was such misery for him, absolute misery. There was no joy in it, no success for him and as a result it was a kind of nightmare.'

Mothers thus found themselves in the difficult position of being expected by the school to listen to their child read when their child was extremely reluctant to do so and found it a very difficult task to do. Many of the mothers asked the school for specific advice on how to help their children, but only 2 out of the 22 mothers said they were given any advice over and above the general advice given to all parents on listening to their children read.

There isn't sufficient room in this book to go into the considerable debate over the teaching of reading and the attendant role of reading schemes. Critics of reading schemes such as Smith (1988) and Meek (1982) have emphasised the importance of 'real books' in the teaching of reading. Turner (1990) has countered by criticising the over dependence on a real books approach and claims that this has led to a decline in reading standards. Bryant (1994) suggests that children need both a real books and a phonetics approach and that the two approaches are best seen as complementary to each other rather than in opposition to each other. The theoretical underpinning for these two approaches comes from the wider debate over whether children are best taught to read using a top down or bottom up approach. The top down approach has been heavily influenced by psycholinguists such as Frank Smith (1988) and emphasises the importance of learning to read through reading for meaning with the use of 'real' books. The bottom up approach argues that complex skills such as reading need to be broken down into their component sub-skills and that children need to progress from the simple to the complex with the use, for example, of graduated reading schemes and the systematic teaching of phonics. Pumfrey and Reason (1991) like Bryant argue that both approaches are necessary and that the needs of individual children are probably best met by differing combinations of these two approaches. Pumfrey (1990b) in a small scale survey of teachers' practice found that most used a mixture of methods and didn't stick rigidly to just one approach. Whether a real books or a reading scheme approach or a mixture of the two is employed difficulties can arise at the early stages where some critics claim there is insufficient linkage between early reading skills such as phonics and the task of being expected to read a simple book. Some reading schemes pay more attention to phonics than others but the experiences of many of these children suggests that they had insufficient skills to progress through the reading scheme at the expected rate and that many of them were left floundering.

KEY FACTORS FROM EARLY IDENTIFICATION

Before drawing some general points from the study sample, some provisos need to be added. Although the results may be representative of parents who identify their children as dyslexic, they may not be applicable to the same degree to all children with such difficulties. These parents may be:

1 More conscientious and alert to difficulties than other parents.
2 Better informed about the nature of such difficulties.
3 A higher proportion may have similar difficulties themselves.
4 Children may have been more likely to attend schools with an approach to reading that exacerbated their particular difficulties.

Within the constraints of these provisos there did appear to be evidence that many of these children had a number of early indicators that they were at increased risk of reading delay or dyslexia. Whilst all these indicators were observable by parents they only became aware of the significance of them once they were familiar with the concept of dyslexia. The most obvious of these were

1 Relative/s with a similar problem
2 Early speech delay or difficulty with no obvious physical cause.
3 Difficulty with verbal sequencing, e.g. alphabet, days of the week etc.
4 Clumsy or slow to learn to ride a bike, swim, tie up shoe laces etc.
5 Difficulty learning nursery rhymes.
6 Poor short term memory, e.g. poor at remembering new names, messages etc.
7 Shows little interest in identifying letters or words for fun.
8 Dislikes and/or is very poor at reading books sent home from school.

There was no evidence at a qualitative level that parents were unrealistic or over ambitious about their children's early development, if anything they appeared to tolerate quite significant delays in certain aspects of their children's development before expressing concern. In a study carried out in the USA (Chen and Uttal 1988) mothers of first grade children said they would only be concerned if their child's performance was close to one standard deviation below the average. Research carried out in the Grampian region of Scotland (Booth 1988) found that 85 per cent of parents whose children had specific learning difficulties were accurate in their perceptions of their children's learning difficulties. Pumfrey and Reason (1991) also found that parents were generally quite realistic in their expectations of how their children would progress. In other areas of special needs such as hearing impairment, parents have been found to be highly reliable in their judgement that their child has a hearing problem (Webster and Ellwood 1985). Webster and Ellwood suggest that, 'a parent's worries should always be taken seriously and as often as not are found to be justified'. Although it can be argued that hearing impairment is a different type of special need to dyslexia, parallels can be found in the difficulties that some parents have in getting their child's problem recognised. Particularly in the past some parents of hearing impaired children were told that they were over anxious and imagining difficulties or that the child would grow out of their difficulties. Even with a relatively easily identifiable condition like hearing loss, it is only in the last twenty years that there has been a shift towards seeing parents as reliable detectors of difficulties.

Given the present interest in developing early screening tests for dyslexia it would seem both desirable and feasible that information from parents be used either to supplement screening or to alert professionals to children at increased risk of such difficulties. Questions based on the eight areas of difficulty noted by parents could be asked either in a verbal or written form. Many reception classes collect information on children in the form of 'All about me' booklets, it might be possible for example to collect the information as an adjunct to this, thus minimising both time and expense. Such information would need to be treated with caution and common sense, but it could alert teachers to some high risk children and suggest children they would want to keep a close eye on or talk to parents in more detail about. Screening always raises problems of false positives and negatives and when based on parents' observations alone issues of reliability are also raised. But despite these drawbacks it seems important that some systematic approach to collecting information on early indicators of difficulty is implemented before children begin to fail, or at very least if a child is showing difficulty with reading or pre-reading skills and that a teacher knows what questions to ask parents about the child's development and knows the significance of the replies that they give.

SUMMARY

1 Many families already have some experience of dyslexia or similar problems, although in the majority of cases adults have not been formally
  recognised.
2 Mothers can with hindsight identify a number of possible early indicators
  of dyslexia.
3 The majority of mothers are realistic in their perception of their child's
  overall development and general level of intelligence.
4 Some children with speech and language difficulties have a higher risk of
  dyslexia.
5 All the children in this sample were considered well adjusted and 'normal'
  by their mothers before entering school.
6 A large majority of mothers in this sample 'knew' that something was
  wrong during their child's time in infant school.
7 The majority of mothers in this sample found that their children encountered considerable problems with the school reading scheme.

Chapter 6

Identifying dyslexia

'I danced down the street. At last we knew what was wrong.'
(Mother of girl with dyslexia)

By the time the children in this sample had been through infant school all the mothers, bar one, felt that something was definitely wrong. The next series of questions looked at the process, from their point of view, by which their child was identified as having dyslexia or specific learning difficulties. Questions were asked about who first suggested that the child was dyslexic or had a specific learning difficulty and what the response to this suggestion was. Mothers were also asked how they came to find out about dyslexia and how they felt when their child was identified as having dyslexia or a specific learning difficulty. In response to the question, 'Who was it that first suggested that the child might be dyslexic?', the following responses were given.

Mother	15
Friend	1
Teacher	5
Professional relative	1

In just over two-thirds of cases a lay person suggested the child was dyslexic and in under a third of cases a professional initially suggested that the child was dyslexic. Out of the 17 mothers who asked the school if their child might be dyslexic, in 11 cases they claimed that the school was dismissive, in 5 cases the school was seen as noncommittal and in one case the school was in agreement. This information only tells us about mothers' perception of the situation. It may be that in some cases schools had their own formulation of the problem, but that there was not effective communication between school and home on the nature of the problem. Whatever the case may be, half the mothers in this sample felt that initially the school was dismissive of their suggestion. Many of these mothers backed up their claim by giving specific examples or quotes of comments made to them by teachers. Mrs Roberts described what happened when she started expressing her concern over how unhappy her son appeared to be at school. She herself wasn't sure what was wrong at this stage but simply wanted the school to look into it.

'Well she said I was neurotic. I didn't get any joy out of them so then I went to my sister-in-law (head of teacher training college). She assessed him and said he was dyslexic and that he hadn't done a thing in the two years he'd been at school. So I decided to send him to the Dyslexia Institute. Of course all this didn't go down very well with the school. I was told, "If you want to waste your money, it's up to you."'

Mrs Slatter was also concerned about her son's lack of progress and his unhappiness at school.

'I thought something was up. I was told I was an overprotective mother and Dean was just a slow learner and there was nothing wrong. And I, being foolish, left it and the next year we went to parents' day and looked at his work and there was absolutely no progress. Again I voiced my opinion and again I was told I was being silly. And I thought, "No, I don't think I am," and so I went about it myself and I got in touch with the Dyslexia place through the telephone. I thought, "In for a penny, in for a pound. We'll try this." My husband agreed that there was something there; he was just stopped solid for two years and the trouble was, with him being intelligent, he knew there was something wrong and he couldn't understand what was wrong with himself. You don't want to stir up the water but you have to.'

Mrs Slatter felt that she encountered a negative attitude to dyslexia at both a school and an LEA level.

'The head wouldn't acknowledge it at all, he said there was a two year waiting list for an LEA assessment. The trouble is, you get more help in some areas than others. I think he (head of LEA) was totally against dyslexia, he didn't believe in it.'

Mrs Carter similarly felt that the school was dismissive of her concerns.

'But the only thing was every time I mentioned dyslexia it was like a taboo word.'

The experiences recounted by these mothers were typical of those recounted by the two-thirds of mothers who initially suggested to professionals that their child was dyslexic.

THE PROCESS OF IDENTIFICATION

For many families identification is a gradual process that goes on over a period of time. The process of identification that is described also follows closely the processes described by Booth (1978) that families with children with developmental delay experienced. In Booth's study he identified four main stages that families went through in getting their child identified. These stages were:

1 the growth of suspicion;
2 seeking professional advice;
3 suspending judgement;
4 the growth of conviction.

In both studies parents began, usually over a period of time, to suspect that something was wrong. In the second stage parents then sought professional advice. In the majority of cases parents were either reassured that there wasn't really a problem, and were typically told that the child would catch up or they were told that they needed to readjust their expectations and accept that their child was a bit slow but again it was suggested that there wasn't any serious problem. Parents then went away temporarily reassured, or at least in deference to the professionals, prepared to give the child the benefit of the doubt. But the child's subsequent lack of progress and in the case of most of the dyslexic children their evident unhappiness convinced their parents that something was wrong. Once parents reached this stage of conviction they were determined not to be fobbed off by professionals and were prepared to seek alternative advice, if necessary, until they received a satisfactory explanation for their child's difficulties. Whilst the dyslexic children's problems were very mild in comparison to the severe problems of some of the developmentally delayed children, the same difficulties in getting some professionals to take parents' concerns seriously appeared to be in evidence. In both cases the absence of physical markers and the reliance on behavioural observations made it important for early identification that there was a good relationship between parents and professionals and that professionals took seriously parents' concerns.

Parents as clients or partners

Wolfendale (1983) argues that traditionally parents have been treated as clients and it is only recently that there has begun to be a move towards treating them as partners. Wolfendale lists a number of characteristics of both the client and the partner concept.

Client concept

Parents are dependent on professional opinion.
Parents are passive recipients of services.
Parents are in need of redirection.
Parents are peripheral to decision making
Parents are perceived as 'inadequate' or 'deficient'.

Partner concept

Parents are active and central in decision making and in its implementation.

Parents are perceived as having equal strength and equivalent expertise.

Parents are able to contribute as well as receive services.

Parents share responsibility.

Although both positive and negative experiences were recounted by mothers, the majority of experiences fitted with the parent as client concept. This may help explain the long delay experienced by most families between suspecting there was a problem and getting it identified to their satisfaction. The average period of time for this was four years and led to the median age for children to be assessed and identified as dyslexic as ten years.

DIFFERING VIEWS AMONG PROFESSIONALS

Many families found that there were differing views among teachers as to the nature and extent of their child's difficulties. Mrs Thompson had noticed that her son was becoming very distressed about school work. She herself had come across various articles about dyslexia and found that he fitted most of the points. She felt that her initial tentative approaches to the school were not productive.

'I didn't get far at all with them. In the early stages it was a case of the usual, "Oh, he'll catch up, some of them are slow," and so on.'

But when her son was seven he had a different teacher who agreed that there was a problem.

'His teacher said, "I don't know what it is, but there's definitely some block there with Ryan, why he can't learn to read and write like the other children, because he's bright enough and there's no reason why he shouldn't." '

For over half the mothers in this sample, conflicting opinions among professionals were reported as part of their experience of trying to get their child's difficulties identified and supported. This conflict could be at the level of the school with different teachers having different views or it could involve outside professionals such as educational psychologists.

'Well, I asked the head if he was dyslexic and she said, "No, I don't think he is," and his teacher said he's not. Then the educational psychologist saw him. She'd taken a course in dyslexia and she thought he was. She told us off the record to get specialist help for him.'

'The school were pretty noncommittal. "It'll come, she'll be all right," and so on. Eventually when she was nearly ten they did refer her to the educational psychologist. She was very supportive; her own daughter was dyslexic. She suggested unofficially that we sent her to the Dyslexia Institute.'

'I was confused by all the dispute among the professionals. His second teacher referred him to the educational psychologist. He assessed him and said it would all come together and there wasn't anything to worry about. Then his next teacher said there definitely was a problem and that he needed help. They're the experts, I felt betrayed.'

Several mothers said that they were told by various professionals including class teachers, special needs teachers, headteachers and educational psychologists 'off the record' that their was child was dyslexic and would benefit from specialist help outside the school. In many of these cases the person in question either mentioned that they had a dyslexic child or had received specialist training in dyslexia. It perhaps says something about the general climate of the school or the LEA, that professionals felt the need to stress that these recommendations were being made off the record. Macbeth (1989) found that when teachers gave opinions to parents on choosing schools, the advice was usually given unofficially. Macbeth suggests that this is because teachers are reluctant to comment on their fellow professionals and states that, 'The closing of ranks by teachers poses an important professional problem.' As far back as 1978, Robinson commented that the current political climate and lack of support left professionals who wanted to practice in a different way, 'in a very exposed position'.

'His teacher thought something was wrong, she suggested we try the Dyslexia Institute. She said she was sticking her neck out in suggesting it.'

Even when a child had been identified as dyslexic by a bona fide professional and this had been accepted by the school at a general level, this didn't guarantee that individual teachers would agree with this.

'And his teacher did say to me once, "I don't think that Mark is dyslexic". And I said, "Well, with all due respect, do you know anything about dyslexia?" And she said, "no." I says, "Well, how are you qualified to turn round and say to me he isn't if you know nothing about it?" I said, "I could bring you in plenty of literature if you'd like to read it," but she declined to do so.'

This comment along with most of the comments quoted so far in this chapter, was made by a working class mother. These comments illustrate the wide variation in parents' views and approaches and warn against the danger of having simplistic and stereotyped views of what parents from a particular social class think. Blaxter and Paterson (1982) suggest that clear and consistent social class differences in child rearing are only present at the extremes of the classification system. Ribbens (1994) argues that it is over-simplistic to divide parents into working class and middle class because this misrepresents the complexity of the data and tends to ignore aspects of the data that show no class differences in child rearing. It also means that the considerable variations within class are often overlooked. This is not to deny that it is highly likely that children from socially or economically deprived backgrounds are more likely to be overlooked or to have their difficulties attributed to other causes. But it does suggest that it is important not to hold stereotyped assumptions about how parents from a particular background will behave. Several of the most assertive and articulate mothers in this study were from a working class background, whereas there were several unforceful middle class mothers who felt they had little power to influence the school. It may well be that overall there are more assertive middle class parents but it is important not to assume that all or even the majority of middle class parents fit this stereotype.

In the seven cases where someone other than the parents first suggested the child was dyslexic mothers were asked what their initial reaction to this suggestion was. In all cases parents were basically in agreement with the suggestion. In some cases they had already wondered themselves if the child was dyslexic but hadn't liked to voice these opinions to professionals. In other cases they knew nothing about dyslexia and reserved judgement until they had checked out for themselves what the label meant.

'I must be one of the few people who hadn't heard about it. I hadn't even come across it, so I hadn't thought about it before. It wasn't until he was getting special help at school that one of the teachers said sort of very diplomatically, it wasn't officially, had I heard about dyslexia. Perhaps it could be the case. I wanted to know if it was possibly the case. At least you've got an avenue to follow.'

The following comment was made by a mother who was herself a primary school teacher.

'I can honestly say I never knew a lot about it which is why I didn't think of it. I just knew he didn't fit into any normal category.'

SOURCES OF INFORMATION ON DYSLEXIA

Given that in fifteen cases mothers said that they were the first one to suggest that their child was dyslexic this raises the question of where they got their knowledge of dyslexia from. In the cases where someone else first suggested the child was dyslexic there was still the question of where mothers got the bulk of their information about dyslexia from. In response to the question, 'where had they initially learnt about dyslexia from?', the following replies were given. Some mothers mentioned more than one source of initial information and some couldn't remember precisely where they'd first heard about dyslexia, although this uncertainty was confined to which aspect of the media they'd first seen it mentioned in.

Magazines (9), papers or books	13
Television or radio	5
Dyslexia Institute publicity or information	4
Teacher	1
Friend	1

Although these figures are best taken as a rough approximation, they do show quite clearly that the media is the major source of initial information. A common pattern was for a mother to first read an article or hear a programme about dyslexia and to think that the outline of dyslexia that was given fitted well with the difficulties that her child was experiencing. As mothers became more convinced that their child might be dyslexic they actively sought further information and, for example, borrowed books from the library or obtained pamphlets from specialist organisations. Many mothers commented that once they were aware of the possibility of their child being dyslexic they noticed increasing coverage of dyslexia in the media.

'Well his remedial teacher first suggested he might be dyslexic, then I read an article in the paper and then I read a couple of books. Just recently Ryan and I watched this QED programme about it together. He said, "Oh yes, that's what I do."'

'I can't remember. I really can't. I'd probably read a little bit, or saw a little bit, but it was only a tiny bit. I knew nothing about it whatsoever, it was only after that, that I made it my job to find out as much as I could. . . . I don't know if it's a case that once you get started, it becomes easier to find more, but obviously over the past few years there has been more realisation about it. It's on the television and the paper did a big thing about it recently.'

'I saw something about it in a magazine and then there was this radio programme I think.'

'The more I read articles and so on the more I thought it described Darren so much, although he didn't have all the elements, he wasn't clumsy or slow to talk. After that I read some books from the library.'

MOTHERS' REACTIONS TO THE LABEL 'DYSLEXIA'

Mothers were asked how they felt when they were told or had it confirmed that their child was dyslexic. Twenty out of the twenty-two mothers described themselves as 'relieved' when they were told that their child was dyslexic.

'Oh god, such a relief! It was the first time he wasn't lazy, wasn't stupid. It wasn't his fault.'

'Really I was quite relieved to know, because it's an explanation. I think you're disappointed for them, aren't you, and a bit anxious about what it means.'

'Well, I was relieved in a way. I wasn't upset at all. Because I just thought, "Well yes, now we've got something to work on." Well, maybe he'd never get rid of the problem, but at least there's specialist help we can get.'

Mothers stressed the importance of having an explanation, of their child no longer feeling stupid, and of practical plans for helping the child being possible once they were identified as dyslexic. One mother who had great difficulty in convincing the primary school that there was a problem, despite her son being three years behind on his reading and spelling, described herself as 'thrilled' when he was finally identified as dyslexic. Another mother who had received conflicting advice from professionals throughout her daughter's primary school and had been told that she wasn't dyslexic, described herself as 'devastated' when at 12 years of age her daughter, at the instigation of her secondary school, was identified as dyslexic. She felt that she had been 'fobbed off' by professionals and blamed herself for believing them. Sixty per cent of the mothers blamed themselves to varying degrees for not having followed their own convictions. Mrs Graham whose son was also assessed on the advice of his secondary school and found to be over 5 years behind in his reading made the following remarks.

'I felt guilty I hadn't followed my own instincts in the first place. I feel really guilty about that. But you know, if you're talking to professionals, you expect them to know. I really wish I'd followed my own instincts.'

So for over half the mothers relief was tinged with regret or guilt that they had not had their child identified sooner.

CHILDREN'S REACTIONS TO THE LABEL DYSLEXIA

Children were also asked what they thought about being called dyslexic. In order to try and guard against children giving the answer they thought the researcher wanted to hear they were deliberately asked the negative leading question of 'Didn't they resent being called dyslexic because it made them feel different?' All the children denied this, and 21 out of the 22 children were positive about the label 'dyslexia'.

'I'm glad I'm called dyslexic rather than lazy.'

'I'm not branded as thick now.'

'I quite like it, I used to wonder why I couldn't keep up.'

'It helps me understand.'

'It's OK. It has helped.'

'I'd rather know I've got dyslexic than think I was an idiot.'

'It's quite helpful. It's better to get it sorted out.'

'Now I know there's a lot of people with the same problem.'

Several dominant themes could be identified from children's comments.

1 Not thinking they were 'thick' or 'stupid'.
2 That it had helped.
3 It had specifically helped them to understand why they had been having difficulties.
4 That there were children with the same difficulty.

Mothers' comments also backed up many of these themes.

'It did help him because he said, "I'm not stupid. I haven't really got a stupid brain."'

'He needs a reason for everything. He thought that some thing was wrong with him.'

'He was pleased because he thought that he was thick, stupid and an idiot.'

The only child to express negative feelings about the label 'dyslexia' was the youngest child in the sample who said,

'I mind a little bit because she (his mother) tells the whole world.'

This raises an important distinction between the private and the public aspects of the label. Whilst as already shown all but one child found the label helpful at a personal level, 50 per cent of the children didn't find the label helpful at a public level (Riddick 1995a), mainly because of teasing by other children.

'I find it helpful, but I'd rather others didn't know.'

Although in this sample numbers are too small to be categorical, two factors did appear to relate to children's willingness to use their label in public. One factor was the general attitude of the school. The two schools in this study that were most open and supportive of the concept of dyslexia both had children attending who were willing to say they were dyslexic.

'Oh everybody knows. I use it quite a lot in fact'.

Whereas some of the schools that were most negative about the concept of dyslexia were the ones where children reported considerable teasing.

'They used to call us (me) "spacker".'

'He used to call us names, "dim", "spacker", "thick". I used to get quite upset.'

This information fits with other research from the special needs area (Swann 1985) which shows that the attitudes of the school and the individual teachers within the school to special needs children are important in determining the attitudes of the rest of the children. Sophie, in the extended case studies in chapter 13, talks about the negative attitude of other children in her school to dyslexia and the problems that this causes her. The other factor appeared to be related to children's level of self-esteem or confidence combined with the verbal ability to stick up for themselves. The two boys who gave the two longest male interviews and both scored high on the Lawrence self-esteem inventory and were rated high in self-esteem by their mothers both said they were willing to talk about dyslexia in school. According to their own accounts and those of their mothers they were willing to fight their corner in a verbal sense and both mentioned independently that they had used the example of Einstein to defend themselves.

'Oh Einstein dead thick, eh?'

WHY LABEL?

It is sometimes suggested that middle class parents opt for the label 'dyslexia' because they see it as a socially acceptable and advantageous label for their children to receive (Dessent 1987, Riddell *et al.*1992, Reid 1994). In the current study over half the mothers thought that teachers and sometimes other parents thought that they were making 'excuses' for their child by calling them dyslexic. In fact several mothers said they didn't use the word 'dyslexia' at school for fear of antagonising the school and making things worse for their child. There were no discernible class differences with equal numbers of working class and middle class mothers reporting these kinds of experiences.

'I was made to feel over anxious and neurotic. Yes it made me feel very demoralised, I even ended up crying.'

'Oh, all the way along I was made to feel that I was making excuses.'

'And I was getting all those knowing smiles that say, "You're the over-fretting, paranoid mother."'

'The teachers in the junior school definitely thought I was making excuses.'

'I keep a low profile for fear of antagonising them.'

These views suggest that for half the parents at least using the term 'dyslexia' had negative as well as positive aspects to it. These parents didn't feel that the term dyslexia was 'socially acceptable' within the context of their child's school. . . . Neither had the label 'dyslexia' given them access to additional or more appropriate resources within the school system. This would suggest that for a significant proportion of parents, more complex or alternative explanations for choosing to call their children dyslexic should be sought. Many mothers mentioned their reluctance or embarrassment at having to make a 'fuss' and many did not want to be seen as a 'pushy' or 'neurotic' parent.

'I'm not that sort of person. I hate to make a fuss.'

Another mother whose son was found to have a reading age of 6 years 9 months at the age of 11 years described her experience.

'I could tell he wasn't learning to read and things very quickly, but then again I didn't want to be too pushy. Because I knew too many people who were always going up, and you think, "Hold on, he'll do it, he'll learn," but then he didn't. Now I feel guilty.'

It can be argued that from the responses given by parents in this study, a label such as 'dyslexia' serves a number of purposes but a fundamental reason for parents choosing this label is its 'goodness of fit' in terms of describing and explaining their child's difficulties.

'The more I read articles and things the more I thought it's just describing Robert so much.'

The majority of mothers went on to add that once there was a label or an explanation it also gave them a much clearer idea of what sort of help was needed.

'We knew what help he needed then.'

'I was relieved, at least something could be done.'

Allied to this some parents saw this as the first real recognition that their child had a problem and that this wasn't just a figment of their imagination.

'I kept saying to my husband, "I wish someone would tell me what is wrong with this child that he can't do the normal things."'

Mrs Wood's son had been coming home from school very distressed and upset and was having behaviour problems at school. Suggestions to his previous teacher that he might have a learning disability had been dismissed. When he got a new teacher she quickly recognised that he had a problem.

'She called me in before half-term and said, "If this little boy isn't dyslexic, I'll eat hay with the horses." I walked out of school on cloud nine because finally someone had said there is a problem here.'

Parents also felt it was important to be able to explain to their child what the problem was.

> 'Dean couldn't understand what was wrong with himself. He kept asking me, "Am I thick?"'

From the point of view of parents they wanted a label which accurately described and explained their child's difficulties and accounted for the puzzling discrepancies in their child's performance. In 50 per cent of cases, parents felt that at an informal level their child had been labelled as 'thick or slow' by the school and in 25 per cent of cases they felt they had been labelled as lazy. It can be argued that this an unhelpful way to view any child's difficulties, but what parents were specifically objecting to was the inaccuracy of these attributions as a total explanation for their child's difficulties. Mrs Andrews described her frustration with being told that her 7-year-old son couldn't read because he was 'slow'. At 8 years he was assessed by the educational psychologist and found to have an IQ of 120.

> 'I'm very frustrated. We could have saved him a lot of heartache. The trouble is people think you're just pushy neurotic academic parents. I'd be the first to accept that my older son isn't academic, but he's not dyslexic either!'

Mrs Faulkner also objected to her daughter's reading difficulties being put down to slowness:

> 'The thing the teacher did say once, that irritates me now, was that she was very slow at school, slow to learn. And basically she's not slow to learn. It was the reading that she was slow to learn. And I think that was a lack of understanding.'

Several mothers talked about their own caution in giving their child a label.

> 'I don't think you should give them labels willy nilly like. You have to weigh it up. But really it was no contest, the state he was in, so much harm had been done, it could only get better.'

Several mothers were told by educationalists that they didn't believe in labelling children. Jordan and Powell (1992) comment that, 'an educational dogma had developed which discredits the labelling of children.' It is important that the validity and usefulness of any particular label is kept under review and the purpose or purposes behind using it are clearly understood. It is also important that the people who have to live with a label have ownership of it and have a major say in what context and for what purpose the label is used. It can be argued that labels of disability can be used to describe or explain an individual's functioning at the biological, psychological and sociological levels. Most people with disabilities want labels that are socially positive and don't reinforce negative or inaccurate stereotypes of themselves. Hence the constant changing and renegotiating of labels that takes place. One fundamental change has been the move away from labels that describe the person in terms of their disability such as blind or mentally handicapped to terminology which puts the person first such as she has a visual impairment or he has a learning disability. Despite this move there is still disagreement and controversy over labels and some people with visual impairments for example prefer to call themselves blind. Thomas (1982) comments on this, 'disability is not only a matter of medical and administrative definition, it is a personal one of how each person with an impairment defines him- or herself.' He also points out that different groups such as the public, professionals and disabled people themselves will have different perceptions of the nature and meaning of disability. In the present study many of the mothers were aware that teachers and especially educational psychologists preferred to use the term 'specific learning difficulties'.

'Basically they were in agreement, except they never called it dyslexia: they called it "specific learning difficulties".'

Most mothers didn't object to this as long as there was clear agreement with the school as to what the child's difficulties were and what should be done about them. Mothers and children preferred to use the term 'dyslexia' as opposed to 'specific learning difficulties'. It could be that this was a particularly biased sample as subjects were recruited through the Dyslexia Institute but in Pumfrey and Reason's (1991) wide ranging survey and in Riddell *et al.* (1992) it was also found that parents preferred the term 'dyslexia' to 'specific learning difficulties'. If we look at these two terms in a wider social and psychological context this is perhaps not surprising. At present nearly all the lay literature, personal accounts, information and specialist support services and role models of adults are accessed through the term 'dyslexia'. In this study it was found that both parents and teachers were confused about what 'specific learning difficulties' meant and to what extent it was exchangeable with the term 'dyslexia'. From the perspective of educationalists 'specific learning difficulties' may seem a more equable and acceptable way of characterising children's difficulties but for children and their families it doesn't offer the same degree of personal understanding, personal identification and personal support. Blaxter (1976), in discussing disability points out that there are inevitable tensions between clinical definitions which can be 'individual, qualified and provisional' and administrative categories which are required to be 'rigid, dichotomous and designed for large groups of people'. Booth (1988) argues that most educational psychologists prefer the term 'specific learning difficulties' because it suggests difficulties with a range of skills and not just reading and it also has less 'emotive' and 'pathological' connotations than dyslexia. Pumfrey and Reason (1991) in their survey of educational psychologists noted that 87.4 per cent said that they found the term 'specific learning difficulties' useful in their work and that 30.4 per cent found the term 'dyslexia' useful. The majority of educational psychologists said that they were aware that parents preferred the term 'dyslexia' and although they avoided the term they did not object to parents using it. Whilst it is important not to get too bogged down in semantics it is important where different groups are using different terminology that there is clear communication between them. In some cases in this study where there was not clear communication about the connection between the terms 'dyslexia' and 'specific learning difficulties', parents thought that educational psychologists were being dismissive of their child's problem and were denying that they were 'dyslexic'.

> 'So this dreadful man came out and did tests with Josh. I don't know what they were; Josh wouldn't talk about them. And then he called me into school, sitting beside the headmistress, who didn't believe there was anything wrong with him except he was thick. And he said, "Well, there's nothing wrong with your child. He's just a very bad speller. I've got a boy who's a bad speller as well, and there's nothing you can do about it." So that was it really.'

In both the large scale inquiry by Pumfrey and Reason (1991) and large scale study in Scotland by Riddell, Duffield, Brown and Ogilvy (1992) it was found that parents were unhappy about the length of time it took for their children to be identified and assessed. They were also unhappy about the lack of specialist support and the lack of training and understanding of dyslexia displayed by many classroom teachers. Reid (1994) concludes on the basis of these studies that considerable improvement in early identification and intervention is required. Booth (1988) reported a study carried out in the Grampian region of Scotland in which all the children referred to the schools' psychological service for suspected specific learning difficulties over one year were recorded. The average age for referral was 9 years 7 months. In over 60 per cent of cases psychologists thought that an earlier referral could have been made by the school. In fairness many schools might argue that the long waiting lists and heavy overloads of many educational psychologists contribute to this problem. The psychologists discussed their assessment findings usually with two members of school staff and in 75 per cent of cases they thought that the school's response was good. Concern was expressed about the remaining 25 per cent of schools where it was felt that there was still poor understanding of specific learning difficulties. Psychologists also thought on the basis of interviews with parents that 85 per cent of them were reasonably accurate in their understanding of their child's learning difficulties and 75 per cent were judged to be realistic in their expectations. The other suggestion put forward (Ried 1994, Riddell *et al.* 1992) as to why parents prefer the term 'dyslexia' to 'specific learning difficulties' is that this is a way of securing resources or provision. Given that many parents are aware that educational psychologists favour the term 'specific learning difficulties' it seems illogical to suggest that parents favour the term 'dyslexia' simply in order to access resources. In the present study all the parents felt they had 'failed' to obtain adequate support for their children at school and using the term 'dyslexia' had not for them been a successful way of accessing either school or LEA resources. It can be argued that many labels highlight likely needs and suggest the kind of provision or intervention appropriate to meet those needs. Most parents whose children are identified as having cerebral palsy for example might expect their children to receive physiotherapy. One wouldn't necessarily argue on this basis that parents seek a label of cerebral palsy simply in order to get physiotherapy for their children. This reasoning leaves out the important role of personal understanding and identification that a particular label can offer.

SUMMARY

1 The majority of mothers initially found out about dyslexia through the media.
2 Identification was for most families a gradual process.
3 In two-thirds of cases mothers took the initiative in asking if their child might be dyslexic and in just under a third of cases a professional first suggested that the child might be dyslexic.
4 The majority of mothers who took the initiative in asking if their child was dyslexic felt that the school was dismissive of their suggestion.
5 Over half the parents experienced conflicting views among the professionals.
6 Ninety per cent of mothers described themselves as relieved when it was confirmed that their child was dyslexic.
7 Ninety-five per cent of children were positive about 'dyslexic' as a personal label for understanding their difficulties.

Parents and teachers

'The myth (of the bad parent) is pervasive and its power should not be under-estimated for it can lead well meaning teachers to treat perfectly able parents with suspicion.'

(Hannon 1995)

Before looking at the present study in more detail it is necessary to consider some of the general issues surrounding research on parents and teachers. The first point is that much of the research is rooted in the concerns of educationalists and inevitably involves institutional or school based perspectives on a given question or issue. Ribbens (1994) in commenting on research into families points out that most of it is concerned with publicly defined social policy issues or professionals' concerns and little of it is from the perspective of family members themselves. A similar situation is found when the extensive literature on special needs education or for that matter education in general is examined. More recently, influences from social research and the introduction of approaches such as 'grounded theory' have emphasised the importance of researching issues from the perspective of the individual involved. In grounded theory for example it is argued that the researcher should have as few preconceived questions as possible in order to allow the participants to define what the issues are from their perspective. Another influence has been the disability rights movement which has emphasised the importance of disabled people speaking for themselves. This has led to publications such as a workbook for teachers on disability and equality in the classroom prepared by a teacher with disabilities and a parent with disabilities (Rieser and Mason 1990). It has also led to a number of 'telling it how it is' books where disabled people talk directly about their lives. Early examples of this are a collection of accounts by women with disabilites entitled *Images of Ourselves* (Campling 1981) and *Conversations with Non-Speaking People* (IPCAS 1984). An issue that arises in looking at children with special needs or disabilities is to what degree their voices are heard and to what degree their parents' voices are heard. The general tenet behind such approaches is that children and parents should be listened to and that their views should influence both research and practice.

Dyson and Skidmore (1994) carried out a survey on the provision for specific learning disabilities in secondary schools in Scotland. These schools were not picked to be a representative sample of all schools but were invited to participate because they had features of interest to the research team. Out of 41 nominated schools 27 schools spread across 5 regions responded. Schools were specifically asked in the survey questionnaire what sort of contact they had with the parents of children with specific learning disabilities. They were also asked how this contact differed from the contact they had with other parents of children with different forms of special needs. They summarise the response to parental contact in the following way.

> For most schools parental involvement was entirely positive, and the need to be aware of potential conflict with parents was minimal.

The majority of schools said that their contact was no different or was much the same as the contact they had with other parents. This was the case even when parents had sought advice from outside the school. A few schools felt that parents of children with specific learning disabilities needed more specifically targeted contact but only two schools mentioned support specifically for parents. It is interesting to note that in researching this issue, five different teacher interviews were constructed and used in case study schools. These included interviews with heads, subject specialists and learning support teachers but at no point were the views of the parents or children themselves sought on provision for specific learning disabilities or on the relationship between school and home. This was a well carried out piece of research but it does illustrate the point that much of what we know is from the teacher perspective.

TEACHER STEREOTYPES

Atkin, Bastiani and Goode (1988) carried out extensive studies on the relationships between parents and teachers and were involved at a practical level in carrying out inservice training in this area. They start by making the point that most work on home–school relations, 'is viewed entirely from the professional perspective'. They also comment that over a period of time they were forced to ask uncomfortable questions about their own assumptions and became aware of deficiencies in their own evidence and perspective.

> In the first place we had become rather suspicious of many of the claims that practising teachers were making about what parents were like. Increasingly, we began to consider that such claims were rooted in teacher lore and staffroom mythology, rather than in first hand experience and direct evidence, being strongest where actual contact was weak or limited.

In the present study the children's specialist support teachers at the Dyslexia Institute were also interviewed. They had all been classroom teachers in mainstream schools before taking their specialist training and changing jobs. One of the questions they were asked was whether their inclination to believe what parents told them had increased or decreased as a result of having more personal contact with parents. The one teacher who had spent half her time on parent liaison when in mainstream school felt that she hadn't changed in that she had always had a lot of sympathy with what parents told her. The other three all felt that they had changed in their attitudes as a result of working more closely with parents and were now more ready to accept the things that parents told them. Riddick (1995a) has commented on the 'myths' surrounding dyslexia and in particular the myths about the parents of children with dyslexia. Like Atkin *et al.* (1988) she found that most of these appeared to be based on folklore and that almost no empirical evidence was offered to back up the assertions being made. There appeared to be a powerful myth of the over ambitious, unrealistic middle class parent who couldn't accept that they didn't have an academic child. Whilst it may be possible that the occasional parent may fit this description it has been over generalised to produce a pervasive and glib stereotype which is neither helpful to parents or educationalists. Not all educationalists hold this type of stereotype but at an informal level it is still quite frequently used. Dewhirst (1995) carried out a series of interviews with teachers on the subject of dyslexia. The following is a brief extract from an interview she conducted with an experienced special needs support teacher. This teacher stressed that she thought it was important to keep up to date and that she had done so by attending inservice training courses.

INTERVIEWER   Have you done any specialist training in the area of dyslexia?
TEACHER   Oh God that! No, no I haven't (pulls a face). Why?
INTERVIEWER   Why did you pull a face when I asked you that?
TEACHER   Well . . . I mean, it's one of those things that has been conjured up by 'pushy parents' for their thick or lazy children; quite often both.
INTERVIEWER   What exactly do you know about dyslexia?
TEACHER   Well, basically they can't read or write. It's supposed to be about problems in communication isn't it? Generally it's children who are either too lazy or haven't got the brains and their parents can't hack it.

This teacher went on to expand that the problems were invariably caused either by over ambitious middle class parents putting too much pressure on their children or over protecting them by using the label 'dyslexia' when in her terminology the children really needed 'a good kick up the backside'. A case of damned if you do or damned if you don't! Kunda and Oleson (1995) describe a range of evidence which suggests that people are good at finding ways of explaining how almost any attribute can be linked to any outcome and as in this example are quite capable of explaining how opposite attributes (too pushy/not pushy enough) can lead to the same outcome. They also claim that this process actually reinforces an individual's belief rather than diminishing it. Later in the interview the following question was asked:

INTERVIEWER   If you haven't any training in the field of dyslexia do you think really that you should be making judgements about it?

TEACHER   Yeah, it's a gut feeling you know, when you have been teaching as long as I have you get to know which kids have problems and which kids are pulling the wool over your eyes.

This raises an important point that those educationalists who are most hostile to or critical of the concept of dyslexia are the least likely to read about or take further training in a condition that they don't think exists. To be fair to teachers like this one many of them received no training on dyslexia or specific learning difficulties during their initial training or received a critical account of it which either implicitly or explicitly put forward the myth of dyslexia as a figment of the imagination of ambitious, unrealistic middle class parents. Many of the parents in this study were aware of this stereotype and as mentioned in chapter 6 were anxious not to be seen as unrealistic, pushy parents. Newson and Newson (1987) drawing on their extensive longitudinal study of child rearing found that parents were generally reluctant to criticise the school or the teachers directly even when their child was making poor progress. They suggest that fear of being seen as a 'difficult' or 'overprotective' parent are often at the root of this and that parents are frightened of making things worse for their children. Mrs Graham, a single parent on a low income, made the following comment.

'I resent them thinking that we're all wealthy neurotics.'

Mrs Slatter had been told in the past by her son's class teacher that she was being overprotective and there wasn't any problem, despite the fact that he was making little progress and was becoming distressed and unhappy.

'To tell the truth I was frightened of her, that domineering teacher. I backed down, I thought, "Ee well, maybe I'm wrong."'

Atkin et al. (1988) note that, 'To this day we maintain a healthy scepticism of teacher stereotypes.' One of the difficulties with stereotypes is that they can be very resistant to change as they appear to be linked to powerful and fundamental belief systems. Stephan (1985) observes that 'stereotypes are notoriously difficult to change.' Even when sound empirical evidence is presented some individuals will keep their beliefs intact by ignoring or criticising the evidence, or where possible, treating the case as exceptional. Kunda and Oleson (1995) found that people attempted to explain away individuals who strongly challenged their stereotypes by claiming they were different in some way from the group as a whole. They conclude by saying: 'On the practical side, our findings have disturbing implications for the likelihood that people will change their stereotypes in the normal course of their daily lives, as they encounter individuals who disconfirm their stereotypes.'

Stephan (1985) also suggests that simply exposing people to individuals who disconfirm their stereotypes is no guarantee that they will revise their stereotype. It has long been suggested that one reason why people hang on to their stereotypes is because they serve important needs such as justifying their own position, authority or behaviour (Allport 1954). More recently it has been suggested that on top of this there may be a cognitive reason in that people tend to defend themselves against anything that challenges their expectations even when it doesn't seem to be related to specific needs. These kinds of findings allied to a lack or avoidance of training may help to explain how some teachers can still dismiss dyslexia by invoking the stereotype of the over anxious, over ambitious parent. On a more positive note it has been found that one of the best ways to change stereotypes is to get people from different groups working together on some common goal or purpose. Hannavy (1993, 1995) reports on an early reading and writing programme for children who are struggling. This involves parent–teacher partnership and has been tried in a number of different catchment areas with different groups of parents from different socio-economic backgrounds with a high degree of success. She noted that one· of the most positive outcomes of the study was that it enhanced parent–teacher relations and that teachers who at the beginning had been dubious about including parents so closely in their children's learning became enthusiastic advocates of such an approach.

DIFFERENT CONCEPTIONS OF PARENT–TEACHER RELATIONSHIPS

Bastiani (1987) gives a useful overview of the different ideologies which he suggests have underpinned parent–teacher relationships. He outlines four major ideologies: compensation, communication, accountability and participation. The compensatory ideology had its roots in the Plowden Report (1967) which stressed the importance of parents' attitudes to their children's education. In doing this it proposed that an important task was for the less supportive families to be made more like the supportive families. This in turn encouraged deficit or pathological models of families to be applied and led to the development of interventions based on the notions of compensation and positive discrimination. Despite the good intentions of this approach based on post war aspirations of educational opportunity for all, critics have pointed out that the Plowden Report was naive in not giving sufficient weight to the powerful influences that political and social factors have in shaping the relationships between parents and teachers. Drawing on the groundwork of Plowden by the 1970s the role of good communication between schools and parents was seen as vital in promoting good parent–teacher relationships. The strength of this communication ideology was that it focused on the practical organisational issues involved in ensuring that good communication took place between school and home. Whilst nearly all those involved in children's education would agree that good communication is an important starting point, critics have expressed concern that the danger is in assuming that what is communicated is unproblematic. They argue that in some cases some parents and teachers may view an issue from very different assumptions and perspectives and that clear communication without a more fundamental shift in attitude will not necessarily lead to agreement. Another issue concerns what is meant by good communication. Bridges (1987) points out that professionals sometimes have a paternalistic model of communication where they see themselves enlightening uninformed parents and don't conceive of themselves as also learning from parents.

With a political shift in the last fifteen years to viewing parents and children as consumers and schools as part of the market led economy has come an accompanying emphasis on accountability and responsiveness to consumer demands and choices. Under the accountability ideology there has been concern to elicit parents' views on home–school relations both as direct consumers of the service and as part of the wider external audience that schools are accountable to. Despite the reservations expressed by a significant proportion of educationalists and parents to treating schools as part of the market place, accountability has expanded our understanding of home–school relations. It can be argued that the ideology of accountability has encouraged research which focuses on the issues and experiences which are of particular concern to parents. The level at which the concerns of parents are delineated is dependent on the type of research employed. With market survey type techniques, figures are presented which can lead to generalisations about groups of parents based on simple divisions such as class or culture. Bastiani (1987) comments that with a move to more in-depth qualitative methods such as open interviews, we can move beyond these relatively crude types of generalisations and begin to appreciate the wide variations in views between parents assumed to be in the same category. In a similar vein the wide variation in views between teachers is of equal importance and needs to be taken into account in any comprehensive picture of parent–teacher relations.

Parents as partners

The ideology of participation or partnership between teachers and parents has emerged out of elements of the ideologies of compensation, communication and accountability. But what distinguishes it from the other ideologies is the notion of parents and teachers as equal partners with equal rights and responsibilities. Wolfendale (1983, 1987) has written extensively on this model and as illustrated in chapter 6 has spelt out in detail the differences between viewing parents as clients and parents as partners. The difficulty with the partnership model is that it presupposes that organisational and social changes based upon adequate resources can be made in order for parents and teachers to spend sufficient time together to work in partnership. Wolfendale (1991) has recently acknowledged that with the present pressures on schools it is hard to see how such a model can flourish. Bastiani (1987) has also pointed out that the major barrier to the participatory model is that not everyone agrees with it. Wolfendale has pointed out that even when the organisational changes are made to facilitate this model one cannot force individuals to adopt it and that practices can be subverted. Barton and Moody (1981) argue that a fundamental problem is that the interests of the school and those of parents of children with special needs are not always the same. Partnership models have been documented as particularly successful for specific activities such as home–school reading schemes (Topping and Wolfendale 1985) and these have been widely adopted by schools. The problem again is that in some cases these appear to have been adopted by schools without sufficient researching and commitment to the partnership model, so that listening to children read at home becomes a task prescribed by the school rather than a partnership between school and home. In the present study 19 out of the 22 mothers said that they had participated in a home–school reading scheme. As described in chapter 5 this caused considerable difficulty in every case bar one. In a small number of cases mothers thought that their concerns were appreciated by the teacher and in some cases the teacher would suggest alternative strategies that could be tried.

'I had a lot of contact with the school and to be honest they were quite good. They would suggest, "Try this sort of thing," or lay off it for a while, or ask him to read a paragraph and you read him a paragraph. They tried different things.'

But the majority of mothers felt that their concerns were not really acknowledged and were disappointed that despite asking for guidance they were given no additional support or advice on how to deal with the situation.

'I was on my own really, they didn't give me any advice at all.'

It is easy to envisage that from the teacher's point of view many of them were struggling to hear all the children in their class read on a regular basis and that finding time to do more than this was difficult for them. This highlights another difficulty with parent–teacher relations: teachers and parents can have differing priorities, so that whereas parents are concerned with the needs of their own child, the teacher is trying to meet the needs in an equable manner of all the children that she or he teaches. Families and schools are organised in very different ways and this can easily lead to differences in perception over the nature and severity of difficulties. Connell (1987) argues that many parents don't see teachers as workers who are influenced by a whole range of workplace factors such as the way the school is organised, but instead judge teachers more as a kind of honorary parent. Given that many parents only meet a particular teacher a few times in the atypical circumstances of a parents' evening it is perhaps not surprising that they are not aware of all the factors that impinge on a teacher's performance. Both teachers and parents are in the position of forming opinions of each other based on very limited and partial information. It is perhaps not surprising in these circumstances that misperceptions and stereotypes can arise. Connel (1987) argues that the stereotypes formed by both teachers and parents have a point. In the case of parents he suggests that these arise out of an attempt to make sense of what is happening at school based on very limited information. In the case of teachers he suggests that stereotypes such as the unsupportive or uninterested home are often used to explain children's performance and behaviour and thus help the teacher to survive in the face of a difficult and demanding job. In a similar vein Carugati (1990) has suggested that some teachers defend themselves against 'failure' by denying responsibility for children who fail. It can be argued that teachers are less likely to use the stereotype of the uninterested parent to explain the failure of middle class children in general or particular working class children where there is clear evidence that parents are interested and involved in their children's education. In this case the teacher has to reach for the alternative stereotype of the pushy and unrealistic parent to either explain or deny the child's difficulties.

Clients or partners?

As already mentioned, Wolfendale has argued that parents can either be viewed as clients or partners by educationalists. Over half the parents in this sample felt that they had been openly blamed by the school in some way for their child's difficulties and therefore felt that the school, in Wolfendale's terminology, saw them as clients in need of redirection or as deficient.

Table 7.1 Parents' perceptions of criticisms levelled at them by the school

Reported blame by the school	Number
Overprotective/over anxious	6
Emotional problems	2
Not doing enough at home	1
Spoilt	1
Child abroad for a year	1
Child moved school	1

In all these cases mothers claimed that some kind of direct comment had been made to them by the school. It could be argued that in some cases this may not have been the message that the school intended to convey, but several mothers were emphatic that they were being quite clearly blamed. When it came to accusations of being over anxious or overprotective these were applied equally to working class and middle class mothers in this sample. The following is a typical account of this.

'I knew something was wrong, but I was told I was worrying about nothing, and that she was just a bit slow learning to read.'

Mothers like this one thus found themselves in a difficult situation. If they carried on expressing their concerns this was further confirmation to the school that they were 'fussing', over anxious mothers. As well as environmental explanations centred on the home, 75 per cent of parents felt that at an informal level, inaccurate within-child explanations for their child's problems had been used by the school. Fifty per cent of mothers thought that their child had been informally labelled as slow or thick by the school and another 25 per cent thought that their child had been branded as lazy.

'She kept saying that he was slow.'

'What they feel is that he has got the ability but he won't try.'

There was some evidence in this study that schools' explanations were linked to cultural stereotypes. Two out of the three single parents were told that their child's reading problems were linked to home based emotional problems and the third was told she was over anxious. One of these mothers described how angry she was when it was suggested to her that it might be an emotional problem.

'They thought it was an emotional problem because he was from a one parent family, which I disputed because he was a happy-go-lucky kid.'

Another mother from a working class background was also annoyed when it was suggested to her that she didn't do enough reading with her son.

'I get the impression they were thinking the mother isn't helping. I find a lot of people think it's because the parents don't sit down and read.'

She resented this suggestion because she had always read to her son and she didn't think this suggestion would be made to a middle class parent. Again mothers found themselves in a difficult situation. They either had to accept the school's explanation that their child was slow or lazy and in some cases both, or risk being seen as an unrealistic 'pushy' mother if they argued that this was not the case. Several mothers pointed out that they only argued that their child was intelligent because they felt that the school was implying that their child wasn't learning to read or spell simply because they were 'stupid'. These mothers also pointed out that they weren't arguing that their children were more intelligent or more special than other children but that they were on a par with other children and that the explanation offered for their child's difficulties didn't fit with their own observations of the child.

'He's of average ability like most of the world, but it's obviously that much harder for him. What I want is for him to survive and be happy in school and feel that he's as intelligent as other children.'

'Well, the psychologist said he didn't expect to find her in the top set, but she didn't deserve to be in the bottom set either, which I thought hit the nail on the head.'

Another mother of a child of average intelligence commented,

'As long as he can achieve his potential, that's fine.'

The mother of an above average boy also commented,

'You don't want Einstein, you just want to see them keeping up.'

It's easy to see how misperceptions can arise on the part of both parents and educationalists. Some schools may not intend to convey the message that a child is slow but if this is how it is perceived by the parents they may in turn feel forced to argue that the child is intelligent. This in turn may be perceived by the teacher as an unrealistic parent with over inflated views of their child's ability. What can be suggested is that where stereotypes already exist such as the 'pushy parent' or the 'uncaring school' there is far more danger of behaviour being perceived in terms of these stereotypes. In summary it appeared that there were two key factors that influenced the relationship between teachers and parents of dyslexic children. One was the general nature of parent–teacher relationships within a specific school and also the way that individual teachers within the school responded within this context. This factor, it can be argued, is not specific to children with dyslexia but affects the way that all parents in the school are related to. But what can be argued is that the effect of viewing parents as clients rather than partners will have greatest impact where there is the most discrepancy in views between the parents and school as to the nature of a child's difficulties. This is related to the second and more specific factor which is the school's view of dyslexia or specific learning difficulties. Where the school is highly negative or sceptical of the concept of dyslexia there is increased likelihood of poor parent–teacher relationships. Inevitably where a school or a teacher sees parents as clients and is thus sceptical of their views and is also sceptical of the concept of dyslexia there is the most danger of disagreement between school and parents. In some cases good parent–teacher relationships were seen by mothers as important when a school had declared itself ignorant or uneasy about the term dyslexia being applied. In these cases mothers felt that schools were willing to acknowledge some of the concerns that they had and to be sympathetic towards the child even though they wouldn't use the term dyslexia in school.

SUMMARY

1 Most research on children's schooling is carried out from the perspective of educationalists and not from the perspective of children or parents.
2 Both teachers and parents can form inaccurate stereotypes of each other based on partial information.
3 Some teachers subscribe to the inaccurate but powerful myth that dyslexia is entirely in the eyes of over ambitious, pushy, neurotic middle class parents.
4 Half the parents in this sample felt they had been stereotyped and blamed in some way by the school for their child's difficulties.
5 Stereotypes can be difficult to change.
6 It is suggested that the model of parents as partners working closely with teachers on shared goals is one of the most likely ways to reduce stereotypes.

Chapter 8

Home life and support

'He wanted to be dead. There was nothing for him. He wanted his tie so he could hang himself.'

This chapter looks in more detail at mothers' observations of children's emotional responses to living with dyslexia and goes on to consider the kind of practical and personal support that mothers gave to their children to try and help them deal with their difficulties. Mothers were first asked what influence if any having dyslexia had had on their child. The following results were obtained.

None   5%
Some   40%
A lot   55%

Many mothers commented that the worst effects had been before their child was identified as dyslexic and offered support. Several mothers said that it had been traumatic in the early days of school.

'He used to wet the bed. He wouldn't get up in the morning and he had to be dragged to school.'

'He obviously looked under so much pressure that he looked pale and agitated.'

'He became much more moody once he started school and he had nightmares.'

'She was like a different child once she started school. There were tears and tantrums, she used to beg me not to send her, it was hell really. I didn't know what to do for the best.'

It can be argued that behaviours like bedwetting and tantrums are common features of early childhood and are not necessarily related to a child being dyslexic. Mothers seemed aware of this point and many were careful to point out those aspects of their child's development which they didn't think were related to dyslexia. One mother, for example, said that her son had always had sleep problems but she didn't think that these were related to dyslexia because they didn't tie in with what was happening to him at school. Another mother whose son was a persistent bedwetter made a similar point. Most mothers only seemed to claim that particular behaviours or emotional states were related to dyslexia where they thought there was a relationship between the child's experience at school and the behaviour or emotion in question. It can still be argued that mothers' personal perceptions were biased in this matter and that only more empirical research can check out the validity of these claims. Whilst this may be true there was a strong ring of authenticity about the accounts that mothers gave and in some cases there was corroboration from other sources such as teachers or educational psychologists expressing concern over a child's low self-esteem. In addition the 81 per cent of mothers with other children also stressed the difference in their dyslexic children compared to their non-dyslexic children in terms of their emotional response to school.

> 'Really, it's never given his sister any problems. I wouldn't even say she likes school that much but it doesn't bother her, it's never made her miserable the way it has him.'

In some cases mothers described reactions which went on over a period of time.

> 'Like in French, if he's not doing terribly well, he finds it difficult remembering his words because of his short term memory, and he gets very cross. He's never going to be academic, that's not in him anyway. But he's got disheartened and upset because he wanted to get good results like the other children and he wasn't. Then he stammers, and it's an emotional stammer. It comes and goes. But really it's more there than the times it's not.'

Several mothers mentioned incidences which tied in closely with what was happening at school such as a child getting very upset before a spelling test or coming home in a state because they'd been asked to read aloud in class (see Sophie and her mother in the extended case studies, chapter 13). One mother recalled a period of a few weeks when her 6 year old son was getting increasingly distressed. He was chewing all his jumper sleeves right up to the elbow so that they could no longer be repaired. In addition she kept finding him asleep on the stairs after he'd been put to bed at night. He generally appeared upset and distressed and his child minder who had known him since a baby was equally puzzled by the tantrums and distress he was displaying after school. At this point he had not been identified as dyslexic. His mother had no idea what was wrong but wondered if he was being bullied at school. She spoke to his class teacher after school one day. The teacher told his mother that she had concluded that her son was intelligent but that despite his good behaviour he wasn't trying hard enough to learn to read and write and she had therefore decided to put him under a period of concerted pressure. Discussion with her son revealed that this pressure was making him very unhappy and as soon as term ended his distressed behaviour disappeared. In another case a mother found that her son would feel sick and stop eating at the beginning of each school term and that it was only in the holidays that his eating really returned to normal. This was related quite specifically by her to his dread of returning to school and having to face tasks he couldn't do. In cases like this, where specific behaviours could be tied to specific events, mothers were fairly clear about what was happening. Where mothers were considering the possibility of more pervasive long term effects they were more cautious in their statements and took time and care to answer the question. A single parent mother whose son was a teenager, mused on the difficulty of sorting out the various causes for her son's behaviour.

'The problem is to fit in what's the adolescent part, what's the dyslexic bit and what's the bit that there isn't anybody else to take it out on. It's difficult trying to sort those out. He stopped going to school. He missed school for eight and a half days. In the end he was put on report. So I take him to the door every day, otherwise he's never there on time. That's the bit that I can't get through to people. People think dyslexia is about reading and writing. It's the whole organisational and motivational thing. If I stood over Luke and told him what to put on he'd get there in time.'

This mother felt that the negative experiences her son had had at primary school where he had been constantly called lazy had had a strong and pervasive affect on his outlook.

'What I find difficult to get through to certain teachers is that he's had so many negatives that the positives aren't enough. The problem is they need to improve his self-esteem or he won't even try. If he thinks he's going to fail then he won't try in the beginning.'

Many mothers spontaneously mentioned lack of self-esteem or confidence in discussing their child's reactions to having dyslexia.

'It was her self-esteem that really suffered.'

'Because he couldn't read and write his self-esteem was dead low when he was younger.'

In addition to this mothers were asked to estimate their child's present level of self-esteem on a 5 point rating scale from very low to very high.

Without comparing these results with matched non-dyslexic controls it is difficult to know if these results are any different to the norm. But what was

Table 8.1 Mother's estimate of child's self-esteem

Very low	2
Fairly low	6 (2 much lower in the past)
Average	7 (4 much lower in the past)
Fairly high	6 (5 much lower in the past)
Very high	0

interesting was that half the mothers spontaneously mentioned that their child's self-esteem used to be much lower in the past. As can be seen from the figures this was most striking among the mothers who now rated their children as having above average self-esteem but some mothers who rated their children average and even below average also claimed that their children had lower self-esteem in the past. Whereas some mothers used the term self-esteem other mothers used the term confidence. Whichever term was used mothers described a similar pattern with children losing confidence or self-esteem once they started school and especially if they had a particularly 'negative' teacher.

'And over the years he changed from being a bright little normal child to losing confidence in himself, and I think he's just beginning to get it back after all those years ruined really.'

'Well I would say he would be average. . . . In the past I would have put it as very, very low. Because it was his self-esteem that really plummeted when he was at school and he couldn't do what the rest of the children did. His value of himself was nil really . . . and he wouldn't try and do anything because he thought he was going to fail.'

Some mothers distinguished between their child's academic or school based self-esteem and their self-esteem outside school.

'Fairly low coming into average but that's when we're talking about school. Otherwise higher because he can do lots of things.'

In other cases mothers felt that their child's feeling of failure was so pervasive that it had started to colour all areas of their life.

'Oh, he couldn't do anything according to Mark. Even football that he loved, it was, "I can't play football, I'm useless."'

'But another thing was he didn't have any friends at school. He was probably afraid that they would find out that he was slow or they would laugh at him or something and of course that made him feel dreadful as well.'

This boy's mother went on to point out that since her son had been identified and supported and his confidence had improved he had made several friends so it does seem plausible that his earlier lack of friends was related to his lack of confidence. Several mothers commented on their children becoming very withdrawn and quiet as they lost their self-esteem and some wondered if their children were depressed. One mother described how her happy well motivated 8 year old son who had always had lots of interests changed when he had a teacher who was very negative and critical of him.

'He cried at the slightest thing. He didn't want to see his friends and he couldn't think of anything he wanted to do.'

Three mothers mentioned that on one occasion or more their child had said they wanted to kill themself as a direct consequence of the problems they were encountering because of their dyslexia.

'He wanted to be dead, there was nothing for him . . . he wanted his tie so he could hang himself.'

'He got himself so wound up that night he said he wanted to kill himself and I thought, "I can't believe this, what the heck is happening here?"'

Van der Stoel (1990) in her interviews with Dutch parents of dyslexic children recorded similar incidences of depression and distress.

'Recently he's been depressed. I simply don't know what to do next.'

'He was really bordering on the suicidal.'

An examination of Osmond's (1993) interviews with parents, adults and children with dyslexia reveals strikingly similar themes of distress and loss of confidence.

'It took three years for Geoffrey to regain his self confidence. He was so used to trying and failing at school that he had just given up.'

'Immediately she began at primary school there was a familiar pattern of stress, frustration, panic and temper tantrums.'

As has already been noted in chapter 3 many educationalists and researchers (Pumfrey and Reason 1991, Miles 1993, Edwards 1994) have acknowledged the serious emotional consequences that dyslexia can have for some children especially when it is unrecognised and unsupported. It should be emphasised that this is not specific to dyslexic children and that many children with a wide range of special needs are at risk of low self-esteem and personal distress. What it does suggest is that more research is needed to look at what factors are likely to lead to loss of self-esteem and distress in dyslexic children. Both personal reports and evidence from researchers (Fawcett and Nicolson 1994, Singleton 1994) strongly suggests that a major factor is lack of identification and support particularly when this leads to teachers having an inaccurate or negative view of the child. What we don't know at present is how this might interact with other factors such as the severity and nature of the child's difficulties, the educational context in which they are trying to cope and their particular personality. We also need more systematic ways of following up the descriptions that parents give us. Parents will obviously vary in the language that they use and the way that they judge the severity of their child's problems. Objective measures of self-esteem, anxiety and behaviour are needed as well as objective assessments of the child's cognitive functioning and educational attainments. Such results need to be compared with those of non-dyslexic children before anything more precise can be said about the particular impact of dyslexia. What is also important is that these factors are looked at on a longitudinal basis as the personal accounts clearly indicate that esteem and personal well being are closely related to the changing circumstances that children encounter. Given the number of complex variables involved it is perhaps not surprising that what also emerges is the reported degree of variability in children's responses with some children showing considerable distress, whilst others show relatively little distress according to their mothers. In the following example, Mrs Falkner, who was the only mother in the main interview sample who said that having dyslexia had had no effect on her daughter, felt that although her daughter was not identified as dyslexic until she was ten, her school had been relatively supportive especially of her personal well being so that dyslexia had caused her little personal distress.

'I mean, she didn't seem to worry about it. I think she was too young to realise there was a problem. Give her another couple of years and she would have realised there was a problem. . . . She takes it in her stride very well.'

Interestingly this girl had one of the larger discrepancies in the sample between her reading age (6.8) and chronological age (11.1) when first identified as dyslexic which would suggest that severity alone is not a reliable predictor of personal distress. As well as the supportive environment of the school another moderating factor for her may have been that her best friend was also dyslexic and they were both identified around the same time.

'Believe it or not, her best friend at school was dyslexic as well, and they found out at virtually the same time, that they were both dyslexic. Which was a help for her.'

Two mothers who both rated their sons as above average in self-esteem thought that having dyslexia had had both positive and negative influences on their development.

'In some ways it's hindered him, because he doesn't fulfill his potential, but in some respects it's made him more aware of other people's problems, so in some ways it's been good for him.'

'I think it has given him a lot of character and push, he seems to want to strive to improve. I think it's made him more positive since he's found out, he's not so airy fairy about it now, he does realise it's going to be twice the struggle.'

Both these boys reported that they had had quite difficult times at school in the past and both felt angry about being thought lazy and stupid by their former schools. This raises the question of how different families choose to view a specific impairment and how the personal qualities of both parents and children influence this process. Did the high self-esteem of these two boys influence their mothers' views or did their mothers' ability to see positive as well as negative aspects to dyslexia help their sons to maintain high self-esteem? In addition, what role do other skills and competencies play in this process? Both these boys were highly articulate, (in fact they gave the 2 longest male interviews in the main sample) and both had a wide circle of friends. By their own accounts and that of their mothers they were both open about their dyslexia and were quite prepared to stick up for themselves at a verbal level.

'I don't think he lets anybody do him down.'

Two mothers mentioned that success at a particular activity (captain of the school football team and winning horse rider), had considerably enhanced their children's self-esteem and helped to counter the negative effects of dyslexia. Scott, Schermann and Phillips (1992) reported a study in which they had tried to find out what distinguished 'successful' from 'unsuccessful' adult dyslexics. In this study they claim that the key factors were a supportive family background, early identification and encouragement of talents and hobbies and a search for self worth. In the current study mothers showed a high level of concern over their children's self-esteem and 80 per cent of them rated improvement in self-esteem as the most important outcome of their child's specialist support at the Dyslexia Institute.

'He's more self confident, and I'm sure that's had a lot to do with coming here.'

'Well, it helped his self-esteem firstly.'

Again it could be argued that mothers were misguided in their perceptions but their views were corroborated by the children and by specialist and in some cases classroom teachers. What is not clear is what aspect of identification and support led to the reported improvement in self-esteem. Does simply knowing you are dyslexic lead to improvement in self-esteem, or is the specific improvement in skills, or the personal relationship with an adult who believes in you and encourages you of equal or more importance? It may well be that a combination of these factors in varying degrees are of importance depending on a child's particular circumstances, age, personality etc. As already mentioned in chapter 3 many researchers have commented on the links between self-esteem and academic performance (Burns 1982) and Lawrence (1985) in particular has focused on the links between low self-esteem and poor reading performance. The issue of how schools offer support and set about enhancing self-esteem will be looked at more closely in chapter 9. In this chapter mothers' attempts to give practical and personal support to their children will be looked at in more detail.

PERSONAL SUPPORT

Mothers were asked what kind of personal support as opposed to practical support they offered their children. This fell into two main categories that often went hand in hand. One was countering the negative thoughts that their children had and the other was boosting their children's self-esteem or confidence by offering encouragement and dwelling on the positives. Mrs Knight, for example, said that her son often spoke of having a stupid brain, she would counter this by telling him,

'You're not stupid. It's just a problem that you have with one part of your brain which is not working properly that gives you difficulty with reading and writing and nothing else. You're good at sport and you've got lots of friends.'

Mrs Roberts also offered her son reassurance when he said he was stupid.

'You're not stupid. You have to believe in yourself.'

Mrs Kerslake described her son as saying 'I'm useless. I can't do anything,' to which she would respond,

'I'd always say, "Have a go at things. It doesn't matter if you can't do it. Just be positive. If you enjoy it, well, maybe you can do it."'

Mrs Thompson made the following comments,

'I just says, "There'll always be things that other children can do that you can't do, but there again there'll be things you can do that they can't," because he's pretty good at skating and things like that, you know.'

Mrs Hanson described the strategies she used when her son came home upset about his homework.

'Cuddle him, "We'll do it together. I know you can do it." Tell him how good he is, but don't pressurise him.'

Mrs Wood said that her response varied according to the situation,

'Sometimes I ignore it or I try to seem relaxed about it. Sort of try to defuse the situation, like make a joke of learning his spellings. His sister joins in she marches up and down pretending to be his teacher and we all have a laugh about it.'

Five mothers specifically mentioned stressing the positives, another five boosting self-esteem, four not being stupid and three offering encouragement. It can be argued that mothers were responding to negative images that children had received largely from outside the home.

Mothers therefore seemed very aware of the combined issues of how to give their children personal support and how to maintain or improve their self-esteem. Whereas with some children it was relatively easy to find things they were good at, for at least a third of the children this was much more difficult to do especially during their early years at school. Those children who, because of their specific cognitive impairments were clumsy or poorly co-ordinated and had poor verbal fluency, appeared to be at particular risk of low self-esteem. One mother pointed out that her daughter, when seven years old, despite having a well above average IQ, could not read, ride a bike, swim, skip with a rope, tie shoe laces, put clothes on the right way round, tell her left from her right, recite the days of the week in order or hold a fluent conversation, neither was she particularly musical or artistic. For children like this their 'failure' at learning to read, write and spell was compounded by their difficulties in mastering a number of other socially expected skills. Another mother whose son had experienced a similar range of difficulties pointed out that he had to spend so much time acquiring these basic skills that it hadn't left much time or energy for acquiring any special skills. Another mother whose son had an IQ in the superior range said that he would often come home from junior school and plaintively say,

'I wish I was good at something.'

His mother went on to comment,

'He was teased a lot by the other kids and often called thick and stupid. I don't think that should happen to any child, but the crazy thing was he was probably brighter than most of them. The thing he's really good at is thinking, but that doesn't cut much ice, it doesn't give you any kudos with your friends.'

Another mother commented that during the early school years,

'His total value of himself was nil really.'

Yet another mother said:

'I think what hurt the most with Malcolm was last year (aged 10) he was even thinking about what he was going to do when he leaves school. He was coming home and saying things like, "I think I'll be a lollipop man because you'll not have to do much written work." And I thought, "You know, you shouldn't even be having to worry." You know really, your school days should be happy and even if you ask him, you know, because his brother is saying he will be staying on and doing his 'O' levels, and Malcolm is saying, "Well, I'm leaving school when I'm sixteen." You know he still can't see what the future might hold . . . that he might be able to go on and do examinations and things like that.'

From these accounts it appears that for a significant proportion of dyslexic children the early years at school can be particularly demoralising and lead to a considerable loss of self-esteem. The majority of mothers thought that being identified as dyslexic and appropriately supported was of key importance in improving their child's self-esteem. What is not clear from a sample like this is what happens to children who are not recognised as having a specific learning problem by their parents. One of the mothers in the sample who was not recognised as dyslexic until she was an adult recounted her own experiences as a child.

'Basically I think they (her parents) thought I was thick. They were always telling me how slow I was and how my younger brother would run circles round me when I was older. I must have been about six or seven when it was pointed out to me that he could write his name and address and say the alphabet. I hated him for it! Of course I thought I was stupid, it's stayed with me for the rest of my life really. That's why I'm determined the same thing won't happen to my daughter.'

PRACTICAL SUPPORT

Mothers were asked a series of questions about what practical support if any they offered their children in addition to help with their reading. The first question was 'What sort of practical support have you tried to offer (name of child) at home, or do you think it's best left to the experts?' The question was phrased in this way to try and ensure that mothers weren't made to feel that they were lacking if they weren't offering practical support and to also lessen the chance of their giving a socially desirable answer. It may also have been the case that some mothers might legitimately feel that they should leave it to the school. The following response to this question by Mrs Carter was a typical reply, in that many mothers had tried a whole variety of things.

'Oh we've done pairs, like with cards. We've got all sorts of little games and things like they suggested. We've bought probably every book that's ever been suggested that might help. Like role playing books, we get through them, and all different sorts of things really, just to try and interest him. We've bought magazines about things he likes. But the thing was this year, I've taken him to the football . . . and I could have really cried because he sat down and started reading the football programme. And I thought, well that's the first time I've ever seen him sit down and read without being told to. We've bought the computer as well for Malcolm so we try . . . not that I've done a great deal with him, but sometimes if he gets his homework, we'll go on up and do a story on the computer. And because it's got the spell check and everything then he can print it out and take it into school. You know, I'll write that he's typed all the words himself, and things like that.'

Mrs Carter was a working class mother with three sons and a husband who worked away from home quite frequently. She by her own account had a lot of regular contact with school and spent a lot of time liaising with the teachers over Malcolm's difficulties. She didn't have paid employment outside the home and this meant that she could visit the school easily and also spend time giving her son practical support. What emerged in this sample was that it was those mothers who didn't work outside the home who generally had the most involvement with the school, and the most time to give practical support and campaign on their child's behalf. This included both working and middle class mothers in this sample and again underlines the importance of not having stereotypes about the degree of support and involvement by families from different class backgrounds. A simple count was made of the various activities mentioned by mothers. Reading was included if it was over and above listening to reading as part of a home–school reading scheme. Many mothers like Mrs Carter mentioned trying a range of reading materials to try and engage their child's interest.

This is not a definitive list as many mothers may not have mentioned all the activities they had tried but it does serve to illustrate the wide range of activities included under practical support. Mothers were also asked how they had decided on what support to offer. Out of the 22 mothers 19 said that they had basically had to decide for themselves as they had not been given any advice or guidance by the school. The remaining three mothers said that they had been given some advice and support by the school. Many mothers said that they were disappointed at not being given any advice by the school especially when their children were younger and were struggling to learn to

Table 8.2 Types of practical support offered by mother (n = 22 mothers)

Reading	11
Games	7
Homework	7
Workbooks	5
Phonetics	4
Storytapes	4
Computer	4
Flashcards	3
Writing	3

read and write. Many felt that in the earlier days in particular it had largely been a matter of trial and error, of using their common sense and seeing what did and didn't work.

'I had to decide for myself mostly through reading up on it and getting pamphlets and such like.'

'I think you have to try whatever you think. I went up a few times asking for help to both schools. I tried buying books, like the phonetic books and what not and we got to the stage where we worked through this particular book and I didn't know whether to go to the next book or whether we should learn them and I used to say, "Look, I don't know what to be doing. I'd be willing to do something but I don't know what."'

'The school never gave me any advice. I was never really sure whether I should be correcting what he did, because I didn't want to make him feel that everything he did was wrong.'

Several mothers mentioned this difficulty of not wanting to discourage their children by picking up on their mistakes all the time. Even within the context of practical support concern was expressed over how this could affect self-esteem or confidence.

'I tried to praise anything worth praising at all, just to try and encourage him. The thing we did most of all was to give Robert confidence above anything else, and he really seemed to gain that when he was about 9 or 10. He just became much more confident. He was a quiet, shy little boy at school before that.'

Mothers were also asked if they came across any problems in trying to offer their children support. Their answers to this included both the support that they had instigated and the support that they were asked to give by the school in tasks such as reading and learning spellings and also the phonetic sound cards that the Dyslexia Institute asked them to do with the children.

19 a lot of problems
 2 few problems
 1 no problems

Mrs Bell whose son was now 13 talked about the problems she'd had over the years in trying to help her son.

'Er, well, it's died a death at the moment. But at the beginning I used to try and help him read his homework. I often offered to help with his homework, but he didn't want help. That's why he doesn't hand in very good stuff, he just wants the homework to be over with. We tried the paired reading scheme (top infants) and he made it clear in subtle ways that he didn't want to do it and then it became such a slog. . . . Well last year we went through a terrible stage where I was trying to get him to do the cards and that from the Institute. I'd ask him to go and get them and he'd disappear for an hour. So we didn't do them.'

'It's more difficult in the lighter weather because they want to be out playing. I sometimes feel a bit guilty, because I think, "Eeh I should maybe be sitting down," and then I think, "Well, all his friends are out playing," and you think it's a shame, isn't it? And then I think he would probably start and resent the fact, and then I think, "Oh well, no, just leave it for a while."'

'He doesn't like doing it. Well you can't do it without them knowing can you? When they're little you can, but when they get to Mark's age, it's, well, work isn't it? . . . and as I say, he doesn't like the fact that he has to do extra work. I mean I have tried to explain it to him as best I can. That it's for his own good.'

Many would argue that these kinds of responses are no different to what may be found in many children of a similar age. What is different is that dyslexic children along with some other children with special needs require extra time and practice in order to access and progress through the curriculum.

'The dilemma is whether home should be a safe haven, somewhere where she can relax and unwind or whether we should be helping her so she can cope better at school. I don't know what the answer is.'

Many mothers were aware of this dilemma and expressed ambivalence and uncertainty about the kind of practical support they should give at home. This uncertainty appeared to be greatest when mothers didn't have specific advice on appropriate ways of helping their child. Mothers were happiest to carry out tasks when they could see the purpose of doing them and felt that they were geared at an appropriate level for their child's needs. The difficulties mentioned in chapter 6 that arose with reading at home often appeared to be the outcome of a mismatch between the task and the child's level of skills. In a similar vein several mothers mentioned considerable difficulties with children having to learn spellings for spelling tests. Mothers thought that the spellings were usually too hard and that the priority was wrong in that there were a great many other simpler and more commonly used words that their child couldn't spell.

'He was coming home with words like "engine" when he still couldn't spell simple words like "was", "that", "bus" and so on.'

'She gave them 20 hard spellings a week. He was worrying himself sick before the spelling test.'

'We used to spend hours learning the spellings. It was so hard for her. She insisted on doing them, cos she didn't want to be shown up in front of the other kids. She used to get in a terrible state about them. The worst thing was, it was a total waste of time because she'd forgotten them all by the next week.'

Another important issue in relation to support was that families varied considerably in the amount of time and resources that they had available. Mothers who worked full time, had other younger children, were single parents or had husbands working away from home all commented on the constraints that this put on their time and energy.

'Time, that's basically the main problem isn't it?'

'It's difficult in a sense because it's always me that has to do it you know.'

Emma was the second of four children. Her mother had started working part time so that they could pay for her two sessions a week of specialist tuition. In addition to taking and collecting Emma from her sessions she had to take her younger sister to speech therapy and help her younger son who had a hearing problem.

'She's missed out really. She's just had to get on with it. I do feel guilty about it, there just hasn't been the time.'

Mrs Williams, a single parent who worked full time and had a 13-year-old daughter, made the following comment:

'When I come home from work knackered, the last thing I want to do is have a fight with Sian about her work.'

In summary a number of issues relating to support were discussed. Mothers were keen for guidance and advice on the sort of support they should give. They first looked to the school for advice. Where this was not available they used trial and error to try and find out what would work. With younger children in particular mothers said that they tried to capitalise on their interests and to use incidental opportunities to encourage reading and writing, for example.

'I've been just lately trying to get him to write anything down. A couple of sentences is a real sweat. He did three or four lines totally on his own last night and I was ever so pleased, because it's the first thing he's ever done on his own in his whole life.'

Once their child was identified as dyslexic some mothers turned to the specialist literature for advice and also to specialist organisations. Many mothers felt that the greatest pressure on them to give support had been before their children were recognised as dyslexic. Once children were being given specialist support mothers felt that this eased the burden on them and also they were given advice on specific structured activities. The nature of support changed with the age and needs of the child. With younger children support for reading and the use of games, tapes and flashcards were common whereas with older children the emphasis changed to help with homework especially reading and checking things through, and the introduction of computers and spellcheckers. From the point of view of mothers the three biggest difficulties with support were:

1 Not being clear what to do.
2 Not having sufficient time.
3 Not wanting to over-burden their children.

SUMMARY

1 Ninety-five per cent of mothers thought that having dyslexia had an influence on their child.
2 At least seventy-five per cent of children were reported to have gone through a period when they had displayed considerable distress of one sort or another.
3 The majority of mothers had been concerned by their children's low self-esteem and saw raising or maintaining self-esteem as one of their major tasks.
4 Mothers considered that one of the main benefits of their children's out of school tuition was that it raised their self-esteem.
5 Mothers found that as well as practical support they also had to give their children emotional support to help them cope with dyslexia.
6 Mothers would have liked more advice from schools on offering appropriate practical support.

Chapter 9

Views on school

'We shouldn't approach dyslexics as broken learning machines.'

(Hales 1994)

For both children and parents, a major part of the interview schedule focused on their experiences of schooling. Children were asked a series of 16 questions starting with what difficulties they thought they had at school both now and in the past, because of their dyslexia. They were then asked how they tried to cope with these difficulties and how they felt about them. They were also asked how other children and teachers reacted to their difficulties. Parents were asked a similar question about what difficulties they thought their child had at school both now and in the past because of their dyslexia. Both children and parents were asked what kind of things were generally found helpful and unhelpful in school and both were also asked to describe the best and the worst teacher that the child had encountered.

PERCEIVED DIFFICULTIES WITH WORK AT SCHOOL

Children's perceived difficulties may not accurately reflect their actual difficulties but given the importance of self-esteem, self-efficacy and self perception in the learning process, it can be argued that it is important to look at children's perceptions of their difficulties. In order to get as clear a picture as possible on how children perceived their difficulties they were simply asked: 'What sort of work do you have difficulty with in school because of your dyslexia?'

As has been noted before on the basis of clinical observation some children appeared to find this an uncomfortable question to answer at an emotional level. Children appeared to have no difficulty in understanding the question at an intellectual level and in fact it could be argued that it was because children understood the question only too well that some of them found it uncomfortable to answer. At a general level children's perceptions of their difficulties fitted well with evidence from other sources such as reports by psychologists, classroom, special needs and Dyslexia Institute teachers.

Table 9.1 Children's perceived problems with school work related to dyslexia

Perceived problem	Primary (n = 10)	Secondary (n = 12)	Total (n = 22)
Spelling	4	9	13
Writing about things	6	3	9
Slow work speed	2	7	9
Maths	3	3	6
Copying off board	3	3	6
Reading	1	4	5
Tests	1	3	4
English	3	1	4
Specific subjects (other than maths and English)	1	3	4
Dictation	0	3	3

Table 9.2 Mothers' perceptions of their children's problems with school work related to dyslexia

Perceived problem	Primary (n = 10)	Secondary (n = 12)	Total (n = 22)
Written work	7	10	17
Spelling	7	7	14
Maths	10	2	12
Reading	6	2	8
Slow work speed	2	6	2
Copying off board	1	1	2
Reluctant to work	0	2	2
Behaviour	1	1	2
Exams and tests	0	2	2*

* Few of the children had encountered exams at this stage but all the mothers rated themselves as very worried about how their child would cope with exams in the future.

Although there was some difference in the details and the way that difficulties were described at a general level there was also reasonable agreement between parents and children on the types of difficulties they had encountered.

From tables 9.1 and 9.2 it can be seen that both children and mothers claim that spelling and writing problems are the most frequent difficulties in relation to school work.

PROBLEMS WITH MATHS OR ARITHMETIC

The high rating given to maths by mothers of primary school children may be because many of the children followed maths schemes such as the Scottish Maths Scheme which required a fair degree of reading accuracy. Several mothers felt that their child's progress in maths had been held up when they were younger because of their lack of reading ability. These mothers also felt that teachers weren't always aware of the degree to which their children's maths was affected by their poor reading. In addition mothers and children mentioned problems with mental arithmetic and the learning of tables. Gillis Light and De Fries (1995) reviewed much of the evidence on what they term as the 'comorbidity of reading and mathematical disabilities'. They concluded from their review that the majority of studies indicate that between 50 per cent to nearly 100 per cent of children with reading disabilities also have difficulties with some aspects of mathematics. This raises the question of whether these difficulties are mainly due to common underlying cognitive deficits or whether they are due to common environmental factors such as poor teaching or a negative attitude to learning. In order to try and answer this question Gillis Light and De Fries have drawn on data from the Colorado Reading Project which was set up explicitly to look at the genetic and environmental contribution to reading disability. With additional funding this has been extended to include mathematics. In this extended study 148 identical twins and 111 fraternal twins were selected because one member of the pair was initially identified as having a specific reading disability. It was found that 68 per cent of the identical co-twins and 40 per cent of the non identical co-twins also had a specific reading disability and that 49 per cent of the identical co-twins and 32 per cent of the non identical twins also had a deficit in their mathematical performance. These findings are statistically significant and the researchers claim that this would suggest that common genetic factors contribute to the poor performance in reading and mathematics. Gillis Light and De Fries don't make it clear in their paper, what aspects of mathematical performance are found to be lacking. They do mention that one of the tests used was the WISC–R arithmetic sub-test, which would suggest that they are talking about arithmetical performance. Another difficulty that they do acknowledge is that tests like this involve word problems and it may therefore be children's poor reading ability that is hampering their performance. In order to try and control for this they tested a sub-sample of the children on the Wide Range Achievement Test for mathematical ability. This is a pencil and paper test that involves no word problems. Despite this it was found that children still performed badly which would support the argument that specific underlying cognitive impairments affect both the reading and arithmetical performance of some children. However, there is also evidence that the reading and computational demands of arithmetic do significantly affect children's performance. Muth (1984) found that by artificially manipulating the reading and computational demands of arithmetical problems up to 50 per cent of the variance in performance could be attributed to these two factors. Many researchers (Ackerman, Anhalt and Dykman 1986, Lerner 1989, Brandys and Rourke 1991), have proposed that the deficits underlying reading and mathematical problems are in short-term auditory memory or in retrieval of information from long-term memory. Henderson (1991), an experienced teacher of dyslexic children, summarises the kind of day-to-day difficulties that children can have. She points out that as well as the obvious difficulties in reading mathematical problems, some dyslexic children may have difficulty in remembering what operations are associated with what mathematical symbols. They may also have difficulty in knowing which direction they should move in when working out a sum and find it difficult to know where to place a decimal point. Reversals of numbers can sometimes cause problems, as in the case of a boy who would often reverse two figure numbers so he would for example write 47 down as 74 as well as reversing the orientation of the 7. On top of all this is the well known difficulty that many dyslexics have in learning multiplication tables (Steeves 1983) and their poor performance on the arithmetic and digit span sub-tests of the WISC. Darren when tested at 9 years of age on the WISC–R showed a profile that was typical of many of the children in the study in that his digit span and to a lesser extent his arithmetic were strikingly poor in comparison to his other verbal skills. Each sub-test is given a scaled score out of 20 with 10 being an average score. A child who got an average score of 10 on each subscale would end up with an IQ of 100. As it can be seen Darren ended up with a verbal scale IQ of 130 despite the unevenness of his profile.

Darren Street WISC-R Verbal IQ 130

Information	17
Similarities	16
Arithmetic	11
Vocabulary	15
Comprehension	15
Digit Span	(5)

What is not clear from the literature at present is what the developmental history of these difficulties might be and what proportion of dyslexic children encounter them. The relative lack of comment about mathematical problems in older dyslexic children might suggest that as they resolve some of the earlier problems of reading, symbol identification, directionality, and reversals combined with less emphasis on arithmetical skills their difficulties decrease. The added use of calculators may also be helpful in diminishing problems. It is important that a distinction is made between arithmetic and mathematics as case studies would suggest that children can have a good conceptual grasp of mathematics despite poor arithmetical skills. An 11 year old boy not in the main study talked about the problems that he had at school with maths. This boy had scored very highly on a mathematical reasoning test and above his age level in the SATs, despite being seen by his class teacher as only average because of his 'slowness' in doing maths.

'Sometimes they put loads of maths on the board with loads of tables. One morning Mrs T (class teacher) put about 20 sums up. I got really worried I didn't get it all copied down. Everybody else had finished and I was still writing them down. They were table sums all of them, and then I got all mixed up and I know bits of tables and they all get jumbled up. . . . There are only 2 true types of sums. Like divisions are just a sort of take away and multiplications are a type of adding sum. I try to find new ways to do sums, else it gets boring.'

Sian (13 years) when asked what she had difficulty with at school responded with:

'Maths, the reading bits, and mental arithmetic.'

Clayton (1994) also endorses the importance of distinguishing between maths and numeracy or arithmetic. She raises the issue of how far we should expect dyslexic children with their poor short term auditory memories to learn numeracy skills and at what point they should be allowed to use aids such as calculators and number squares. Mothers therefore seemed to be reflecting research findings in mentioning difficulties with specific areas of maths. They may have stressed these difficulties because they are a less expected and less publicised outcome of having dyslexia.

WRITING, SPELLING AND SPEED OF WORK DIFFICULTIES

Riddick (1995b) has commented on the relative prominence that children give to writing and spelling difficulties as opposed to reading difficulties. This may well be a function of the age of the children who were interviewed as the average age of even the primary school children was 10 years. Many of them had improved considerably in their reading, possibly as a result of their specialist support and several did mention that they had problems with reading in the past.

'I used to have problems reading, but now I read big books. Sometimes I get mixed up on things. A lot of hard words that I've forgot. I only have a little problem now' (Graham 11 years).

'In the past reading, I was on a really low book, I used to resent it' (Emma 12 years).

It may well be the case that if 7-year-old dyslexic children were interviewed, reading would rank first or high in their list of difficulties. In fact the only primary child to mention reading difficulties in relation to school was the youngest child in the sample. This boy was 8 years of age when interviewed and had only been receiving specialist support for 3 months. When assessed

3 months previously he had scored on the first centile on the WRAT reading test despite an IQ of 123, and was still in the process of learning to read. He said he never read unless he had to because he found it too hard. Two of the secondary children who mentioned reading difficulties had discrepancies of over 5 years between their reading age and chronological age when initially assessed. Neither had been identified as dyslexic until quite late on and were still therefore working on their reading. The other two secondary age children mentioned reading difficulties in relation to specific tasks and subject areas. One said that she had problems with reading in maths because of the need for complete accuracy and the other said that he had problems with subjects where a lot of reading was required because he couldn't read quickly enough. This highlighted the issue that concerns over speed and accuracy of work in a wide range of tasks (dictation, copying from the board, free writing, spelling, reading) tended to increase with age. Whether this is because of children's increasing awareness of their difficulties with age or because of the more stringent demands of the secondary school environment or some interaction between these two factors is not clear.

'Like copying off the board, I get frustrated cause it slows us (me) down. Like the teacher will be speeding ahead and my writing's slow' (David 12 years).

'It's difficult to get things down fast enough' (Kathy 12 years).

Some children also spoke of the dilemma of whether to go for speed or accuracy in their work as they were well aware of the trade off between them.

'If a teacher dictates work I can't write fast and neatly' (Luke 13 years).

At a more general level children spoke repeatedly about the constant pressure of 'keeping up' and the constant humiliation of always finishing last or getting the lowest mark in spelling tests.

'I usually finish my work last' (Graham 11 years).

Some children spoke of their frustration at being told to hurry up or be more tidy in their work when they felt they were already doing the best that they could.

'Just saying like, "Hurry yourself up," and things like that when I cannot go any faster' (David 12 years).

Other children spoke of their upset at being called lazy or careless for not spotting spelling or punctuation errors or words missed out.

'If I knew I'd spelt it wrong I wouldn't spell it the way I had to start with. It always looks all right to me' (Mandy 11 years).

Some children like Ewan were upset when they were accused of not having done homework such as learning a list of spellings or part of their tables.

'Spellings and tables I always used to get them wrong. Then I used to get wronged (told off). They said I didn't do them but I couldn't.'

Ewan's mother confirmed this independently in her interview by talking about the hours that she had spent in the past trying to help him learn his spellings. Again children spoke of the worries they had about exams and tests, these centred on not being able to read the questions accurately and fast enough and not being able to write fast enough.

'I don't like tests. I get very nervous and I don't do well, because there isn't enough time to get things down' (Stephen 14).

'I get really nervous about exams because of reading the questions' (Sam 11).

What this did emphasise was the need to see dyslexia as a developmental disorder which manifests itself in different ways at different ages and stages in a child's development. Whilst early intervention and support for reading are of vital importance for most dyslexic children it is important that the longer term difficulties with areas like writing and spelling are not overlooked. It is also important that we have a good picture of how the difficulties appear from the child's perspective. Children were particularly concerned about visible public indicators of their difficulties such as finishing last or being required to read out loud. This was underlined by their responses to a further question which asked if there was anything in school they really dreaded having to do. Seventy per cent of the children said that there were things that they dreaded having to do in school. We don't know from this data what percentage of 'non-dyslexic' children also dread doing certain things in school but what was striking was that all the activities mentioned were related to their specific learning difficulties. The most frequently mentioned were reading aloud in class, spelling tests and exams.

'Reading in front of the class; anything that shows me up and makes me different.'

'I get upset in exams when I can't read something, my palms go sweaty.'

UNDERESTIMATING DIFFICULTIES?

What was noted both in the children's interviews and independently by mothers was that some of the younger children in particular tended to underestimate their difficulties and appeared reluctant to acknowledge them. So, for example, Mark when asked what difficulties he had with his work at school started by saying:

'I don't really have any problems.'

Table 9.3 Total number of named difficulties with work because of dyslexia

	Primary (n = 10)	Secondary (n = 11)
Children	24	34
Mothers	34	33

And when asked how much he wrote compared to other children he said:

'I just write the same.'

Whereas his mother said:

'Spelling is the bane of our life, it's horrendous. One or two times they've had this thing like dictation. Calling something out and the kids have to write it down. That's just like the horrors for Mark, because he comes out with something that's totally incomprehensible. Sometimes getting something down quickly, he can't get it down quick enough. And his short-term memory causes problems for him. I don't think he realises how far he has a difficulty.'

Some additional evidence for the defensiveness of some children may be the smaller number of difficulties mentioned by primary age children compared to their mothers and to secondary age children, although other factors such as embarrassment or poorer ability to generate answers may be responsible.

Children were asked whether they wrote more, the same or less than other children. Their mothers were also asked the same question. Several mothers commented spontaneously that whereas they thought their child wrote a lot less than other children their child probably wouldn't agree and would be more likely to say they wrote the same amount as other children. In fact all the mothers thought that their children wrote less than other children, whereas only 50 per cent of the children thought that they wrote less than other children. Mothers' views were backed up with specific examples and corroboration from other sources such as school and the Dyslexia Institute. It also fits with Mosely's (1989) finding that children with spelling problems tend to write less. So for example Mandy on being asked how much she wrote said:

'The same as other children.'

Whereas her mother said:

'I think she writes a lot less than other children, because she takes twice as long to write it.'

This raises the question of why some children responded in the way that they did. Were they genuinely unaware of the extent of their difficulties or were they personally aware but not willing to admit to them, or had they consciously or unconsciously minimised their difficulties in order to keep their self-esteem intact? Returning to the case of Mark his mother made the following comments:

> 'The reason he started getting some extra help in the junior school was because at that point his self-esteem and confidence was rock bottom. And that's why they recognised the need to do something. Not specifically, I don't think, because of the academic side of things, because as a child he had no confidence or self-esteem.'

As indicated in chapter 3 some researchers have suggested that children may progress from a more global self-esteem to a more differentiated one as they grow older and there may also be individual differences in how self-esteem is structured. It could be argued that where children are operating at the level of more global self-esteem, any difficulties may be threatening to that self-esteem whereas if their self-esteem is differentiated into different areas they can afford to admit to specific difficulties without this affecting all areas of their self-esteem. This is highly speculative at present but more understanding of how and why children construe their difficulties in the way that they do is an important area of future research. Another reason why this is an important area to consider is that there is probably a relationship between the feedback that children receive on their performance and the way that they perceive their difficulties. Both mothers and classroom teachers spoke about the dilemma of how you pointed out mistakes without demoralising children and damaging their self-esteem. As described in chapter 3, one experienced primary classroom teacher spoke about her bewilderment when confronted by the first piece of free writing of the year from a 10-year-old dyslexic boy.

> 'Well I just didn't know where to start. I'd never seen anything like it before. I had to get him to come and read it to me, because I couldn't make a lot of it out.'

This teacher like many good teachers decided on a strategy of giving as much positive feedback as she could on the content of the story and just picking up on a few of the most basic errors. She admitted herself that she relied mainly on 'commonsense' in deciding on what errors to pick up on and that this was a somewhat arbitrary strategy. This strategy appeared to work in terms of encouraging this boy to write and giving him the confidence to say what he wanted to say, but didn't really tackle his underlying difficulties in any systematic way. As Pollock and Waller (1994) point out, arbitrary spelling and grammar corrections are of little use to the child who needs to be given structured coherent feedback. Another classroom teacher who had been on a specialist dyslexia course described the feedback she was giving to a dyslexic child.

'Well I try and turn the whole thing on its head. Rather than pointing out mistakes I try and put it in a positive light. So I'll say, "Now you're doing so well, I think you could try and have a go at putting 'ing' and 'ed' endings on your words" (something this girl rarely did). I'll give her some structured work to do to practise it first and then say she can have a point for each time she uses them in her free writing. I try and encourage her and make it fun.'

Mothers also spoke about the difficulties of giving feedback both on specifics and at a more general level.

'It was very difficult choosing your words. Trying to say that although he was doing very well . . . you try to build him up . . . but! and how to put this "but" over as best you could. That he was having a few problems with his spellings and to try and help him . . . and we never said you know, "You've got a problem with reading." It's always "You've got to have this help." It was a case of being very delicate, picking your words extremely carefully so that he wouldn't object to it.'

This does raise some important questions. How far do children need to be aware of their difficulties in order to progress or to accept help? What appears to be important is the framework and the context in which difficulties are considered. It can be argued that difficulties need to be presented within a highly positive framework where the child is given explicit strategies for dealing with them so that they can feel they have some control over them. Doran and Cameron (1995) discuss the importance of metacognitive approaches which encourage the child to be aware of their learning strategies. It also raises the question of how far children should be viewed as having difficulties and how far the environment should be seen as 'disabling' the child. Writers on disability have argued strongly that it is the environment that produces 'disability'. Others would argue that in a highly literate culture it is very difficult to completely avoid the need for literacy skills and that it would equally being doing the child a disservice not to try and improve their skills as much as possible. What seems important is that there is a balance between these two points of view and that they work together in harmony to provide the best possible outcome for the individual. These arguments may seem rather abstract and removed from the nitty gritty of the everyday classroom but they do have a direct impact on the type of special needs interventions that take place. Much of the interest in early interventions such as reading recovery is based on the assumption that children's difficulties can and should be remediated. Whilst few would argue with the desirability of early intervention it is important that this doesn't lead to an exclusive focus on remediating early within-child difficulties. No doubt arguments will continue about the efficacy of various forms of early intervention but what seems clear is that some children will have longer term difficulties. For example Wheldall, Freeman, Outhred and McNaught (1995) claim that in a one year follow up study of the reading recovery programme in 10 primary schools, 35 per cent of the children were not 'recovered'. This then raises the question of what sort of support these children are offered and how far the focus should be on improving difficulties and how far environmental changes should be considered. Mrs Slatter felt that even though her son Dean had improved considerably environmental changes would be of additional help to him.

> 'I think it's a very biased system, all the tests he's going to have, are going to be written tests. They should be given an option. I still feel that orally he's a lot better than his writing. I think also the testing early on should be like that. The junior one he scored very low on the written test, and she gave him the same test orally, and he scored on the right line. I think there should be a lot more oral tests.'

Whilst a whole range of environmental adaptations such as extra time in exams, taping work, photocopied notes are possible these, as many teachers will know, are not without their difficulties. Many children with special needs, especially as they grow older, try to cover up or disguise their difficulties, especially from their peers. Not surprisingly anything that they think will show them up or make them different from their peers can be threatening and unacceptable. Environmental interventions have to be handled with skill and delicacy and need where possible to be negotiated on an individual basis with the child. What might be quite acceptable to one child may be highly unacceptable to another child and much might depend on how obtrusive or unobtrusive the intervention is. Sophie, a thoughtful and articulate 16-year-old, interviewed in a later study spoke about her experiences of being given extra time in exams.

> 'Yes, that's helpful. I would say that's helpful. I didn't think it . . . well, in some things it isn't, but then in others it's been really helpful.'

She continued by explaining:

> 'I have to go and do it in the Sixth Form so everyone knows. It's awful really. They don't consider your feelings that much. They made us get up, we had to walk out of an exam and go into another room, and there was like a hundred people watching us walk out.'

On a longer term basis there are also questions about how much time and energy an individual should devote to overcoming their 'difficulties' and 'improving' themselves. Tim a third year university student was asked as part of a pilot interview if he had used the new literacy support centre at the university. Tim had been identified as dyslexic whilst at primary school and had received support over a number of years. He said he hadn't used the new centre because this would only involve him in more work and that he felt he'd spent enough of his life doing extra work. He added that he'd got to a point where although his difficulties still limited his performance to some extent he was prepared to accept this and felt that he wanted to concentrate on other more positive aspects of his life. Pollock and Waller (1994) also stress the importance of teachers highlighting what children can do rather than what they can't do. One mother talked about the difference in attitude between her daughter's primary school and the secondary school she was about to transfer to:

> 'At her primary school they never really acknowledged that she had dyslexia. It was always homilies about "be more careful," don't be lazy, don't be careless. It was like she wasn't valued; she was never picked for anything. I couldn't believe the difference when I went up the comprehensive to tell them about her problems. They took the problems seriously, they didn't try to sweep it under the carpet. They had specific plans about what they would try and do. They said it sounds like she's got a lot to contribute to this school. It was so positive, it was just such a different way of looking at it.'

HOW CHILDREN FELT ABOUT THEIR DIFFICULTIES

When children had talked about the various difficulties they had with their work, and other people's response to their work they were asked how they felt about these difficulties. Many of them also added comments at other times during the interview. The children described themselves as disappointed, frustrated, ashamed, fed up, sad, depressed, angry and embarrassed by their difficulties.

CHILDREN'S STRATEGIES FOR DEALING WITH DIFFICULTIES

Children were asked what strategies they used to try and deal with the difficulties they had described. Because in its abstract form this was a difficult question for children to answer they were asked some specific questions about how they dealt with their writing and spelling difficulties. In this case they were presented with a list of strategies such as avoiding difficult to spell words or getting help from a classmate. This list was compiled from strategies already documented in the literature, such as avoiding difficult to spell words and strategies named in the pilot interviews such as putting off writing. It was not thought that the children were simply agreeing with the interviewer in answering the list because children were quite selective and quite emphatic about which strategies they did and did not use. So, for example, when asked whether they avoided certain words several children gave a similar answer.

> 'Every day.'

'I avoid lots of words I can't spell.'

'Yes, all the time.'

'Yes I do that nearly all the time like "was" and "because".'

'Yes, I try and make a different sentence out of it.'

Whereas a small number of children were quite certain that they didn't avoid words in their writing which they found difficult to spell.

'I just give it a try.'

'No, I just carry on. I try and use like my A and E (sounds).'

The information in table 9.4 on avoiding difficult to spell words fits well with research which shows that both children (Mosely 1989) and adults with spelling difficulties restrict their vocabulary because of this. What is not clear is how far these difficulties exacerbate any difficulties that children may already have with sentence structuring or how far they may be producing difficulties with sentence structuring. It is not hard to imagine that if a child is constantly trying to construct sentences without using words like 'was' and 'because' this will lead to difficulties with sentence structuring. Pollock and Waller (1994) who are both experienced teachers of dyslexic children highlight the dilemma that children face. If they are very careful in choosing words they can spell then they will often appear to be immature in their vocabulary and mode of expression. If on the other hand they ignore their spelling and get on with writing what they want to say they are in danger of being accused of being careless, especially as they may be able to correct their mistakes when they have been pointed out. One of the mothers in the study gave an example of this:

'She (class teacher) said she tells him not to be careless. When he brings her a piece of work she tells him, "Don't be lazy. Go away and do it prop-erly." She says well he can do it because he brings it back with less mistakes.'

Table 9.4 Children's reported coping strategies for dealing with spelling and writing difficulties

Coping strategies	Primary (n = 10)	Secondary (n = 11)	Total (n = 21)
Avoids hard to spell words	5	11	16
Writes less	3	8	11
Gets classmate to help	4	6	10
Puts off starting or avoids doing writing	2	6	8
Total number of strategies named	14	31	45

This mother was very concerned because in past years when her son had sympathetic and supportive teachers he had been willing to write even though it was a struggle for him. Now he appeared very unhappy and had said all year that he couldn't stand school any longer. The boy himself when interviewed said:

'I dread having to do writing. I draw pictures instead if I can.'

Another girl commented about writing:

'I'd choose to do anything else.'

Numbers are small so any conclusions have to be tentative. What does seem clear is that for whatever reason older children are more explicit about their difficulties and the strategies that they use to cope with them. By secondary age all the children claim that they avoid difficult to spell words and over half of them claim that they put off or avoid doing writing. It has been suggested that whereas primary school teachers are basically optimistic about children with special needs and still expect them to improve or overcome their difficulties, by secondary school, teachers are more pessimistic in their attitudes and no longer expect children to show substantial improvements. It seems that by secondary school the emphasis of the intervention is based on teaching children to cope with or circumvent their difficulties rather than directly tackling their difficulties. It could be argued that the increased number of strategies named by secondary children is partly a response to this shift in ethos. The children themselves, in consciously writing less, avoiding writing and limiting their written vocabulary, appear to be adopting coping and avoiding strategies. Nearly all the secondary children had been put in bottom sets for some or all subjects. Many of them spoke of feeling rejected and ignored and resented the low expectations that they thought that many teachers had of them, these sentiments were also reiterated by their mothers.

BEST AND WORST TEACHERS

Although children were asked what sort of things they generally found helpful and unhelpful in school it was found in piloting the interview that this was a difficult question for many children to answer. Whereas they responded quite enthusiastically to the more personal question of describing the best and the worst teachers that they had encountered. Similarly with parents it was found that they responded in more detail and more confidently to the question about best and worst teachers. As was discussed in chapter 7 this is probably because parents and children often don't have insight into the many structural and organisational issues which impinge on a teacher's role and they therefore have to judge teachers largely independent of context and on their face to face performance. Parents did temper their comments in the more general question and many of them showed awareness and expressed sympathy for the context in which teachers were working.

> 'It's not so much the worst teachers, he's had very interrupted teaching through his school career. He's been first of all in a very big class that had like the top number that you can have. So obviously they were pressurised with coping with that. And then just throughout the whole of infants as well he had like somebody was off ill for a long time, and then there was the supply. Somebody was off pregnant, and then there was another reason, and it went on and on. . . . I think they generally did care. I don't think anybody knew exactly what it was and as he got higher up the school I think they did try to work around him. Well I know they did try. I don't want to write them off. They did try to help him.'

There was close agreement between mother and children pairs in describing the best and worst teachers they had encountered. In the case of four pairs it was thought that there had been no 'best' or 'worst' teachers, with all the teachers described as fairly supportive or alternatively as fairly indifferent. So one mother when asked about the best teacher her daughter had encountered said:

> 'Nobody in particular. There's not one who's really thought about it.'

Both mothers and children thought there were close links between the ways in which teachers related to children and how they coped with their dyslexia at a personal level. Mothers in particular emphasised the close relationship between their child's self-esteem or confidence and the way that teachers treated the child.

> 'He had one who made no allowances. She gave them twenty hard spellings a week. He was worrying himself sick before the spelling tests. In fact he started bedwetting because of the pressure of the spelling tests and other things. She destroyed his confidence completely, she used to systematically put red lines through everything.'

> 'The second year juniors he had a very good class teacher, she really took him under her wing. It was her project to get him up and going by the time he left her class. She took a great interest in him, yes and she dwelled on the positive aspects of everything good he could do. He had very low self-esteem before that but his confidence seemed to really start to build in her class.'

From table 9.5 it can be seen that both children and mothers underline the importance of giving praise and encouragement allied to understanding as key qualities of the best teachers. Mothers in particular emphasised the support and encouragement offered by these teachers and often spoke of the teacher 'believing' in their child.

Table 9.5 Children's and mothers' perceptions of the best and worst teachers they had encountered

Best teachers			
Children's perceptions (n = 18[1])		*Mothers' perceptions (n = 18[1])*	
Encourages/praises	9	Encourages/praises	12
Helpful/adapts work/explains	7	Knows strengths	8
Understanding/doesn't show up	6	Positive/supportive	7
Doesn't shout	2	Believes in child	7
Sense of humour	2	Boosts self-esteem	7
Knew child was dyslexic	1	Understands dyslexia	7
Treats as intelligent	1		

Worst teachers			
Children's perceptions		*Mothers' perceptions*	
Cross/impatient/shouting	7	Doesn't understand difficulties	6
Criticises or humiliates	6	Puts down or humiliates	5
Not helpful/negative	5	Negative attitude/no praise	5
Ignores/thinks useless	4	Low expectations/ignores	7[2]
Not understanding/insensitive	4	Lacks tolerance/no allowances	3
Blames you/thinks you are lazy	4	Shouts at child	3
Red lines through work	3	Red lines through work	4

Notes:
1   As 4 out of the 22 mother/child pairs said they hadn't encountered any best or worst teachers only the remaining 18 pairs are represented on this table.
2   6 out of 7 at secondary school.

'She was so supportive, and she was aware of Mark having problems, and she you know recognised that, and she tried to help us. But apart from that if you ask Mark he'll tell you she was his favourite teacher anyway.'

'His year tutor last year picked up on David's problems. He was really committed to helping David. He encouraged him with his marking and takes a personal interest.'

'Mr H. He was the chap that really built his confidence up and encouraged him. He was great.'

Mrs Salter and her son Graham, as can be seen in the next two quotes, were both very positive about the 'best' teacher to have taught him.

'She was wonderful, she encouraged him, praised him and rewarded him. She boosted his self-esteem and he progressed a lot with Mrs M. She enjoyed teaching him.'

'Mrs M. She knew I was intelligent. She used to encourage me and she used to help me with my work.'

Malcolm and his mother were in agreement that his current teacher was one of the best he had encountered.

'The relationship is quite good with her because she knows when to encourage him when he's done well, and she does. And she can see areas where Malcolm's quite good at, like, model building and things like that, and she'll get him to show the other kids in the class how to do things like that. So he does feel, "Well, I mightn't be good at that, but I am good at this." . . . She's really good with him.'

'She's really kind to people, she's encouraged me a lot.'

Both children and mothers mentioned the importance of not being shown up or humiliated by teachers.

'Like she makes allowances for me and she doesn't show me up. She praises me and gives me gold stars.'

'She's understanding. She encourages you and always smiles at you. She's nice even when you get something wrong.'

Some children as well as commenting on these supportive attitudes also mentioned more practical aspects of support. Kathy in her first year at secondary school when asked about the qualities of the best teacher/s she'd had so far named several of her subject specialists and added:

'If the work's hard they help a lot.'

When it came to worst teachers there was close agreement again between children and mothers on who fell into this category and why. Mrs Salter described what happened when her son Graham entered the first year of junior school after a year spent in America.

'He had this bad teacher for two years who humiliated him for two years. She had on the second day we had come back from America, prodded him in the stomach and told him to go down to the kindergarten to get a book to read, right in front of the whole class. She found it an irritation having a child who couldn't read in her class. She had no tolerance at all.'

'Mrs N. She never noticed anything. She just liked the ones who knew everything. It was very off putting.'

'There was one in the primary school I won't mention her name. She said I was useless at everything and I couldn't do anything. My mum was very angry.'

'His second teacher was a battleaxe. There was red writing all over his books and no praise at all.'

'She had no understanding at all. She put him down for the least little thing and put red lines through all his work.'

'She kept saying "You're lazy." It's awful to say to a kid all the time "You are lazy." I think he lived up to expectations. I don't know how if you down a kid all the time you expect to get any good work from them.'

'I don't like being shown up in front of the class. The spelling tests are the worst. I'm not frightened of the shouting, but I don't like it when they get the class to laugh, like one teacher used to do.'

By secondary school both mothers and children felt that on top of teachers who criticised and humiliated them there were teachers who ignored them and had low expectations of them.

Several mothers commented that irrespective of IQ and motivation their children were put in the bottom set for most subjects. Stephen (14) despite being well behaved and well liked by his teachers and having an IQ of 113 was in the bottom set for all subjects.

'At school they think he's great, but he's in the bottom set for everything. He's not being given any homework, he's probably not being stretched enough. Some of the teachers think that because they're in the bottom set that they don't matter, they ignore them and give them less attention.'

Mrs Andrews reported similar problems despite her son having an IQ of 119 and according to his school reports being a quiet thoughtful boy who was well behaved.

'His present maths teacher is the worst I think. . . . She said, "Josh won't be able to take O level you know." He says she doesn't like him. I said, "Well, why do you think that?" And he says that she doesn't take any notice of him.'

Sian's mother also commented on her 13 year old daughter being put in the bottom set for everything and continued by saying:

'She's had teachers who've yelled at her, crossed everything out, labelled her slow and had low expectations of her.'

In summary the worst teachers were thought to be negative in attitude, critical, humiliating and lacking in understanding, in addition, especially at secondary school, some worst teachers were thought to ignore or underestimate children. As stated before the best teachers were seen as positive, encouraging, understanding and helpful. These results are similar to those found when children in general are asked about good and bad teachers (Burns 1982) and the more negative aspects are similar to those reported by children who are failing or having difficulty in school for a variety of reasons. Burns (1982) has also reviewed a wide range of literature which suggests there is a link between how supportive and encouraging a teacher is and how positively they are rated by a child. In addition it has been suggested that there is also a strong link between the teacher's attitude and the child's level of self-esteem. Opie (1995) looked in detail at the practice of five exceptionally successful teachers of reading in terms of both their personal qualities and their teaching approaches. In her summary she gave the following description:

> 'All the teachers studied emerged as valuing positive and trusting relationships with their pupils and having high expectations with regard to progress. They stressed the importance of enabling their students to experience success, improving their confidence and raising their self-esteem.'

These teachers were also reported to be well organised and prepared and enthusiastic in their approach. They all stressed the importance of structured phonics teaching and a multi-sensory approach allied to keeping children on task as much as possible as well as making lessons enjoyable. One teacher who worked with a class of children with special needs emphasised that children have to believe they can be helped in order to progress. Edwards (1994) in her interviews with eight adolescent dyslexic boys at a specialist boarding school found that the boys emphasised the need for a warm trusting relationship with their teachers and that many of them stressed the importance of an 'outstanding' teacher with whom they'd had a special relationship. It may be that the 'best' teachers identified by children and parents are not necessarily the 'best' or most effective teachers in terms of children's educational performance. But it can be argued that there appears to be considerable overlap in the qualities described by parents and children and those describing effective teachers of reading.

Discussing 'best' or 'worst' teachers or effective and ineffective teachers is a difficult area. The first point is that different children may have different views on who best and worst teachers are. A second point is that negative feedback or criticism is often threatening and difficult to handle. To look at it more positively research (Fry and Coe 1980, Galloway 1985) suggests that individual teachers and how they interact with children has more influence on their progress than organisational differences such as whether they are in a mixed ability class or not. Ainley and Bourke (1992) give a useful overview of research into quality of school life issues and in their own research point to large differences in how fair and helpful different teachers are perceived to be by children. Galloway (1985) also suggests that these teacher differences in classroom interaction may have the greatest impact on children who are experiencing difficulties in learning. In the present study there were several instances where children and their mothers felt that they were in 'the firing line' because of their specific difficulties.

> 'He says she shouts at all the children and so on. But he probably gets more of it, because she's always telling him off for being untidy or being slow or getting his spellings wrong.'

A difficulty for teachers may be that some children with specific learning difficulties are more sensitive than usual to criticism. So that a comment which is intended to be helpful such as praising a piece of writing but telling the child to put capital letters in may be seen only as criticism. This may sometimes be the result of cumulative criticism that the child has received over the years and from a number of quarters. Meryl, an outgoing and positive 16 year old talked about this in relation to her written work.

'I get really exasperated people never comment on the ideas first. They say, "Oh look, you've spelt this wrong and this wrong." My best friend at school does it; she leans over and points out my mistakes. I could kill her sometimes! The teachers are just the same and my mum's no better. It really bugs me.'

Edwards (1994) detailed over sensitivity to criticism as one of the common features in the eight boys that she interviewed. One question that arises is whether at an objective level children with dyslexia do receive more criticism about their work than other children or whether they simply perceive themselves as receiving more criticism. It may well be that both factors are in operation although parents and children strongly felt that they did receive more criticism. Robert, for example, by his first half term in secondary school had received negative written comments on the untidiness and supposed carelessness of his work from a range of subject teachers. It was found that half the homework he had done so far had negative comments of this kind and in some cases a subject teacher had given negative comments on several occasions. Many of these comments were tempered with 'good but . . .' and teachers may well have intended their comments as helpful feedback. But Robert was already becoming upset by these criticisms and wrote the following at half term in an account of his new school.

'The science teacher only marks for neatness and tidiness. I liked science, but I don't now.'

Robert, like several children, stressed that what upset him was the 'unfairness' of this criticism and from his point of view the impossibility of doing anything about it .

'I already write as neat as I can.'

To be fair to Robert's teachers his writing was appalling and his frequent attempts to correct his spelling added to the messiness of his work. He attended a school with a good special needs department and a generally positive approach to specific learning difficulties. But his experiences of marking do emphasise the need for all the teachers involved to be aware of a child's difficulties and to be aware of the cumulative effects of the feedback they are giving.

Some of the children in the study described in this book had displayed many of the features of depression when at their lowest point. It has been found that depressed individuals are more likely to remember negative rather than positive feedback (Cole and Jordan 1995) and are therefore more likely to be adversely affected by it. The need for appropriate feedback has already been discussed in chapter 3, and the views of children and mothers in this study support the importance of giving careful consideration to how feedback should be given. With older children it may be possible to discuss with them the kind of feedback they find most helpful and the form they would like to receive it in. One difficulty appears to be that particularly when children are in a negative frame of mind it can take years of encouragement to get them to view themselves more positively.

> 'It's taken years to convince him that he's not stupid and to be more positive about things. When he was really low nothing seemed to be able to shake him out of it. He'd come home with praise for a piece of his writing and still be negative about it. One day he came home and complained that he'd only got 49 out of 50 for a maths test! He blamed himself because he'd got one sum wrong.'

What was encouraging in this study was that where teachers did have positive and warm relations with children they were reported to bring about big improvements in children's self-esteem. Opie (1995) suggests that it is important that teachers set aside time for building up good relationships with children when teaching them to read and that factors like self-esteem and motivation are kept in mind. Solity (1995), Wheldall and Glynn (1989) suggest that teachers need the time to be able to reflect on their own behaviour in the classroom as a basis for building up positive interactions with children. Where classes are large and teachers already overworked this obviously becomes more difficult for them to do. On the other hand in this study there was no indication that 'best' teachers spent appreciably longer helping the dyslexic children than 'worst teachers'. It was the way they related to the children that was seen to be of greatest importance.

In conclusion best teachers appeared to combine a warm positive outlook with good specific understanding and skills.

SUMMARY

1 Late primary age children as a group see writing about things as their greatest difficulty.
2 Secondary age children show increased concern with the speed and accuracy of their work.
3 There was a fair amount of agreement between children and mothers on the kinds of difficulties they had.
4 Mothers of primary age children placed more emphasis on maths and reading problems and several thought that their children tended to underestimate their work related difficulties.

5 Children were particularly concerned with visible public indicators of their difficulties such as finishing work last.
6 Children reported using a range of coping and avoiding strategies to deal with written work.
7 Both children and mothers thought that individual teachers had a big influence on their self-esteem and ability to cope with difficulties.

Chapter 10

Children's views on dyslexia

'They said I would always be dyslexic cos they can't cure it, but I can be great at
my work.'

(Darren 12)

'Well, people think you're being stupid to be quite honest. That's the whole attitude of it.'

(Sophie 16)

In chapter 6 children's reactions to being labelled dyslexic were discussed, as
this was felt to be a critical part of the labelling process. It was concluded
that whereas the majority of children found the label dyslexia helpful at a
personal level, half of them didn't find the label helpful at a public level.
This chapter looks in more detail at their views on dyslexia and the ramifica-
tions of these views for various aspects of their life. A number of questions
that children were asked, explored their understanding and attitude towards
both their difficulties and the term 'dyslexia'. They were asked, for example,
what dyslexia meant, who had explained it to them, and whether it made
sense to them. They were also asked if they met other children with similar
difficulties, and whether this was helpful or not to them. In addition they
were asked if they'd had adult dyslexics pointed out to them and again
asked if they found this helpful or unhelpful. Another series of questions
overlapped with their views on school but focused specifically on social
issues such as whether they thought other children noticed their difficulties
and if so how did they try to explain their difficulties and how did other
children react to them. Finally their long term expectations were questioned
by asking if they thought they would still be dyslexic when they were an
adult.

In order to ask children about their understanding of the term 'dyslexia'
in a non-threatening way the question was put in the following form:

If somebody asked you what dyslexia meant, what would you say?

Children responded to this question with a wide range of answers which
could be divided into the following categories.

Table 10.1 Children's definitions of the term 'dyslexia'

	Primary	Secondary	Total
Reading, writing, or spelling problem	5	5	10
Learning difficulty	2	3	5
Slow at work/learning	1	2	3
Can't explain or doesn/t know	2	2	4

Only two children (one primary and one secondary) characterised dyslexia primarily as a reading problem. Given what is known about the long term difficulties accompanying dyslexia and the priority that children of this age had given to problems with school work other than reading, this is perhaps not surprising.

'It's when you find it hard to read and things like that. It takes a long time to overcome.'

In contrast to this answer most children in the first category mentioned reading in combination with writing and/or spelling and one child described it solely as a spelling problem.

'You have trouble with reading and writing.'

'Not good at reading and spelling.'

'Somebody who can't spell as good as the rest.'

Children in the second category rather than mentioning specific literacy difficulties referred in some way to the learning disabilities underlying these difficulties.

'I tell them like it's problems with learning words, it's a learning difficulty. Like the other way I use to describe it is, like, my memory, my short term memory is like a broken camera, like the flash isn't working.'

'People who have to learn in a different way.'

Perhaps not surprisingly given that 'keeping up' was a major preoccupation of many children, two children actually described dyslexia in terms of slow speed.

'Basically a bit slow at your work.'

Another child who said he didn't really understand what dyslexia was described himself as a slow learner.

'Just probably I don't know or a slow learner or something.'

This boy had been very demoralised by his experiences at school and scored low on self-esteem.

In contrast the boy who scored highest in self-esteem and also had good verbal fluency was the only child to mention intelligence.

'Intelligent, but can't read and write.'

It has to be born in mind that these comments only give a snapshot of children's views on dyslexia at a given moment in time. It may also be the case that what you choose to say in explaining dyslexia to others may not fully reflect your own understanding. One boy looked very frustrated and said:

'I know what it is, but I can't really explain it.'

Trying to explain dyslexia in brief, concise terms is quite a difficult task and much might depend on the verbal fluency and confidence of the child. One child pointed out that it's difficult to explain dyslexia to children who are basically hostile or disbelieving. The mother of another child talked about a recent incident at school. Her son was in the last year at primary school.

'They had to fill out this form describing themselves for the next school to look at. He'd put this bit about how he was slow at his work but he didn't know why. I asked him why he hadn't said he was dyslexic. He said he was worried that he might be asked to explain what it is, and that he wouldn't be able to.'

This boy was able to explain what dyslexia was quite adequately to the interviewer and thought that knowing he was dyslexic was helpful. His mother felt that he had picked up on the critical and disbelieving attitude of his primary school and that this combined with his lack of confidence and poor verbal fluency made him very defensive and wary of any situation which might expose him to critical questioning or ridicule. This again reinforces the idea that whereas children find the concept of dyslexia helpful at a personal level they don't necessarily find it helpful at a public level, especially if the public level is seen as hostile or critical of the concept. Those educationalists who argue that labelling is harmful are right in a sense, in that labelling children in a public situation especially one that is critical of the label probably is harmful. But where they are probably wrong is to go on and deny the use of the label altogether. As argued before, labels have to be used in the right context and only when they are of help to the individual concerned. It's important that both parents and teachers discuss with children as they get older if, when and where they want a particular label used. It should also be accepted that children's views on this might sometimes be complex and contradictory and that as children change and develop so might their views. It can be argued that children's understanding of dyslexia is probably heavily influenced by how it is explained to them. In order to examine this issue

Table 10.2 Who, according to the children, explained dyslexia to them

Mother	12
Mother + father	2
Mother + father + dyslexia teacher	1
Mother + dyslexia teacher	2
Mother + dyslexic friend	1
Mother + doctor	1
Dyslexia teacher	2
Assessing psychologist	1

children were asked who had explained to them what dyslexia meant and whether the explanation had made sense to them.

It can be seen that in over 50 per cent of cases mothers alone explained dyslexia, and in another 7 cases mothers explained dyslexia in conjunction with someone else, in 3 cases with the child's father, and in 4 cases with a professional. Thus in over 80 per cent of cases mothers were primarily involved in explaining dyslexia to their child. In 3 cases a professional was seen as the primary explainer. In these last 3 cases the children in question were all of secondary age and it maybe that judgements about the appropriateness of who should explain change with age. What emerged from the interviews was that in some cases there was an ongoing dialogue between the mother and child and/or specialist teacher about what was meant by dyslexia whereas in other cases children were reluctant to speak about the subject so there was little opportunity to clarify or discuss with the child what dyslexia meant. What was striking was the heavy responsibility that mothers had and the total absence of any explanation from within the mainstream school environment. This may be a function of this particular sample and in areas where schools and LEAs are more supportive of the concept of dyslexia, more explanation might come from within the school setting. Children's recollections of who explained dyslexia to them may not necessarily be accurate in a strictly objective sense but they do reflect their perceptions of who was significant in this process. Given that the manifestations of dyslexia change over time and the types of difficulties encountered change with time, it may be important for some children that they can revise or update their understanding of dyslexia. So a child in early primary school may understand dyslexia as a difficulty in learning to read whereas by secondary school they may see it as a difficulty in spelling. In addition to having dyslexia explained to them by an adult, two children mentioned that watching a television programme on dyslexia had increased their understanding.

'I once saw a programme on dyslexia, that helped me to understand it.'

Following on from the question of who had explained dyslexia to them children were also asked if this explanation had made sense to them.

Table 10.3 Children's understanding of the explanation of dyslexia they had received

Did it make sense to you?	*Primary (n = 10)*	*Secondary (n = 11)*	*Total (n = 21)*
Yes	9	9	18
No	1	0	1
Not completely	0	1	1
Forgotten	0	1	1

As can be seen from these figures the majority of children thought that the explanation given to them made sense. Sian (13 years) who said: 'I suppose I'll never fully understand it.' was the child oldest in age when identified as dyslexic. She said that knowing she was dyslexic was helpful but was resentful of her mother having her assessed even though this was at the school's suggestion. She went on to say that she would like to talk about it more but not with her mother.

'Not to my mum, because she's my mum like.'

Luke (13 years) who as mentioned previously had been called lazy throughout his primary school and was very demoralised by the whole experience said that although he'd probably had dyslexia explained to him that he'd forgotten what it meant and that he would like to ignore the whole thing anyway.

Harry (8 years) the youngest child to be interviewed, when asked if dyslexia made sense to him, said:

'No it doesn't, it's a funny word.'

Despite this response, Harry had in fact given a good explanation of dyslexia. It seemed more the case that he, like Sian, was responding more to the question of whether the idea of dyslexia made personal sense to him. He and Sian had only been receiving specialist support for the last 3 months and they both appeared to be grappling with what it meant for them. All three mothers of these children commented independently in their own interviews that their children were still coming to terms with the idea of thinking of themselves as dyslexic. Harry's mother had in fact written down verbatim some of Harry's thinking on the subject.

As a result of many of the poems/prose in the 'as I see it' book produced by the Dyslexia Institute, Harry and I had a long chat about 'getting to know' and I asked if he would mind if I wrote down whatever he said – these are Harry's words:
'When I was told I had to go and see a man about my reading I was gobsmacked. But then I supposed I had to get used to the idea. On the

journey there I felt funny: I didn't know this man . . . When we got there, we sat in a waiting room. Then the man came and called mummy and daddy. He came back and asked for me. After a while of doing lots of tests – I was very bored – he asked to speak to mum and dad. Much later mum and dad came back to the waiting room and we went outside. I said, "What did all that mean?" When we were outside the building and in the car mummy said that it meant that I was dyslexic . . . I didn't like it . . . I didn't like the idea of seeing a specialist (Dyslexia Institute teacher) every week either, but mum and dad said not to worry and, "Let's go to Mc-Donalds to celebrate."

After a few days I began to feel a bit better about being dyslexic. Dyslexic people can't remember words, and they don't know how to use words on paper. They can't do writing and spelling very good either. They may not be very good at all those – reading, writing, spelling, but some things they are good at, like, they're intelligent and can do other things like maths . . . and swimming.'

Harry's mother independently in her own interview gave an account of how they first told him he was dyslexic.

'We told Harry immediately. He wanted to know everything. We told him in a very congratulatory way that we were delighted. We're so pleased because we know what the problem is and we can help you.'

Sophie, a 16-year-old who was interviewed in a later study, also commented on the difficulty of coming to terms with thinking of yourself in a new way. She had been assessed as dyslexic at the age of 13 at the instigation of her new school.

'When I found out I was really upset because I thought it was incurable like. Like if you were a bit slow, you think "Oh well, I can do this and then I'll catch up." But when I found out like, everyone was saying, "Oh I thought you'd be happy," but I wasn't, I was shocked. Because everyone had been saying for so many years that I'm not dyslexic, I'm just slow. And it was frustrating that they'd never picked it up and I might have been able to get a bit better than I am now.'

Sophie's mother confirmed these views in her interview, when asked how she felt when it was confirmed that Sophie was dyslexic:

'Relief. Sophie didn't. I felt, "Oh great! That's found it!" I thought Sophie would be pleased. Sophie was disgusted. "Oh no!", you know. I think she'd rather have been a slow learner.'

Given Sophie's initially negative reaction to the label it was interesting to check on how she felt about it three years later.

INTERVIEWER   How do you feel about the label now? Does it help you understand or do you resent it for making you feel different?

SOPHIE   Yes it does, it helps me. Because there's things about it and stuff you can relate to, and that makes you feel a bit better that there's someone out there going through the same thing.

At a speculative level it could be suggested that whereas the majority of mothers had suspected for some time that their child was dyslexic and had been gradually seeking out information on it, for some children the idea may have been much more a bolt out of the blue. Sian, who as already illustrated, was still coming to terms with the label 'dyslexia', made the following comment.

'The first I'd heard of it was in January when I went for the test.'

Alternatively some children may have built up a very negative image of dyslexia based on the attitude of the school to it. Sophie felt very strongly that the children in her school had a negative image of dyslexia.

'Well, people think you're being stupid to be quite honest. That's the whole attitude of it.'

In summary, it appears that the majority of children feel that they do understand what dyslexia is even though some find it hard to describe it to others. Where children don't think that they understand dyslexia this appears to be related more towards how they feel about the label than any simple lack of understanding.

TELLING OTHER CHILDREN

When children had been asked about the kinds of difficulties they had with their work at school, they were then asked if they thought other children noticed the difficulties they had. As can be seen from the following figures only two children definitely thought that other children didn't notice their difficulties.

Table 10.4 Dyslexic children's thoughts on how aware other children are of their difficulties

Do others notice?	Primary (n = 10)	Secondary (n = 12)	Total (n = 22)
Yes	6	8	14
Not sure	3	3	6
No	1	1	2

Table 10.5 Children's explanation of their dyslexia to other children

	Primary (n = 10)	Secondary (n = 12)	Total (n = 22)
Doesn't explain	5	3	8
Only tells best/close friends	4	4	8
Teacher explained	0	1	1
Yes will explain	1	4	5

A major reason given for other children noticing their difficulties was their slow work speed.

'Cos I usually finish work last.'

Another reason given was that other children noticed when they when they were withdrawn for specialist support either within school or out of school.

'Yes, because I went to see a special teacher.'

This then raised the question of if, and how, children explained their difficulties to other children.

As can be seen from these figures over two-thirds of children either didn't explain their difficulties to other children or only explained them to their closest friends. The overwhelming, and in fact only reason given for this reticence, was their fear of being teased by other children.

'I don't want to tell anyone, because I think they'll tell everyone else, and then everybody might tease me.'

Emma's mother made comments quite independently in her interview that underlined what Emma had been saying.

'She doesn't like going in school time. She doesn't want anyone to find out. In fact she tells them she's going swimming, she really doesn't want other children to know. It's the same in class, she doesn't want any obvious help in class.'

The next reply by Graham was typical of those given by children who just told their friends.

'Some people I do tell, some I don't. Most of them would just make fun of me.'

Some children like Mark said they only told their best friend.

'Only my best friend knows.'

Sean (8 years), who had experienced considerable teasing at school, said he had started by telling other children to mind their own business. With support from his mother he had told some of his friends. Because of the negative attitude of his class to dyslexia, his mother had recently asked if someone from the Dyslexia Institute could come in and talk to the children about dyslexia and was waiting for this to happen. Among those children who said they did explain their difficulties some limited themselves to brief practical explanations. So Robert, for example, said that when other children asked where he was going he would reply:

'I'm going for a bit more English help.'

Only three children claimed that they directly explained what dyslexia was to children in general. As has been noted earlier in this book, the two boys in question scored highest on self-esteem and verbal fluency out of the children in this sample and the girl in question went to a school that was highly supportive of dyslexia. In several cases mothers had discussed with children the issue of whether they should tell other children about their difficulties, especially if their child was being teased about them. What clearly emerged was that nearly all the children were left to fend for themselves with mothers offering what support they could in the background. The one boy who said that his teacher had explained about dyslexia to the class was appreciative of this support.

'Well, the teacher said a bit about it. That was helpful.'

In another case although the boy in question didn't mention it, his mother mentioned that a class discussion on dyslexia had taken place.

'They have discussed it in the class (secondary school) why David comes here, which I think is a good open attitude. I was really pleased with that.'

Interestingly, David was one of the few children who said he was willing to talk to children in general about dyslexia.

Although there would be issues about how and in what context dyslexia is explained and it would need to handled with great sensitivity, it is important, that if children wish, they are given help and support, and are not left solely responsible for explaining their difficulties to other children. In some cases children needn't be singled out, but the school could inform and educate both teachers and children about dyslexia and create a more informed and sympathetic environment. This in turn could be part of a school's overall special needs policy and would not be treating dyslexia as a special case but as part of a comprehensive approach to special needs. Sophie (16), who was interviewed in a later study, spoke of her frustration at the negative attitude of children in her comprehensive school to dyslexia. She felt that the school should have been educating children about dyslexia and changing their attitude towards it. She said that her secret dream was to give a talk in her school about dyslexia.

'I've always wanted to do like a big talk on it. Just to tell them what it means and everything. They don't understand at all.'

TEASING

Half the children in the sample said they had been teased specifically about difficulties with their work related to dyslexia.

'She kept saying I was thick because I was always last on our table (to copy things down).'

'They said I was dumb and a nerd because, like, I couldn't spell things.'

O' Moore and Hillery (1989) reported that in four Dublin schools, children in remedial classes were more likely than other children to be bullied and were almost twice as likely to be bullied frequently (once a week or more). Whitney et al. (1994) found that in a survey of eight schools in Sheffield, children with special needs were at a higher risk of being bullied and that the degree of risk varied with their type of special need.

They didn't include a category of children with specific learning difficulties but they did have a category of children with mild learning difficulties, where 55 per cent of them reported bullying. They don't clearly explain who is included in this category but do later make passing reference to dyslexic and clumsy children who it may be supposed were included in this category. It was also found that children perceived children who were shy or in need of help as being in increased risk of bullying. They found that teachers tended to underestimate the amount of bullying of children with special needs, especially at the junior age. Edwards (1994) reported that all eight of the boys she interviewed said they had been badly and frequently teased in their mainstream schools and she saw this as one of the main reasons for them ending up at a boarding school for dyslexic boys. What was noted in the present study was that many of the children lived with the constant fear of being teased about their difficulties and put a lot of their energies into covering up their difficulties or trying to divert attention away from them.

DYSLEXIC FRIENDS

Several children made spontaneous reference to friends with dyslexia during the interview and towards the end of the interview all the children were asked if they met other dyslexic children, and if so was this helpful to them.

Table 10.6 Meeting other children with dyslexia

Do you meet other children with dyslexia?	Primary (n = 10)	Secondary (n = 12)	Total (n = 22)
Yes	10	12	22

In fact, all the children had teaching sessions in pairs at the Dyslexia Institute so in this setting they all met at least one other child with dyslexia. Although exact figures are not available, what was clear from the interviews was that for some children this was the only opportunity they had to meet another child with acknowledged dyslexia. It appeared that particularly in schools where dyslexia was not acknowledged, children could feel very isolated. In some cases they suspected that certain other children might be dyslexic but because the school didn't recognise dyslexia and children tended to keep it secret this made it difficult for children to identify each other.

'But they tend to keep it hush hush. . . . Where at my school, like, you don't meet each other and stuff. It's like private.'

Following on from this question about meeting other children, they were then asked if they found this helpful or not.

Table 10.7 Children's views on meeting other children with dyslexia

	Primary (n = 10)	Secondary (n = 12)	Total (n = 22)
Yes	9	10	19
No	0	0	0
Not bothered	1	2	3

These figures would suggest that the large majority of children in this sample did find it helpful to know other children who were dyslexic or had similar problems.

Children's answers gave more details on the kind of contact they valued.

'It's helpful knowing there's someone else.'

'It's more enjoyable knowing someone else has the same problem.'

'Because then I feel it's not just me.'

Children appeared to particularly value either having someone in the same class with similar problems, whether these were recognised as dyslexia or not, or having a close friend with dyslexia. Jason and Malcolm, for example, both mentioned boys in their own classes who had similar problems.

'It's OK, cos there's someone with your own difficulties.'

'I'm not very embarrassed now because there's someone the same as me.'

Other children mentioned the positive value of having close friends who were dyslexic.

'Two of my friends are dyslexic, we're like closer friends because of it.'

'Well my friend Tim's dyslexic you know. We joke about it and call each other names and that, but it does help us (me).'

Some children also made positive mention of sharing their session with another dyslexic child at the Dyslexia Institute.

'I share a lesson with Rachael. I like that better.'

The Dyslexia Institute teachers in their interviews also spoke of the positive advantages of children being able to share their problems and talk them over in these sessions.

In summary there appeared to be three major aspects to knowing others with dyslexia.

1   Having a close friend/s with the same problem.
2   Having other children in the class with the same problem.
3   Sharing specialist support with children with the same problem.

As well as this face to face type of contact, some children and mothers spoke of more distant types of 'knowing' which gave support. As has been previously mentioned in discussing the issue of labels, children spoke of the advantage of knowing at a general level that there were others with the same problem and of seeing illustrations of this on television or in books.

Whereas having a friend with dyslexia seemed to focus on positive factors such as supporting each other and sharing experiences, knowing there was another child in the class who did as badly or worse than you sometimes appeared to be based on the more negative strategy of simply comparing yourself with someone the same as or worse off than yourself.

Although the majority of children said that knowing other dyslexic children or children with similar difficulties was helpful, they varied considerably in how helpful they seemed to find this. So that responses varied from the highly positive, to the more lukewarm, to the frankly indifferent.

'Yes, yes, definitely.'

'Yes, it's a little bit helpful.'

'I'm not really bothered.'

The variation in responses may be partly a function of children's mode of expression and the experiences they were reflecting on. But as we know from many areas of disability people vary considerably in how helpful they find it to align themselves with others with similar experiences. Whereas many derive great benefit from doing so, some people do not find this at all helpful and have no wish to do so. These individual differences need to be borne in mind in any plans to enable dyslexic children to meet or support one another and would suggest that they need to be optional and responsive to feedback from children. Having said this, the majority of children in this sample did find that knowing other children was helpful, especially in their own school. This would suggest that ways of enabling dyslexic children to meet either individually or in groups should be considered as part of special needs support. Meryl, another 16-year-old interviewed in a later study, described how dyslexic children tended to know one another and informally get together in her comprehensive school. This school had an open and supportive attitude to dyslexia as part of a wider special needs policy which appeared to enable this personal support to flourish. Schools, it can be argued, can by their ethos and organisation either facilitate or hold back various types of peer support.

ADULT ROLE MODELS

Both children and their mothers were asked about the significance of adult role models. Out of the 22 mothers, 21 said that they pointed out adults with dyslexia to their children. The one mother who didn't do this was the one who had already said that they didn't use the term dyslexia at home. The children were asked if they had heard of famous or successful adults with dyslexia. They all said that they had heard of adults apart from the boy who didn't discuss dyslexia at home. Following on from this children were asked whether they found this helpful or not.

Table 10.8 Children's views on adult role models

Does this encourage you or not?	Primary (n = 10)	Secondary (n = 11)	Total (n = 21)
Yes	10	9	19
No/not bothered	0	2	2

Some children responded to this question at a general level whereas others named specific role models.

'Yes, it's encouraged me a lot.'

'Yes it does, if they can do it, so can I.'

'Yes Duncan Goodhew, cos I used to like swimming.'

'Tom Cruise, Cher, Michael Heseltine. Yes, it helps, like Michael Heseltine is an MP. It's nice to think you're not the only one.'

This 13-year-old girl was keen on pop culture and wanted role models that she saw as current and relevant to her.

'Einstein, Roald Dahl wrote the *Vicar of Nibbleswick*, and Michael Heseltine.'

This boy was very keen on politics and wanted to be leader of the United Nations when he grew up. He was therefore particularly pleased that there was a role model from the political world that he could refer to. He was also interested in science and as described earlier in the book, said that he sometimes defended himself when teased, by referring to Einstein.

'I brag at school actually . . . like Einstein was dyslexic . . . so that means dyslexics can't be thick, that stops that.'

Apart from Einstein who according to a recent survey is a popular cult figure with young people, all the role models were of living people recently or currently in the public eye.

Table 10.9 Role models named by children

Duncan Goodhew	(olympic swimmer)	6
Tom Cruise	(film star)	5
Einstein	(scientist)	4
Michael Heseltine	(politician)	4
Cher	(pop singer/actress)	2
Ruby Wax	(comedienne)	1
Susan Hampshire	(actress)	1

(These were all people that the children believed to be dyslexic, whether this was the case or not.)

Some children described people whose names they had forgotten.

'That presenter on children's TV. The one with peroxide hair, she said she was dyslexic.'

What appeared to be important was that role models were relevant to children's values and interests. One girl complained about the lack of current women role models, and one of the mothers mused on the lack of current sporting role models.

'Duncan Goodhew is quite a long time ago now. It doesn't mean that much to him. Now if it were Kevin Keegan (ex captain of the England football team and current manager of Newcastle United), that would be a different story.'

Luke, when asked if he had heard of famous or successful adults, replied,

'There used to be some people on the noticeboard (at the Dyslexia Institute). Duncan Goodhew I think was one, and there were a few other people.'

When asked if this encouraged him or not he said,

'Not particularly . . . I somehow don't think . . . what's swimming got to do . . . Duncan Goodhew I mean . . . what's it got to do with dyslexia. It's like you learn it off by heart.'

INTERVIEWER   He said the reason he started swimming was because he wasn't any good at most of his school work, so it was like a way of proving you know that he could be really successful, and that's how he got into swimming.

LUKE   That's a bit like me that . . . I sort of like bikes.

Luke was classified as one of the two children who didn't find role models helpful, but his comments do raise questions about how role models are introduced to children. He was critical of the idea of simply learning a list of names and the conversation with him suggests that talking about role models in more detail may be of more value. It may well be that there are individual differences in how children identify with and use role models. At a general level it seemed to be the case that role models served two purposes. One was to encourage children and improve their self-esteem, the other was to give them a way of defending themselves when teased by other children. Several children spontaneously mentioned a dyslexic parent or relative as a positive role model, despite the fact that a question was not directly asked about this.

Mark commenting on his dad's difficulties said:

'If he can get past it, I can get past it.'

Given that half the children in this study had a parent with similar difficulties and several more had uncles and aunts or older cousins with similar difficulties the importance of family members as role models should not be overlooked. Children didn't seem to be concerned with their parents having prestigious roles: what seemed to be important was that they could relate to an adult who they saw as competent at coping with dyslexia who had survived school! Two children mentioned their dyslexic mothers who had left school early because of their difficulties and had been largely housewives with occasional part time work.

'Like me mum's dyslexic and she's survived it.'

A girl interviewed in a later study spoke of her delight when one of the teachers at her comprehensive school also admitted to being dyslexic.

It may well be that a range of more familiar everyday role models would be helpful to many dyslexic children. At present this process is hampered because of the under identification of adults with dyslexia. In this study several of the fathers were not openly acknowledged as dyslexic and examples of dyslexic adults in a range of local jobs were not available to children. Lewis (1995) talks about a unit set up for dyslexic children within a comprehensive school. He points out that one of the advantages of this is that older pupils and pupils who have left have acted as positive role models for younger children. Criticism is sometimes made of famous adult role models because, as with physical disability, it is suggested that it encourages the notion of the 'super cripple' and gives children unrealistic goals and expectations to live up to and also gives the public at large unrealistic expectations of what should be achieved. Whilst this has to be taken seriously there was little evidence from the interviews that children viewed role models in this light. For most children they appeared to be a minor but important part of the elaborate defences that they used to survive school and also gave a small but much needed boost to their self-esteem. It can also be argued that by giving children a wider range of more everyday role models that this would counterbalance the influence of 'super' role models.

DO YOUR PARENTS UNDERSTAND WHAT IT'S LIKE TO BE DYSLEXIC?

Children were asked this question and were then asked to choose between three categories.

Table 10.10 Children's perception of whether their parents understand how it feels to be dyslexic

	Primary (n = 10)	Secondary (n = 11)	Total (n = 21)
Definitely do	6 (4*)	3 (2*)	9 (6*)
To some extent	4 (1*)	6 (1*)	10 (2*)
Not at all	0	2	2

Note: * Denotes the proportion of children who spontaneously and specifically mentioned feeling understood by their dyslexic parent.

As can be seen from these figures the majority of children think that their parents do understand at least to some extent. This might reflect the nature of this particular sample of parents, in that the parents had to believe in the concept of dyslexia sufficiently to send their child to the Dyslexia Institute for extra support. Whether children who were initially identified by the school system would feel similarly understood only further research can tell. Perhaps not surprisingly primary age children felt more understood than their secondary age counterparts.

'My dad does most, because like, he used to go through a hard time because like there was no help around. So I think he knows what it's like.'

'My mum's dyslexic so she knows what it's like.'

'Yes they definitely do, because my mum used to have difficulties.'

Those children who chose the 'some extent' category were more ambivalent in their answers.

'To some extent. Sometimes I think they do and sometimes I think they don't.'

'I'm not sure if they know what it's like, although they know what it is.'

'My mum might think she knows what it feels like, but she doesn't fully understand it.'

In several cases it was thought that mothers were more understanding than fathers.

'My mum understands a bit more than my dad.'

Only two children felt that they weren't understood at all.

'She thinks she knows what it's like but she doesn't.'

As well as the six children in the 'definitely do understand' category who specifically mentioned a dyslexic parent another two of the children in this category also had dyslexic parents. Therefore eight out of the nine children who felt definitely understood had a dyslexic parent. Whilst more research is needed to verify this, it would suggest that children are more likely to feel understood by a dyslexic parent, especially in families where the parent openly acknowledges their difficulties. Darren's mother who had been identified as dyslexic as an adult spoke about what happened when she helped him with his homework.

'Well he dictates it to me and I try and type it out on the word processor. He thinks it's really funny when I'm damning and blasting because I've spelt something wrong or I don't know how to spell it. I ham it up a bit because I reckon it's good for him to see that a grown up makes mistakes and that I have to struggle and work at it. We have a good laugh, it's something we can share.'

Darren had spoken of feeling definitely understood by his mother and had also cited his mother as a positive role model. Darren's mother thought, although her non-dyslexic husband was basically sympathetic, especially before Darren had been identified, he used to get more exasperated with him.

'I felt that because I had some inkling into the problems he was having, so

I was a bit easier with him. I think as far as Mike's concerned he used to get annoyed because sometimes it appeared that he could do it.'

In this sample it was almost entirely mothers who helped children on a day to day basis but despite this some children still felt more understood by their dyslexic fathers. Mark, as already shown (first quote, this section), felt especially understood by his father even though his father worked away from home for long periods of time and he valued the day to day support that his mother gave him. Another boy whose dyslexic father worked away from home said:

'Aye me dad's alright, he understands. He works on the oil rigs.'

This is not to say that children didn't value the support and understanding of their non-dyslexic parent and much might depend on the general quality of the relationship that a child has with their respective parents.

There has been little discussion in the literature on the role of dyslexic parents and what there is tends to view them rather negatively as adding to children's difficulties (Ravenette 1985, Thomson 1990). This appears to be based on speculation and assumption rather than firm evidence and, it could be argued, fits with the general tendency to pathologise families (Falik 1995). Whilst more research is needed, the evidence from this study suggests that dyslexic parents can be a positive asset in providing role models and understanding to their dyslexic children.

TELLING PARENTS

Children were asked if they talked to their parents about any problems or difficulties they had at school because of their dyslexia. They were then asked to rate their responses according to four categories.

Table 10.11 Degree to which children tell parents of dyslexia-related problems

	Primary (n = 10)	Secondary (n = 10)	Total (n = 20)
Usually	5	0	5
Sometimes	2	4	6
Rarely	2	5	7
Never	1	1	2

It is commonly held that children in general vary considerably in the amount that they want to talk about school and especially any problems that they are having at school. Research on bullying (Smith and Sharp 1994) suggests that children often don't tell their parents about this especially as they grow older. In this sense these figures may not represent anything out of the ordinary. What may be more significant is that where schools are unaware of problems such as a dyslexic child being teased, having difficulty copying down homework, dreading spelling tests or reading aloud, it was often parents in this sample who brought these problems to the attention of the school. Obviously parents can only bring problems to the attention of the school if they are aware of them in the first place. At the same time children's need for independence has to be respected as they get older. It can be tentatively suggested that children seemed to take this issue into their own hands by becoming more selective about what they told parents as they grew older but it has to be borne in mind that these results are from a small sample of children.

Those children who sometimes told their parents stressed that it depended what it was and how important they thought it was.

'Sometimes not if it's not important.'

'It depends what it is.'

Five of the seven children who said that they rarely told their parents said that this was simply because they didn't like talking about school and not because they deliberately wanted to keep things from their parents, although this may have sometimes played a part.

'I don't like talking about it unless I have to.'

'I don't like talking about school.'

'I usually say school's boring all the time and I think it is, so when I come home, I usually just forget about it.'

Luke went on to explain that because he found much of school boring and stressful the last thing he wanted to do when he came home was to talk about it and that his way of coping was to blank it out of his mind as much as he could.

Luke's mother when asked if he talked about his problems simply said 'no.'

Mark on the other hand seemed more concerned about the reaction of his mother.

'I would keep it to myself, because I don't want my mum to know because I think she would say, "Why don't you do the proper work?" and things like that.'

Mark's mother, when asked if he would talk about problems at school or did she have to drag them out of him, said:

'Drag it out of him. I know there's something wrong by his mood, and I sort of like, I don't go on at him all the time. I ask him. But I mean, the more you go on the more he won't say anything. So I sometimes leave it and then he will eventually sort of like say, "Mum, I've got like . . .".'

The majority of mothers appeared to be aware of the degree to which their children were communicating or not communicating with them. The problems arose when a mother thought something was wrong but had to wait until their child was ready to talk about it. Several mothers spoke of their children bottling things up. Ewan's mother recounted an incident in which her son in his first year at secondary school had been having problems with his homework that she was not aware of, although she was aware that something was wrong.

> 'Ewan bottles it up. He didn't really talk about it. He got quieter and quieter and it all boiled to a head before last Christmas. About the October half-term I got an official letter from them saying Ewan had seven defaults and they were for not doing his homework, and every single night I'd been saying are you alright with your homework, I'd no idea this was going on. So I asked for a homework book because I thought this would help him. Next thing Ewan comes in from school absolutely distraught, in a dreadful state because some teacher had said to him, "Here's a homework book for you, Bell, because your mum's asked for it." What I didn't know, was that they were often given as punishment. So he thought I'd asked for him to be punished. When he came in it was the worst night of my life. He cried and he was upset; he couldn't believe that I'd asked for this punishment.'

It transpired that Ewan was struggling with the written work at his new school and was having particular problems in copying down homework and had gradually become overwhelmed by the difficulties he was having.

Ewan, in his interview, said that he rarely or never talked about his problems at school with his parents, when asked why he said:

> 'I just didn't want to talk about them.'

Ewan did go on to say that on rare occasions he did talk to friends at school about his difficulties. Edwards (1994) noted in her study that five out of the eight boys she interviewed said that they had great difficulty in talking about their feelings of distress and unhappiness to anyone and often hid their problems at school from their parents. Whilst there may be no easy solutions to children who are reluctant to talk about their problems, it can be suggested that, particularly as they get older, opportunities at school should be made for them to discuss any difficulties. One comprehensive school arranged a contact teacher for special needs children who met them regularly on an individual basis to check on any difficulties or worries that the child had. The use of peer counselling or peer support groups might be another way of enabling some children to talk about their problems.

THE FUTURE

The final question that children were asked was whether they thought they would still be dyslexic when they were an adult. The purpose of this was to get more information on how children were viewing both themselves and dyslexia. Some critics have argued that voluntary organisations such as the Dyslexia Institute give both children and parents false expectations by implying that dyslexia is something that can be 'cured' if given the right treatment. This criticism seems at variance with the definitions given by such organisations which emphasise the constitutional basis to the cognitive deficits underlying dyslexia. The organisations, in their defence, would probably argue that they set out to improve and not to 'cure' dyslexics. Nonetheless this debate does raise the question of what sort of expectations children should be given and what sort of balance between optimism and realism should be struck.

Table 10.12 Children's responses to the question, 'Do you think you'll still be dyslexic when you're an adult?'

	Primary (n = 10)	Secondary (n = 11)	Total (n = 21)
Yes	1	3	4
Not sure/don't know	5	5	10
No	4	0	4
Hope not	0	3	3

Although with small numbers such as these, evidence has to be interpreted cautiously, there was some indication that children became more realistic about the possibility of long term difficulties as they got older. The two youngest children in the sample both replied with vehemence to this question of whether they would still be dyslexic when they were an adult.

'No definitely not!'

'No way!'

Two other primary children replied 'no', on the basis that they would improve with help.

'I don't think so, cos I'm getting a lot of help.'

Children in the 'not sure' category varied from those who thought they probably would be dyslexic as an adult to those who thought they probably wouldn't, to those who felt they had no idea.

'I might be, I'm not sure.'

'I don't know, probably not, cos I'm not that bad.'

'I don't know, I'm going to try to get rid of it.'

'I don't know whether it gets better or not.'

By secondary age some children seemed to realise that there was a possibility that they would have difficulties as an adult despite the fact that they wished it to be otherwise.

'I hope not, I want to overcome it but I don't think I can.'

Some of those children who thought that they would still be dyslexic when they were an adult framed this in positive terms. In fact the two boys highest in self-esteem and verbal fluency both thought that they would be dyslexic as an adult, but were positive about their ability to cope with it.

'They said I would always be dyslexic cos they can't cure it, but I can be great at my work.'

'More than likely, but I think I'll learn to cope with it.'

Whereas some children were less positive about the idea of still being dyslexic:

'Well, my mum says you cannot grow out of dyslexia, like, you've got it. You've got it twice as hard as anybody else, to be able to catch up with everybody at work. It would be nice not to have it. Like, for it to wear off. Like, to find a cure, you drink enough diet coke and it's gone!'

As can be seen there were a wide range of responses to this question, only further research can tell whether this variation is largely due to individual differences in personality and experience or whether it indicates various points on some sort of developmental process in coming to terms with a possible long term disability. It may also be the case that children's expectations vary with the severity of their difficulties and/or all these factors combine to provide a distinctive developmental history for each child. What does seem to be important, is that a clear distinction is made between the difficulties underlying dyslexia which may persist, and the ability to develop positive coping strategies and improve performance. The two boys who expressed positive opinions on being dyslexic as an adult appeared to already be doing this. McLoughlin *et al.* (1994) in counselling adults with dyslexia argue that awareness and understanding of one's difficulties are the first step in taking control of them and developing effective compensatory strategies. They suggest that 4 levels of awareness can be identified:

1   No awareness – no coping strategies
2   Aware – no coping strategies developed
3   Aware – unconscious coping strategies
4   Aware – conscious coping strategies

One of the important aspects of specialised support for children may be that it gives them the belief that they can apply effective strategies to their work and that over time they can gain more control over their difficulties.

'He was writing something recently, and as usual he'd left several words out. When he read it to me he realised what he'd done. At one time he just wouldn't have noticed or he'd have got upset and gone off in a state. He was a bit exasperated, he said "I'm always missing words out, but I'm trying to think of a way of not doing it anymore." I was really pleased: a few years ago he would never have said that. It's as if he's getting more insight and more confidence that he can tackle things.'

SUMMARY

1 Over two-thirds of children could give a reasonable explanation of dyslexia.
2 In eighty per cent of cases mothers had a major role in explaining dyslexia to their children.
3 The majority of children felt that the explanation they were given of dyslexia made sense to them.
4 The majority of children thought that other children noticed the difficulties they had with their work.
5 The majority of children were not willing to explain their difficulties to children in general because of fear of teasing.
6 Fifty per cent of children said they had been teased because of their work-related difficulties.
7 Knowing other children with similar problems was rated as helpful by most of the children.
8 The majority of children said that role models were helpful.
9 Most children thought that their parents understood at least to some extent what it was like to be dyslexic.
10 Children may become more aware as they grow older of the possible long term nature of their underlying difficulties.

Chapter 11

Mothers' views

'But the real costs are to the spirit, the sorrow of observing a child's bleak despair, the anguish and alarm when the despair turns to rage.'

(Donawa 1995)

Various aspects of mothers' views have already been presented in several chapters in this book. The purpose of this chapter is to look more closely at their overall views on living with a child with dyslexia and how they think this has affected them and the rest of their family.

RESPONSIBILITY

At a day to day level all the mothers in this sample thought that they had the major responsibility for dealing with their child's dyslexia. This may be partly because this was an atypical sample with several fathers working away from home for long periods of time and several more regularly working away from home for shorter periods of time. In addition there were three single parent mothers. Van der Stoel and Osmond in their interviews both document detailed views from fathers on their dyslexic children, Edwards on the other hand also notes the lack of input from fathers in the eight case studies of dyslexic adolescents which she presents. Scott, Scherman and Phillips (1992) found in their research that mothers were the most likely adults to support their dyslexic children. Several mothers in this case study said that their husbands gave them support on specific occasions such as open evenings or an important meeting in school and generally felt that their husbands supported what they were doing despite their lack of regular involvement. It may therefore be that some fathers have a higher profile in the public arena than they do on a daily basis at home. Edwards wonders if some fathers are less involved because their own experiences of dyslexia make this a painful area for them to cope with. Whilst this is a possibility there was no direct evidence from this study to support this hypothesis. There appeared to be no consistent difference in involvement between dyslexic and non-dyslexic fathers in this sample and dyslexic mothers were just

as involved as non-dyslexic mothers in supporting their children. In the
health area we know that mothers are often the 'guardians' of the family's
health and take the responsibility for monitoring family health. In this
sample within the family it was exclusively mothers who first realised something was wrong and took the initiative in identifying the problem. For
many of them their day to day support appeared to be an extension of this
early initiative.

> 'Dave (husband) says, with him not being sort of like academically in-
> clined at all, he didn't realise at the beginning that Mark really had a prob-
> lem. He just thought, 'Oh well, maybe Mark's slow to pick it up like I
> was." And I says, "Well, I think we should do something about it as soon
> as we could." And so we did. I mean, I help with his homework and every-
> thing like that . . . and sometimes I think he has difficulty understanding
> what Mark's supposed to be doing, so it's difficult in a sense because it's
> always me that has to do it you know.'

Mrs. Thomson had commented in her interview that she was the only one
for a long time who had suspected her son might be dyslexic. She was asked
what her husband thought about this.

> 'I don't think he'd been able to give it a thought. Like most husbands, al-
> though they love their children and they try to be around it's you who are
> there and who have the dealings with the children. You're the one when
> they bring homework and whatever. So I don't think he was really that
> much aware.'

Mrs. Knight felt that she and her husband were in fairly close agreement but
that she saw more of the day to day difficulties.

> 'He's much the same as me really I suppose, although he's not so much of
> a worrier as I am. He tends to be a little bit more philosophical and opti-
> mistic at times, although he does have his moments when he worries about
> it. Well, it's me that does everything with him as well. So it's me that sees
> him when he's had a bad day and he's getting his spelling pack wrong and
> so on.'

Several mothers in this sample pointed out that their husbands either
worked away from home or worked very long hours so with the best will in
the world they were not able to give the level of support that their wives gave
to their dyslexic children.

> 'Well he (husband) does what he can, but he has to work away from home.
> I think people don't always appreciate that you have a lot on your plate
> when your husband isn't there you know.'

> 'My husband is supportive, but he basically leaves it to me. He works long
> hours.'

Other mothers, even when their husbands were at home, made it clear that they saw it as their role to deal with this kind of issue. A few of the mothers who worked did express resentment that the major responsibility seemed to fall on them. Despite this the majority of mothers were at pains to point out that their husbands were very concerned for their children. Again this may be an atypical sample, because given the cost of the Dyslexia Institute lessons it could be assumed that fathers would have to be committed enough to agree with their wives that this was an appropriate use of family funds. Mrs. Schaffer was typical in emphasising her husband's interest.

'I think I had closer contact with the school and what they were doing. It's not that he's not interested. We both constantly went up the school.'

Other mothers whose husbands were not involved with helping their dyslexic children on a day to day basis nonetheless valued the general emotional and social support that their husbands gave. Mrs Street who had struggled with dyslexia at school herself, valued her husband's support if she went up to school to talk about any difficulties that her son was having.

'The only thing is I find I get quite emotional about it because I had experienced it in the past. So sometimes my husband comes with us.'

In the three cases where mothers reported differences of opinion between themselves and their husbands these were not over their child being dyslexic but over what should be done about it and the degree of concern that should be expressed.

'He (husband) does care, but he doesn't see the state he comes home in after school. He doesn't worry about it as much as I do.'

'He (husband) hated school from day one, you know, and he can understand how he really feels. Part of him lets him backslide you know, so the trouble is it's always me that has to make him do it.'

Some mothers felt that even though their husbands were supportive at one level they still didn't fully understand the problem and could still get impatient and exasperated with the specific difficulties that their dyslexic child had.

'Well he's the same as me. He was a bit annoyed really that it had taken all that time to find out. But then he's so busy with the business to be honest. I mean he gets frustrated with Sophie. He thinks she doesn't try and that's not the case, she can't do it.'

Sophie, when asked if her parents understood what it was like to be dyslexic, replied:

'I don't think my dad does. But my mum is more understanding. My dad thinks I'm lazy.'

Some mothers therefore felt that as well as shouldering the major responsibility for helping their dyslexic child that they also had to mediate between their husband and child or between their dyslexic child and their non-dyslexic brothers and sisters.

'His younger sister's always correcting his reading or telling him if he's spelt things wrong, you can imagine how that goes down!'

UNCERTAINTY

For all parents their thoughts on their child cover the present, the past and the future. It's also the case that all parents and children face some degree of uncertainty in envisaging the child's future, even when it is limited to school and the first few years beyond. It can be argued that for many children with special needs there is often greater uncertainty and apprehension about what the future will hold for them. Several mothers commented at various points in the interviews about the uncertainty and anxiety that they felt about their child's future.

'It's like steering a ship through uncharted waters really, you just don't know what rocks you're going to hit next.'

The mothers in this sample were asked a short series of questions focusing on their child's future. They were first asked whether or not they worried about their child's future progress at school. They were asked to rate this on a 5 point scale.

Do you worry, or not, about (Emma's) future progress in school?

a lot   5   4   3   2   1   not at all

The average score for mothers of primary age children was 4.6 and for mothers of secondary children was 4.4. with 65 per cent of mothers overall scoring a 5. Without comparing these scores to mothers' ratings of non-dyslexic children it could be argued that all mothers worry a lot about their children's future development. Only further research can answer this point but at a qualitative level several mothers claimed that there was no comparison between the concern that they had for their dyslexic, as opposed to non-dyslexic, children.

'There's no comparison really, it's just not the same. With her sister we've never really had to worry. She's had her ups and downs, teachers she doesn't like, friends she's fallen out with, but nothing serious. She's just average but she seems to just sail along. There's none of that misery and despair that her sister's had, none of that dreading going to school, feeling sick every morning crying and so on.'

Another mother commented,

> 'I don't think until you've had a child with a problem you've any idea what it's like. It's totally different, it's this constant worry. Oh, please God give him a nice teacher, don't let him get that depressed again. How will he cope at secondary school? How on earth will he do the homework or manage in exams? With my other children I just don't have those sort of worries.'

Perhaps as a hangover from not wanting to be seen as neurotic or over anxious many of the mothers were apologetic or fearful that the degree of worry that they expressed would be seen as inappropriate. Typical responses were,

> 'Yes, I'm afraid I do worry a lot.'

> 'I know I shouldn't but I do worry a lot.'

It thus appears that for some mothers in addition to worrying a great deal they were also made to feel that this was inappropriate or not legitimate.

Mrs. Salter said that when she had tried to discuss her concerns with the school,

> 'They just laughed at me.'

The kind of things that mothers worried about obviously varied with the age and stage of the child. Mrs. Forest whose 8 year old son was still learning to read and had had a difficult start in school said,

> 'I try not to think about it.'

Mrs. Salter felt that her son's school had a particularly competitive ethos.

> 'I do worry about it a lot, they're so competitive there.'

The mother of a primary age girl listed the following worries:

> 'I worry about whether she'll be able to get things down quick enough, whether she'll be able to spell things, copy things off the board, learn her tables, be able to play skipping in the playground without being laughed at or told she can't join in. All those sorts of things. They may sound silly but she's been told off or laughed at for all these things already. It's not that I want her to do them for me, I want her to keep up so she's happy in school, so she can enjoy it.'

Mrs. Kerslake in the following comments encapsulated many of the worries that mothers of secondary or near to secondary age children expressed:

> 'I worry about him going to secondary school. I worry about the amount of work he's going to have to cope with. I worry about how he'll cope with exams when these come along. I worry that he'll sort of lose interest in school, and not want to go. Playing truant. I worry about everything!'

It can be argued that the worries that Mrs. Kerslake has expressed are quite reasonable and legitimate. Evidence suggests that poor readers are more likely to play truant at secondary school and are more likely to display disruptive behaviour (Hinshaw 1992, McGee *et al.* 1992). Other evidence suggests that dyslexic children often do take longer to complete written work and the time concessions for public exams are an open acknowledgment of the difficulties that these present to some dyslexic children. Concern over exams was a major concern at secondary level, although mothers stressed that this was on their children's behalf.

> 'I suppose I worry in the sense of the exams. That's the part that bothers me. If he can't get his exams and it stops him doing what he wants to do.'

Another major concern especially for boys was that they would become disruptive and alienated at secondary school. Mrs. Bell had already had experience of this when her son Ewan started to struggle badly at secondary school,

> 'Because in the other class they say he was misbehaving and then he was one of the naughty boys and that's not really him. I mean he's often been a clown as a means of distracting I think, but he was really naughty.'

Mrs. Carter was worried in case something like this should happen in the future,

> 'I think the only thing that really gives me cause for concern, I mean, like, I say Malcolm's never been disruptive or anything like that, but I know it can get to a stage where they feel totally isolated and I wouldn't want to see any decline in his behaviour when he goes to senior school.'

Several mothers also pointed out that the degree to which they worried fluctuated depending on how things were going at the time and what picture they had of future provision.

> 'It varies really, it's very up and down. Sometimes things go well for a while and you start to get more optimistic about the future, then something will happen at school and you feel right back where you've started. You can never completely relax and say right that's that sorted, its like a long term campaign.'

> 'I feel sad for him. It varies for me between the depths of pessimism to feeling if he's had a good day quite optimistic for a time, and thinking things aren't going to be so bad, he's going to manage.'

Mrs. Graham's son David had been put into a special needs class when he entered secondary school as he could barely read. The school hoped that with special help his literacy skills would improve and allow him to do himself justice. Mrs. Graham felt uncertain as to how things would go and what her expectations should be.

'I'm never sure for myself, at school they have great hopes for him, they say whatever happens he'll get on.'

Mothers' worries it appeared were based on past experience of the difficulties their children had encountered and realistic projections about the difficulties they were likely to face in the future. Allied to this, several underlined their degree of uncertainty about their child's future academic progress. Some mothers were at pains to point out that although they worried, they did their best to keep these worries from their dyslexic child. One mother who was dyslexic herself said:

'I think it's affected me more than him. I don't let him know I'm worried. Graham's quite oblivious as yet. He's got a very easy going temperament he doesn't mind too much about it.'

'The trouble is, I think some teachers think that because you talk about your worries to them that you've made your child all anxious and neurotic. It's not like that at all. It's him that comes home from school with the worries, we tell him not to worry, that it's not that bad, that we'll help him sort the problem out.'

'We never talk about our worries for her in front of her.'

'The problem is getting the balance right between not making him worried, but at the same time acknowledging his worries and not dismissing them.'

'He's due to start secondary school in a few months. He's full of optimism, he seems to think that because he's going to a new school all his problems are going to disappear. I think that's what he wants to believe because he's had such an awful year at school. I haven't let him know about my worries. I'm in a quandary though, I mean I don't want to put ideas in his head, but should I prepare him just a little bit otherwise it might be an awful shock to him?'

'Well, the thing is, you only talk to teachers when things have reached a crisis, when you are really upset and worried. They don't see you the rest of the time. I think they get a distorted view.'

Although worry and anxiety are used widely in informal explanations for the detrimental effect that parents can have on their children, there's almost no formal research on this issue. The assumption often seems to be made that where you have an anxious, worried child and anxious, worried parents, it is the parents' anxiety which has led to the child's anxiety. Of course the opposite assumption that the child's anxiety has led to the parents' anxiety is equally plausible. A third possibility is that there is an interactional cycle with both fuelling further anxiety in the other. As discussed in chapter 7, the belief that anxious parents are responsible for the anxieties and unhappiness displayed by dyslexic children seems to be based more on myth than reality. Dewhirst (1995) reports that the parents that she spoke to argued that the best way to overcome family stress is to acknowledge dyslexia and give effective support so that children don't become anxious in the first place. Some of the mothers in this sample said that they had been called over protective by teachers. This is a term which is widely used to comment on the behaviour and attitudes of parents of children with a wide range of disabilities. MacKeith (1973) has argued that this is a judgemental term and that we should talk instead of very protective parents, a term which he feels doesn't necessarily imply criticism. In the same vein it can be argued that it is more appropriate to talk about very worried or very anxious parents. Another implicit assumption appears to be that worry or anxiety is automatically harmful, whereas in reality, worry may lead to a number of different outcomes. Worry that leads to seeking information and help and leads to forward planning is very different to worry that leads to pessimism and lack of action. A certain level of worry, it can be argued, is an integral part of parenting and a parent who didn't worry would be equally criticised for not showing the appropriate concern for their child. Mrs. Knight's 11-year-old son had in the past been refusing to go to school, bedwetting and falling a long way behind on his reading and spelling. Both his teachers and the educational psychologist had expressed concern about his academic performance and his emotional response to it.

'Given the state he was in you'd have to be a very odd mother not to worry.'

It can also be argued that where worries are dismissed or not taken seriously this is more likely in the long term to exacerbate them, whereas acknowledgment can at least be the starting point for dealing with difficulties. Mrs. Knight went on to discuss what happened when she talked to Jason's class teacher at the end of his second year in junior school.

'He still couldn't read or write properly then, so I asked her whether I was right to worry about how he'd cope when he got to secondary school or was I just making a fuss about nothing. She said that speaking as another mother she would be concerned about him. In a funny sort of way I was pleased she said that because I knew he'd got problems and at least it gave me confidence in my own judgement, made me decide I must carry on doing what I could.'

Meryl, a 16-year-old girl with dyslexia, was asked if she worried about her work because her parents worried about it, or was her worry related to school.

'No, it's definitely not because they worry about it, I worry because of school.'

Goodnow and Collins (1990) talk about parenting as a public performance with many different onlookers who feel that they have the right to judge or comment on the quality of the performance. Whilst this applies to all parents, it applies even more strongly when something is thought to have gone 'wrong'.

'Even my mother-in-law started asking if I was reading enough books to him.'

Hannon (1995), in discussing parents' involvement in their children's literacy development, talks about the myth of the 'bad parent'. He goes on to say, 'but the myth is pervasive and its power should not be underestimated for it can lead well meaning teachers to treat perfectly able parents with suspicion.'

THE FUTURE AT WORK

Mothers were asked a similar question about whether they thought having dyslexia would affect their child's career choice and were again asked to rate their degree of concern on a 5 point scale.

a lot   5   4   3   2   1   not at all

In this case, the mothers of primary school children scored an average of 4.5, and the mothers of secondary children 4.2.

Mothers felt that having dyslexia would restrict their children's choice of job either because they wouldn't be able to do the job or they wouldn't be able to pass the exams needed for the job.

'I often think "Ee, I wonder what he'll do eventually." Jobs are so hard to come by now. Nowadays they're so fussy, people with 'O' and 'A' levels can't get jobs so it will be a big impact.'

'Obviously there are jobs she won't be able to do because she's dyslexic.'

Some mothers felt that their children were already limiting their expectations to jobs which required no literacy skills.

'Oh definitely, he'll go for something totally mechanical.'

'I think she wants a job in Sainsbury's packing shelves.'

'He sees himself leaving without an examination to his name. If he could leave school tomorrow I'd let him.'

Whereas in some cases mothers were worried about children limiting their expectations, in other cases mothers were worried that their children were going to be disappointed.

'I worry about his future. He won't be able to choose what he wants to do. He wants to go to university and he wants to do this, that and the other and I know it probably won't be possible, or you know, perhaps he'd find it very difficult.'

Mrs. Glover, the mother of 16-year-old Sophie who was interviewed in a later study, made the following comments,

'I think she puts too much emphasis on the fact that she might not be able to go to university. That she might not get A and O levels, and I say they're not the criteria for success in life. I mean they are for some but not for everyone.'

Research on the careers of dyslexic adults has come up with mixed results but does suggest that overall they don't do as well as non-dyslexic adults from the same background (Rawson 1968, Rackham 1972). This would suggest that mothers' worries are well founded. Maughan (1994) points out that low achievement motivation is commonly correlated with poor reading. Oka and Paris (1987) claim that whereas low achievement motivation is usually seen as a negative factor, it may be that some children use this as a coping strategy. In this case it is suggested that they pick 'safe' goals that they can attain in order to keep their self-esteem intact. Maughan (1994) argues that evidence from adult follow-up studies (Bruck 1985) suggests that poor readers may use these same strategies when it comes to choosing careers or further education. Again though, it can be argued that this could sometimes be seen as a positive strategy which minimises the risk of disappointment or failure. What is not always clear when looking at these adult follow-up studies is what degree of support, if any, children received for their dyslexia whilst in school, nor do we know if or how this might influence career choice. In the present studies several mothers suggested that their children were limiting their choice of future career because of their dyslexia. Both Sophie (16 years) and her mother spoke independently about how she had already restricted her career choice.

'I think it's limited her to what she'd like to be. I think she would have liked to have been a lawyer or something like that you know; and I think she would have been good, because she's quite articulate and she loves arguing, and she loves nit-picking.'

'If I wanted to do acting I couldn't. Like at school I would like to have had a go. But I've never had the opportunity because it would have taken us(me) longer to learn the lines and everything.'

The issue is whether Sophie has been realistic in limiting her choices or whether she and those factors that influenced her have limited her unnecessarily. The question of career choice is highly complex for anyone and it can be argued that a great many children have their career choices influenced or

limited by a wide variety of factors. What is at question is how far dyslexia interacts or adds to the limitations or influences on career choice.
McLoughlin *et al.* (1994) give a useful summary of the different theoretical
approaches to career choice and their particular relevance to dyslexic individuals. They maintain that dyslexics often choose or exclude certain career
choices because they make incorrect assumptions about the skills required
especially in terms of literacy. They point out as examples that dyslexics
often assume that they cannot enter the legal profession because it involves
too high a demand on literacy skills (as Sophie had), whereas they assume
that video production work doesn't involve literacy skills. They advise that
dyslexics should not automatically exclude themselves from jobs that require
literacy skills and that career counselling should not perpetuate the idea that
there are a lot of jobs that dyslexics should avoid. They also claim that many
dyslexics are surprisingly unaware of their own strengths and weaknesses
and that as well as dealing with the primary cognitive difficulties that they
have they should be given insight and support for their frequent lack of
confidence or low self-esteem. Miles and Gilroy (1986) suggest that is important for dyslexics to develop self-knowledge. McLoughlin (1990) also argues
that there is no evidence that dyslexics as a group are better at either spatial
tasks or working with computers than are non-dyslexics although this assumption is often made. What is not clear at present is whether dyslexics are
over represented in some fields of work and if so if this is because they are
less good at other types of work and therefore avoid them. McLoughlin
concludes that: 'Essentially, dyslexics should pursue occupations and careers
for which they are appropriately equipped in terms of their abilities, apti-
tudes and interests.'

Whilst in theory this is sound advice, the problem in practice is that by the
end of schooling many dyslexic children have been negatively influenced
both in terms of expectation and opportunity. As illustrated in an earlier
chapter one mother found that even when her son was at primary school he
was limiting his expectations to jobs like being a lollipop man on the
grounds that this involved no reading and writing. Nearly all the secondary
children had been placed in the lowest ability groups for some, or in many
cases all, subjects, thus limiting both their expectations and their chances of
exam success. Maughan (1988) and Fogelman (1988) both report in follow-
up studies that the outlook for most severely dyslexic children is poor with
few of them obtaining educational qualifications. Andrews (1990) followed
up fifty students aged between 14 to 19 years who attended the Barts Dyslexia Clinic for assessment. These students were found as a group to be
above average in intelligence and to have average levels of reading although
their spelling was still nearly a standard deviation below the average and
their writing speed was slow. Out of this group twenty-three went on to take
'A' Levels. It was noted that all but three of this group took 'A' Levels in
maths or science. This is not the distribution that would normally be

expected even when taking the predominance of boys in the sample into account. This suggests that even when children are seen as 'successful' in formal examinations for some their choice of subject has been curtailed. One mother whose son had an IQ in the superior range on the WISC, with similar scores for the verbal and performance scales, made the following observations:

'He's a good all rounder really. In a funny sort of way I actually think he's quite good at English! He chooses like the best word to express something and his comprehension has always been excellent. He got almost a 100 per cent for comprehension in the SATs (11 year old), but of course his writing and spelling let him down. But I've noticed he gets marked down for things like history and geography because his writing's so poor, anything really where he has to write he's disadvantaged. So the thing is what he gets the best marks for is maths. He's not really that interested in maths and he says he doesn't like maths. But I can see him ending up doing maths simply because he won't manage anything else. I know in a way it's lucky that at least he can do maths, but I think it's a shame if he ends up without a real choice and without doing something he's really interested in.'

Even in science subjects some mothers thought that their children's poor literacy skills held them back.

'I think he seems to quite understand them, but it's always the presentation. He can't put it down and he can't describe what happens in the experiments and all the rest of it.'

It thus appears that by the time some children with dyslexia come to make career choices that a number of factors, over and above those normally operating on children have already influenced the choices that they can make.

Several mothers emphasised that what they wanted was for their child to reach their potential and be happy in what they were doing.

'As long as Graham can achieve to his potential and do something in life that he's happy in that's fine. That's all I want at the end of the day. I don't want him to be a physicist or whatever! I just want him to be able to get where he wants to be . . . and I said to my husband the other day, "If he wants to work on a production line making cars, as long as he's happy, what's wrong with that?"'

PRESENT FEELINGS

One of the last questions in the interview asked mothers how they felt at the moment about their child having dyslexia. Not surprisingly mothers' answers varied depending on the progress their child was making, the stage they were at in their schooling, the attitude of the school, the age at which they were identified, the severity of their problems and how the child was coping with them at a personal level. Mrs. Carter in answering this question summarised several themes that had arisen during the interview.

'I don't know really now . . . I think I'm relieved like I said before, that you know what it is and you can do something about it. But I don't think, you know, that there's a magic cure. I think he'll be as dyslexic at seventy as he was at seven. But as long as he learns to cope with it. Probably when he was in the infants, I probably thought there was no hope at all, but when you come here and you see them progressing. I'm quite happy with things the way they are as long as he continues to make progress.'

'Right now I'm not as worried as I was originally. He was really down and low, now he's coping well. He's catching up quick. He's more positive he's enjoying life a bit more.'

'I feel sorry for him that he's had to struggle.'

'I just wish she wasn't!'

'Just something that we have to get on with.'

'I admire him the way he deals with it. Considering the problems he's had he's been very strong.'

'I've given up trying to push him, but now I feel guilty. I can get very negative at times, it's all left to me.'

'I'm quite concerned with coming up to GCSEs. I can't see him getting anything. People have made comments to his sister, "Your brother's simple." It must be very hard for him.'

These comments reflect what mothers feel at a particular point in time, but what also emerged from the interviews is that, for both the children and their mothers, they were dealing with the difficulties related to dyslexia on a long term basis. The nature and extent of the problems changed with time and circumstance and they all had to learn as they went along to make sense of their current difficulties and try and find the best way of dealing with them.

' I suppose I've come to accept now that she's always going to have difficulties and that I'm always going to have to support her, at least while she is at school.'

Donawa (1995), an educationalist herself, reflects on the difficulties of bringing up her son Gabriel who has dyslexia, in what she describes as the formal and competitive school system of Barbados.

'Much of my energy of the last 15 years has been devoted to negotiating a safe passage for my son.'

Donawa goes onto talk about both the financial and emotional costs of bringing up a child with special needs.

'Even at the least painful level, that of financial cost, there is an unending stream of lost thermoses, books, shoes, glasses; the extra tuition; the jettisoned career.'

'But the real costs are to the spirit; the sorrow of observing a child's bleak despair, the anguish and alarm when the despair turns to rage.'

Whilst few of the mothers in this study had encountered such severe difficulties as Gabriel's mother, the majority could point to a time when their child had been deeply unhappy because of their difficulties and many mothers had in turn been distressed or worried by their child's unhappiness. Half the mothers in this sample described themselves as feeling 'sad' for their child during their interview, even if they were basically optimistic in outlook. All of the mothers said that they would have liked more support, especially when their children were younger.

Support for parents

'Initially I would have liked more support. I'd have liked help in sorting out what the problem was and I'd have liked to talk to other mothers.'

None of the mothers in this sample named school as a source of support, and therefore all the significant support that they received was seen to have come from outside the school system. Some mothers specifically mentioned that they would like more support from school.

'I'd like the school to be a lot more supportive.'

The most frequently mentioned source of support was from voluntary organisations such as the Dyslexia Institute. This was either on a direct or indirect basis. Indirect support in the form of meeting other parents in the waiting room whilst children were having their tuition was the most frequently mentioned form of support. This was also considered one of the most valuable forms of support and many mothers spoke in very positive terms about it.

' Oh definitely. Talking to the other parents is a big plus, they understand how you feel.'

Direct support would include support from specialist dyslexia teachers and arranged parents' groups. Both parents' groups and specialist teachers were again seen as a valuable source of support by some mothers.

'It really helped at the parents' group to talk to other mothers.'
'Mrs. G. (dyslexia teacher) has been very supportive.'

Mothers of older children and working mothers who didn't use the waiting room and therefore didn't have the chance for informal contact with other parents often regretted this.

'I just drop him off unfortunately, but I came to a parents' course, I found that a great help.'

Some mothers pointed out that as well as giving them personal support meeting other parents also had an educative function.

'Meeting other parents and having informal chats with them. You get ideas, suggestions, it's made me more patient.'

Hannavy (1995) describes the piloting of a simple reading and writing programme which can be followed by parents of children who are progressing slowly in these skills. She comments that an unexpected outcome of the parents' meeting together is the considerable amount of help and support they give each other, especially in solving problems about how to get their children to work. Apart from two mothers whose daughters both attended the same highly supportive school, none of the other mothers had the opportunity to meet other parents whose children had similar problems through the school. Another major source of support for mothers was from friends or workmates who had similar problems.

'I talk to this woman at work who's got a grown up son whose dyslexic. I do find it a help to talk things over with her.'

In summary, the mothers in this sample drew on a wide range of support largely outside the school. This may not be typical of what happens in all areas but Dyson and Skidmore (1994) also found in their survey of 27 Scottish secondary schools that only one instance of support for parents was recorded. Schools may well argue that with all the pressures upon them there isn't time to offer support to parents as well. But if dyslexia/specific learning difficulties are taken seriously then it does raise legitimate questions about how parents can best be supported. The support that mothers most wanted from school was help and understanding in identifying their child's difficulties and acknowledgement of their worries and concerns.

'I just want recognition of the nature of his difficulties. I don't expect magic.'

Given that parents draw much of their support from voluntary organisations outside the school it is also important that they don't feel criticised by the school for doing so, as happened to several of the parents in this sample. Where schools don't feel they have sufficient time, resources or expertise to offer support, they can encourage parents to contact parent support groups or voluntary groups or perhaps consider any form of organisation which will enable interested parents to meet and support each other. Part of what parents derived from support was information and understanding on how to help their child in a variety of ways. As the role of parents is seen as critical in how children cope with their difficulties it is important that parents are educated and informed about their difficulties and are given support and encouragement when needed. The mothers in particular in this sample made it their business to be well informed. There may well be cases when difficulties are first identified by the school where parents will not be as well informed and this raises the question of how such parents can best be informed and supported.

Overall, many mothers in this sample had found that as well as dealing with their child's difficulties they had also had to deal with the hostility, disbelief and blame of others. Edwards (1994) comments that: 'The parent of a dyslexic faces the continual strain of having to watch helplessly, while your child suffers, often while the authorities blame you for the problem, which would be unthinkably brutal with any other form of handicap.' Far from blaming parents it can be argued that educationalists should be thinking about how best to support parents in a constructive and enabling manner.

SUMMARY

1 The majority of mothers felt that they had the main responsibility within the family for supporting their child, especially at a day to day level.
2 Mothers had legitimate worries about their children's future academic progress in school.
3 Mothers said they worried a lot about their child's specific learning difficulties narrowing down their future career choices.
4 There were indications that some children were already restricting their career choices as a direct result of their specific learning difficulties.
5 Mothers obtained support for themselves entirely from outside the school system.
6 Mothers found the support of other parents particularly helpful.
7 Many mothers would have liked more support from the school especially in initially identifying and understanding the problem.
8 Given that parents are a major source of support to children with dyslexia, it is important that they are in turn given the information and support that they need to enable them to support their children as effectively as possible.
9 Many parents had supported their children over a number of years and had gained insight and understanding of their children's difficulties; it is important that this 'expertise' is recognised and utilised.

Chapter 12

Case studies

'People jump to the wrong conclusions and they should be educated about what dyslexia means. It's just been one of my dreams to tell them all what it means.'

(Sophie 16 years)

One of the problems with using the case study approach to any issue has been in deciding how 'typical ' or 'representative' the case studies described are. As was discussed in chapter 3 this is especially difficult in the case of dyslexia or specific learning difficulties because in many areas identification is still patchy and variable in nature. This means that a representative sample of all the children in a given population with dyslexia is almost impossible to obtain as not all children are identified. It has to be borne in mind that identification in a loose sense is not an all or nothing phenomenon. Teachers, like parents, may think that something is wrong and offer some level of support even though they don't recognise the child as having specific learning difficulties. In looking at the case studies presented by the likes of Osmond, Van der Stoel, Miles and Edwards it is easy for the unconvinced in particular to say 'Yes, but aren't these exceptional cases? Perhaps these children are particularly vulnerable, or particularly severe or particularly unlucky in the experiences they've encountered.' These are valid points but the sheer weight of case studies reporting similar experiences makes it hard to consign them all to the category of exceptional cases. In reality we do need to know more about the range of experiences that dyslexic children encounter and the range of responses that they make to these experiences. The present study although still open to criticism of sampling bias tried to go some way to addressing this problem by selecting a representative sample of children who attended the Dyslexia Institute. It can still be claimed that these children are not representative of dyslexic children in general but given that they were selected from 80 children attending over 70 different schools in 6 different LEAs they do represent a wide range of experiences and degrees of difficulty. These children may well be typical of the dyslexic children who are recognised by either the school or their parents as having a specific problem, but the sample excludes an unknown proportion of children whose parents cannot afford private tuition or whose problems go unrecognised. A particular aim of this study was to look at a group of children whose parents had explicitly chosen to understand their children's difficulties in terms of the label dyslexia and had chosen to seek extra support outside the school system for their children. The three case studies looked at in more detail were again not picked to show exceptional or extreme responses, but merely to flesh out the range of experiences that children and their families came across. If anything, in presenting two out of three case studies which had good outcomes so far, these represent the positive end of the spectrum of children interviewed and don't dwell on the more negative experiences of many of the children. Some of the comments made have already been quoted in other chapters but were included here when they were an important part of a wider picture or part of an ongoing thread or theme running through an interview. These are shortened extracts from the full interviews.

SOPHIE, AGE 16

Sophie had been fully assessed by an educational psychologist when she was aged 14:5 and the following results had been obtained.

WISC–R Standard: High Average	Full Scale IQ	111
	Verbal Scale IQ	105
	Performance Scale IQ	115
Macmillan Graded Word Reading Test:	Reading age	8:9
Neale Analysis of Reading Ability	Accuracy	7:6
	Comprehension	8:11
	Rate	9:6
BAS Spelling Scale Age		9:3

These test scores confirmed the results of more informal testing at school which had put her literacy levels at around 9 years of age.

Thus at the age of 14 years 5 months Sophie was clearly over 5 years behind in her reading and spelling.

Mother's account

Sophie has attended her present comprehensive for three years. Before that she attended a middle school. She had two older sisters who had no problems at school. Her mother thought that Sophie's father and uncle and niece and nephew had all had similar problems, although less severe.

'I suppose my husband was a slow reader you know. He used to be in front of the telly and he couldn't read it, and he didn't read books till he was in his mid teens, and also my husband's brother was a very poor reader and needed specialist help.'

When asked when she had first realised Sophie had a problem she simply said,

'Straight away. . . . There was no question about it.'

'She found it so difficult to read and she didn't like it. She had trouble with the first teacher as well . . . she didn't like Sophie, and she smacked her on the leg the second day there. And she was always saying she was lazy and stupid. And she was straight away put in a class for slow children. I didn't think she was slow, I just thought she couldn't read.'

Mrs Glover said that looking back with hindsight Sophie was probably clumsy as a young child and had difficulty with skills like learning to tie her laces. She hadn't learnt her alphabet until about 12 and at 16 still didn't know her times tables. Mrs Glover thought that she'd probably read about dyslexia in magazines and newspapers and when Sophie was about 7 she started asking the school if she might be dyslexic. She was asked what happened when she suggested this to the school.

'They tested other kids! That's what got me. I just couldn't understand it. Probably because they knew the other daughters were OK they couldn't accept that Sophie could be different.'

INTERVIEWER   So how did they explain her problems to you?
MRS GLOVER   Well they just said, "You get children like that. She's a bit slow. She'll catch up."

Sophie's middle school accepted that she had problems and gave her additional help but according to her mother were still emphatic that it was not dyslexia.

'They were always, "No, no, no. We don't believe in that, it's not recognised."'

It was only when she entered her comprehensive school at 13 that it was recognised by the school that she was dyslexic. In fact the special needs department at the school took the initiative and phoned Mrs Glover to suggest that she might be dyslexic.

'I said, "Well, thank goodness." You know, someone at last had listened!'

The school told Mrs Glover they would make a programme for Sophie but she felt that despite good intentions they had done very little. Finally out of desperation she talked to Sophie about going for sessions at the Dyslexia Institute. Sophie was reluctant to do this because the only vacancies were during the school day, she went a few times but stopped going when she'd run out of excuses. Although the school thought that Sophie was dyslexic and actually suggested to her mother that she had some private tuition they were very negative about her attending the Dyslexia Institute.

'They thought it was a waste of money, the school. I'll tell you that now. She shouldn't go because they take your money and they take you. He got this tutor for me, Sophie goes there on a Thursday, and I think she only goes there for a natter and a cup of tea. . . . She's got no idea about dyslexia this woman, she admitted it.'

Mrs Glover then talked about the sorts of difficulties Sophie had.

'If you ask her to read something, she'll die. She says, "Don't ask me to read or write anything," because she'd rather die than do anything like that.'

This had led to particular problems at school because on several occasions she had been asked to read aloud to the class.

'And they've done it time and time again. I've got so cross I've nearly threatened to get her out of the school. And when she comes home she's so upset. She gets stressed out. She cries. The first few times she did it she was so frightened she just burst into tears and was completely humiliated. Everyone laughed. I think that's awful. Before the term's started I've always rung up and said, make sure she's not allowed to read aloud. But it's part of the curriculum. They seem to pick on her now because I've told them not to.'

'But really when I've got cross at this, at the end of the day it's not really made much difference. They've still done it again about two weeks later and you just despair, and you think I've made all that fuss and palaver and they do it again!'

To be fair to the school, Sophie's general willingness to talk in public may have made her understandable fear of reading aloud less obvious to those who weren't fully aware of her problems.

'Now if you said to Sophie, "Oh, tomorrow you've got to stand and talk on something," oh, she'd love it. She'd stand in front of the class and she'd do it. She'd revel in it. Yes, it seems that one thing is different from the other. In fact a school mistress said she would have made a good television reporter.'

Something that arose several times during the interview was the extra amount of time and effort that Sophie put into her work.

'If she's doing her work she can start at six and she can still be doing it at eleven. She'll hardly have done anything. It's like having teeth pulled out without an anesthetic. I mean the older girls are saying "Oh, Sophie's got homework, I'm going out. Bye. See you later." It takes her for ever to do anything. She's miles behind now with everything.'

'They just have to work doubly hard really . . . I mean, she puts 10 times more effort into everything than the other girls did.''

Another issue that arose was that like nearly all the secondary age children in the main study, she was in the bottom sets for everything and allied to this, no attempt was made to explain the specific difficulties of dyslexic children to other children in the school.

'Well, she's in all the low groups and everything which she doesn't like. Some of the kids in her class are really you know, bad. I think there's six boys who have extra time a week. We're presuming they might be dyslexic as well but none of them discuss it. I would have thought the school could do more by bringing it out in the open. . . . Like them six children that are in Sophie's year. I mean they could all get together, and there might be a few more who are as well. You could have like, say, a half an hour free period to discuss your problems. . . . They should explain to other kids that it's not their fault that it's a handicap. It's no big deal. But they don't tell the kids this. And then the kids just say "Oh she's dyslexic, she's stupid."'

Despite these criticisms, Mrs Glover was appreciative of the efforts that the school were making on Sophie's behalf.

'It's quite a good school. They're doing OK for her.'

She talked about various forms of support that Sophie had been offered such as someone to read exam questions to her and write things down, and also extra time in exams. Mrs Glover felt that the difficulty was that as Sophie had hidden her problems from all her peers she was reluctant to accept any form of help that would single her out. She described what happened when Sophie was offered extra time in an exam.

'Of course, it was an absolute trauma trying to get her to do that. But in the end she did. Because she had to go and sit the exam in the 6th form. She'd told none of her friends she was dyslexic, with them all being in different grades, she could get away with some of it. But one of them she couldn't. She had to tell one girl she'd got extra time. But I think the girl was quite sympathetic. But they should tell them you're dyslexic.'

INTERVIEWER   So she doesn't tell her friends?
MRS GLOVER   No, not even her best friend.
INTERVIEWER   Has she talked to you about why she doesn't tell others?
MRS GLOVER   Well I think she thinks that they'll think she's stupid, if she's dyslexic. She has said to me 'Oh, so and so were discussing someone that they thought was really thick and stupid, and they said they must be dyslexic or something.'

In contrast, although Sophie hadn't been recognised as 'dyslexic' at her middle school her difficulties were openly acknowledged.

'All the time she was in middle school she had special tuition. A lady she went to two or three times a week, and Sophie accepted it. I mean all her friends knew she had learning difficulties and helped her, you know, with her assignments or whatever she was doing.'

Mrs Glover mentioned several times during the interview that Sophie was more concerned about doing well at school, formal examinations and further education than she and her husband were.

'She's just took her mocks. She was really upset when she didn't do well. You know, she got some bad marks. So I've said, "So what?" You know we're not one of those parents who thinks they've got to have a bit of paper and that's going to be success for life.'

Mrs Glover was asked how she felt at the moment about Sophie having dyslexia.

'Well I'm sad that she's got it. I'd sooner she didn't have it really! But she can cope with it. She's coping with it alright. I think she does quite well. . . . She's got quite an outgoing personality, and she's got, like, the support of her family which a lot of kids might not have. . . . I mean them advantages more outweigh, you know the fact that she's a bit dyslexic.'

She was finally asked if there was anything else that she thought important or relevant that she wanted to add.

'Just the negativeness that I was bit worried about. If you come across more of that, if there's anything you can do to get her out of it? Feeling so negative about things.'

Sophie's account

Sophie presented in the interview as a pleasant and articulate sixteen-year-old with a good sense of humour. Understandably given the degree of her literacy problems she appeared depressed and frustrated when talking about some of her experiences and was close to tears on occasion. Despite this, at the end of the interview, she said she hadn't minded talking about her experiences and was glad to have the chance to give her point of view.

Sophie was first asked about what sort of interests she had out of school.

'Well, I've just started making clothes and things. I find that interesting. And art. But really that's the only thing. I don't like reading books. Not at all. I don't mind magazines and things like that.'

She went on to say that the only thing she enjoyed at school was art.

She then talked about the difficulties of going for Dyslexia Institute lessons during school time.

'It's school. Because it's one thing learning to read, but you're missing out on the other things. It's like fighting a loosing battle really.'

INTERVIEWER   How did you explain it to other people?

SOPHIE   I used to make up all lies and stuff. I was going to get my eyes tested, going shopping. I would say anything. . . . It was stressing us (me) out trying to think of excuses.

INTERVIEWER   Would it have made a difference if it had been out of school time?

SOPHIE   Yes, I would do it after school like. That's what I'd like to do. But there's no space really.

Sophie was then asked about what difficulties she had in school because of her dyslexia.

'Reading out. In lessons they make you read out all the time. My mum does complain sometimes but the school doesn't listen. They don't know how much it affects you. I think it, like, frightens you, it really frightens you. Being put through the traumas of it. And like sometimes you have to read like paragraphs and stuff, and you're not as fast as other people. You feel embarrassed, it's not easy.'

INTERVIEWER   When you're writing, do you find that's all right?

SOPHIE   Well if they dictate to you it totally confuses me.

Sophie then went on to say that she wrote less than other children, and that she avoided words she couldn't spell and that in consequence she got less marks for her projects. She was then asked how she felt about having these types of problems.

'I hate it. I really hate it. It's frustrating.'

INTERVIEWER   Do you think other children notice the difficulties you have?

SOPHIE   I think some of them do. Some of them close round me. Like some of them know now, and they've said, 'Oh well it explains a lot of things you've done.'

INTERVIEWER   Have you told them, or have they just found out?

SOPHIE   They found out. I wouldn't never really have told anyone.

INTERVIEWER   How do you feel about them knowing?

SOPHIE   Well, people think you're stupid, to be quite honest. That's the whole attitude of it . . . I try not to let them notice, as best I can do.

INTERVIEWER   What about the teachers at school. Do you think that they understand the difficulties you've got?

SOPHIE   No. Not all of them. No, I don't think they're aware of it at all. They don't understand what it is. They don't know what it's about, they don't. I think they think things are backwards. That's what everyone thinks. Some of them are more understanding though.

Sophie was then asked if she thought she'd had a best teacher, and if so what this teacher was like.

'Mrs F. I had her for a year, and she never asked me to read once. She used to be very helpful. If I couldn't hand in a project or something, she would say "Well Sophie, I understand, I'll give you some extra time." She was nice. But it's just because she was probably a nice person.'

By contrast she was also asked about the worst or least helpful teacher she'd encountered.

'Like the head of department I didn't think he was very helpful. I think it's because he hasn't much time ... it's only, like, him running the whole thing. I understand, like, there's a lot of people that he's got to help. But he's just not helpful at all.'

INTERVIEWER   Is that because of his attitude or what?
SOPHIE   I think it's mine as well, because I don't want help probably. Because he wanted to take me out of lessons to help us, but it's like the same thing. The embarrassment and I'm missing out on other things I need to learn.
INTERVIEWER   So has he talked over the way you'd like the help?
SOPHIE   Yes, I told him the way I would like it to be, but he says, 'you can't have that way, it's impossible.'

Sophie was then asked about teachers' attitudes towards her

'Teachers have called us lazy. Because I'm slow. Like homework; I hate doing it because I can't do it. French is my worst. I can't do French at all.'

INTERVIEWER   Do you find homework in general a struggle, or is it this in particular?
SOPHIE   Everything, I, think is hard going. I'm so wrecked. Tired after the day, and just worn out from all the effort.

Sophie was then asked what she thought about being called dyslexic.

'When I found out I was really upset because I thought it was incurable like. Like if you were a bit slow, well you think, "Oh well, I can do this, then I'll catch up." But when I found out, like, everyone was saying "oh, I thought you'd be happy" but I wasn't, I was shocked. Because everyone had been saying for years that I'm not: I'm just slow. And it was frustrating that they never picked it up and I might have been able to get a bit better than I am now.'

INTERVIEWER   How do you feel about it now?
SOPHIE   It helps me. Because there are things about it and stuff you can relate

to, and it makes you feel a bit better that there's someone else out there going through the same thing.

Sophie was asked if she would or would not like the chance to talk to other dyslexic children.

'I think I would to be quite honest. Because they're the people who are going through the same thing as you. Because no one can know until they've actually been through the trauma of it. But they tend to keep it hush hush. Like at my school you don't meet each other and stuff. It's, like, private.'

Sophie was finally asked what sort of help would be most useful for people with dyslexia.

'Just to make people more aware of it so that you don't feel like you've got some horrible disease. People just jump to the wrong conclusion and they should be educated about what dyslexia means. It's just been one of my dreams to tell them all what it means.'

Key points to emerge

Many of the points that arose have already been discussed in other chapters, so just a few of the main ones are commented on here. Both Sophie and her mother thought that there was a negative attitude towards learning difficulties including dyslexia on the part of other children at Sophie's comprehensive. This meant that the attempts of the special needs department to provide her with support were undermined to some extent by the overall ethos of the school, and this underlines the importance of having a whole school policy, which as part of its remit considers the general ethos of the school and the opinions and attitudes of others.

Another point of note is that even though the school took the lead in identifying her as having a specific learning difficulty they were still dismissive according to Mrs Glover of the idea that the Dyslexia Institute could offer appropriate support. Whilst there may be valid concerns about the effectiveness of out of class support, the school itself wished to withdraw Sophie for support and had suggested an out of school tutor to help with Sophie's literacy. It appeared from Mrs Glover's account that it was more ill informed prejudice rather than rational criticism that led to the school's comments. All the Dyslexia Institute teachers have a recognised specialist diploma in teaching children with dyslexia on top of their ordinary teaching qualifications. It was also the practice of this branch to advise parents to try and first get a free assessment by an LEA psychologist and to try and get support in school. Again it may be that schools have genuine concerns about parents having to pay for tuition, but Mrs Glover, by her own account, could comfortably afford the fees. Given the degree of Sophie's literacy problems and the obvious concern of the school, it appears that it was mistrust of specialist dyslexia organisations and the general 'mythology' that surrounds dyslexia that was influencing the school.

A more general problem that this did raise, was how best to offer support to a secondary school child who was very behind in her literacy skills because of a specific learning disability. In a case like this it is hard to imagine that within-class support alone would be sufficient and yet Sophie herself was reluctant to miss out on her 'normal' school timetable. If there had been a much more positive attitude to dyslexia and special needs in general on the part of other children and Sophie had been able to miss one of her least favoured subjects such as French, it is possible that withdrawal could have worked combined with good in-class support.

In many ways Mrs Glover fitted the stereotype of the 'dyslexic' parent that some educationalists seem to hold. She was middle class, articulate, financially well off, a successful business woman and a graduate. Yet like many parents in this study she stressed that she had not pressurised her daughter in terms of academic success and that she felt relatively powerless in trying to influence the school. While it may be true of parents in general that some do put pressure on their children for academic success it's important that this isn't used as an automatic explanation for the anxieties that some children display and it's especially important that it isn't over used as an explanation for the anxieties of children with dyslexia. It could be argued that what parents do and what they say may be two different things and that some may unintentionally convey certain expectations. This is hard to prove either one way or the other but in the present study not a single child mentioned pressure from their parents for academic success as an issue.

A problem that can arise for any child with a specific learning difficulty, but may be more frequent among girls is one of isolation in terms of meeting others with a similar problem. Given the much smaller numbers of girls with dyslexia there is more risk of this happening, as in Sophie's case where she didn't have anyone she could share her problems with.

The fear that many dyslexic children have of reading aloud has been well documented (Edwards 1994) and some children like Sophie become highly anxious about it. Reading aloud especially to the whole class is a totally public performance which clearly reveals all your deficiencies, real or imagined, to a large audience. It is important that all teachers are aware of the misery and humiliation that reading aloud can cause some children. In the case of Sophie's school, the educational psychologist concerned thought that this was probably an organisational problem rather than wilful intent on the part of the school. She collaborated with the special needs department in briefing all the subject specialists about children with special needs at the beginning of each term. She pointed out that in the case of Sophie's year, seventeen different supply teachers had been used in the space of one term, and that under such circumstances it was easy for important information not to get passed on to everyone. Whether or not this was the reason why Sophie was asked to read aloud on several occasions, it is easy to see that this situation may be seen as one of personal fault rather than organisational difficulty by Sophie and her mother. It also highlights the need for all classroom teachers to be responsible for special needs and to review their own approach to asking children to read aloud. A child like Sophie needs to feel safe that she is never going to be asked to read aloud in public as living with the fear, dread and anticipation that this might happen can by all accounts seriously affect a child's well-being, ability to learn and overall attitude to school.

This case clearly highlights the point that other people's reactions to difficulties can be as much or more of a problem to an individual than the difficulties themselves.

DAVID GRAHAM, AGE 12:10

At 12:3 David was assessed by a chartered clinical psychologist.

Wechsler Intelligence Scale   Full scale   IQ 113
Reading Age   6:10

At 11:10 David was assessed by the head of the special needs department at his secondary school.

Reading age Holborn   6:9
Reading age Blackwell   6:0

He was estimated by his teachers to be of average intelligence and was considered weak in reading, spelling and arithmetic compared to his age group. Under special abilities it was noted that he was verbally intelligent, and had many interests.

His behaviour in class was deemed as co-operative, friendly, responsive and over-sensitive. His attitude to work was considered to be enthusiastic, and his attitude to adults as obedient and normal. His attitude to others was considered to be friendly and normal and he was popular with other children. In summary it was stated that David had extremely good general knowledge and excellent verbal skills. He was thought to be a very friendly boy who still worked well despite his problems. David presented in his interview as outgoing and highly articulate with a generally positive and enthusiastic approach to life. He was the only child of a single mother although an extended family network gave considerable support. Money was tight and he was only able to receive tuition at the Dyslexia Institute through its bursary fund for low or no income families. He was attending a Roman Catholic secondary school which although it had reasonably high academic expectations was considered to have a caring ethos and a good special needs department. At the time of the interviews David had been attending the Dyslexia Institute for an hour twice a week for the previous eight months.

Mrs Graham

Mrs Graham, like many of the mothers in the larger sample, thought something was wrong during David's first year at school. She felt that far from progressing he seemed to be deteriorating and had lost some of the spark and enthusiasm that he had prior to going to school.

'At his first school they kept saying he was sensitive. But I suppose you would be sensitive if you kept being treated as a moron and you're not.'

Like most of the mothers in the sample, Mrs Graham encountered considerable problems when she tried to help Graham learn to read.

'Oh terrible. I used to sit with him to learn him to read, I even bought him all the reading books (the school had no reading scheme). I was so close to him I was really getting angry with him. He used to go round to my sister. One time he'd read it fine and the next page he couldn't. I used to say, "David, that's the same word." It was a continuous struggle.'

David made no progress in learning to read and could write nothing legible when he entered the junior school. Mrs Graham eventually suggested to the primary school that David might be dyslexic.

'I mentioned it a long time ago at primary school. He was checked by the local authority but they thought it was mainly an emotional problem because he was from a one parent family, which I disputed because he was a happy-go-lucky kid, he was a social child.'

Mrs Graham had several meetings with David's class teachers and the head of the school.

'I felt I was always being fobbed off. I always felt with the primary school, that they thought I was blaming them. But I mean you go to see different doctors for different kinds of things so why not different kinds of teachers.'

After Mrs Graham had persisted it was agreed that he should have 'remedial' support at school. By the time David left primary school Mrs Graham thought that they had realised that he wasn't 'slow' and his difficulties weren't all attributable to emotional problems.

'So we discovered he wasn't emotional and on leaving primary school they apologised that they'd always had him down as a slow learner.'

'David is interested in Watergate and what it's all about. He's mad on J.F. Kennedy and wants to know all about him. At the moment he's mad about

Malcolm X. He loves history. He's interested in politics. He knows who the president is and he wants to know the difference between the democrats and the republicans. He's not a dull child and why they couldn't see that at primary school I do not know. They're in charge of your child's future, it's kids' lives they're playing with.'

As soon as David entered secondary school at eleven years of age it was recognised that he had serious difficulties and in consultation with David and his mother, plans were made to try and deal with these. At this point David was approximately six years behind in his reading and spelling and was thus barely able to read and write at all.

'His year tutor at high school was the first to realise there was a problem. He wanted to know why he couldn't read as he was obviously intelligent. I was thinking about the Institute, I'd got information on it. I said, "Do you think I should get David tested?" and he said, "Yes I would." So it was all my worst fears confirmed really . . . I felt guilty I hadn't followed my own instincts in the first place. I feel really guilty about that, but you know if you're talking to professionals you expect them to know.'

Mrs Graham was very pleased with the support that David's secondary school had provided. It had been agreed to keep him in a small special needs class where he could be given help with his literacy skill. He was also given some individual sessions at school by someone trained in dyslexia as well as the sessions at the Dyslexia Institute. The hope was to return David as quickly as possible to a mainstream class. Mrs Graham felt that in the nine months David had been receiving special support he had made considerable progress.

'Since he's been to secondary school the support he's had has been unbelievable. . . . It wasn't till he came here he could really read. I mean this time last year he was picking up real little books.'

'I think his year tutor last year was a big influence on both of us; he commented straight away. Those teachers seem to really strive for them kids. They're great, their attitude towards them is really good. The headmaster takes them for history and he keeps saying he has high hopes for David.'

Mrs Graham was asked how she felt about David having dyslexia.

'I think it's a damn shame he's got it. We're always positive, and I always talk positive to David about it. But, you know, academic achievement is so much these days, I'm really frightened.'

She was also asked how she felt David had responded over the years to his difficulties.

'We have quite a close relationship, we're quite pals. He's quite open about any difficulties he has unless he's hiding it from me very well. He's quite a happy go lucky kid. I don't think there's much gets him down for long.'

Mrs Graham rated her son's self-esteem as fairly high and added to this,

'He doesn't seem to let himself be put down at all.'

Mrs Graham also noted that he was friends with children in the top grade although a couple of recent incidents suggested that David did encounter some difficulties. He'd recently experienced some resentment from the other children in the special needs class because of his general enthusiasm and keenness to answer questions.

'He's stopped going to circuit training at lunch time, because they're all in the top grade. So he is really aware.'

But overall Mrs Graham felt the school had done their best to counter any negative attitudes.

'They have discussed in class why David comes here, which I think is a good open attitude. I was really pleased with that.'

Mrs Graham emphasised that both she and David had a lot of support from a large extended family. She was asked whether or not meeting other mothers of dyslexic children was helpful.

'Oh definitely. You talk to other girls and you think, "Oh, good I'm not the only one who's going through this, I'm not neurotic," and sort of getting it confirmed that you are not neurotic.'

Mrs Graham talked about the fact that without the bursary fund it simply wouldn't have been possible for David to have tuition at the Dyslexia Institute. She strongly resented people making the assumption that parents of dyslexic children were all wealthy neurotics. She also felt, like many mothers in the sample, that she had been forced into the role of being 'pushy'.

'How many have fallen by the wayside. How many parents aren't pushy. I suppose in some ways I have been pushy, but you've got to be.'

DAVID

David was positive about all the support he was getting. He said he liked his sessions at the Dyslexia Institute and thought that they had helped him to sound words out and read more fluently. He said that at school he still had difficulties with reading and spelling and that he got frustrated quite often, especially with words that he couldn't read. He said that he wrote less than other children, avoided writing if he could and avoided words he couldn't spell on a regular basis. David appeared to be able to transfer what he was learning in his specialist sessions to the classroom situation, because when asked what kind of things he found helpful in school he first said:

> 'Me cards help (systematic sound cards taught in specialist sessions).
> Like I use them to remind me, like, I say, "Has 'h' ".'

He valued specific practical help given to him by various teachers in his secondary school such as being given the spellings of various words for his geography lessons. He felt that on the whole his teachers had quite a good understanding of his difficulties. When asked what sort of thing he didn't find helpful in school he said that copying off the board was the biggest problem and that he got frustrated because he was too slow. He said that in the past in particular he had been frequently called slow and lazy. He said that what particularly annoyed him was being told to hurry up when he was already going as fast as he could, especially as he liked to be tidy and knew that if he went any faster he would then be told off by one teacher in par-ticular for being untidy. When asked about how he felt about these criticisms he said 'angry'.

David said that the thing he most dreaded doing in school were exams and that he worried about these for weeks in advance:

> 'It's the reading of the questions and I generally worry about them.'

In his last exams it had been arranged for someone to read the questions to David and he had been happy with this arrangement. David was asked what he thought about being called dyslexic. He said he was pleased to have this label and to know what his problems were. When asked if he didn't resent it for making him different he replied,

> 'Like some people are ill, like me mum's got arthritis and people like arth-ritics, they're not really bothered about having a label. . . . It's helped us get me own back on some teachers. No teacher now brands me as thick, cause I've told them I was dyslexic.'

INTERVIEWER   So did you think that some of your teachers in the past thought you were thick?

DAVID   Yes, very much so.

INTERVIEWER   How did you feel about that?

DAVID   I felt like punching them, because I was feeling like, I'm not thick cause I know these things. They wouldn't believe that I knew them but I did. It was like one great big knot and, like, the knot's now starting to come undone.

David was asked if he explained his difficulties to other children and what affect, if any, this had on his friendships. David said he was willing to ex-plain his difficulties to other children and said that he still had friends in nearly every class in his year.

'Two of my friends have got it as well. We're closer friends because of it.'

David said that he just ignored or told other children to shut up if they tried to tease him. He said there had been some teasing but that this had stopped since the teacher had explained to the class about dyslexia.

When asked how he thought he compared with his class mates in terms of intelligence, David said,

'Like more for talking, cause like with being dyslexic it's not really shown through.'

David was enthusiastic about the various adult role models he had heard of. He was particularly keen on Michael Heseltine because of his own interest in politics and his ambition to be leader of the United Nations one day. David was finally asked if he thought he would always be dyslexic,

'More than likely, but I think I'll learn to cope with it. Although I think I'll still get stuck on things.'

Postscript

Soon after this interview a statementing process was started and nine months later Mrs Graham received a proposed statement. This said that David would be best remaining in his mainstream school but needed to receive highly structured and sequenced learning in a one to one or small group situation in addition to following much of the national curriculum. It was acknowledged that his literacy difficulties made it difficult for him to access the national curriculum at a level matching his intellectual abilities but that this should be done as far as possible. It was pointed out that David was already responding well to a multi-sensory approach (programme followed by the Dyslexia Institute). It was also recommended that his self-esteem should be monitored and that he should be given the chance to talk about his difficulties or strategies for dealing with them if he so wished.

Key points

It is interesting to contrast the experiences of David and Sophie because they are similar in IQ and also in the extent of their literacy difficulties and were both considered to have good verbal skills. On the other hand any comparison has to take into account all the variables on which they also differ, these include gender, class, age, personality, schooling, and family circumstances to name a few. It also highlights the importance of having more systematic longitudinal research which can give us more idea about how different variables influence a child's long-term adjustment. Is David's confident attitude to telling others about his problems an outcome of his personality and relatively high self-esteem or in part due to a more receptive and sympathetic environment? Does having close friends with similar difficulties help? Will David retain his optimism as he gets nearer to public exams and to making decisions about his future? Is the fact that David was properly identified and given the structured support he needs at an earlier age than Sophie of significance? Did David's strong verbal skills and confidence in speaking up plus his friendly and enthusiastic manner give teachers a more favourable impression of him than a shy tongue-tied dyslexic child who might have greater difficulty in convincing teachers of their intelligence? This is all speculation, but research and observation, which tells us about those children who cope well and in which circumstances, is important in informing future practice.

It was interesting to note that David's school had good relations with the Dyslexia Institute and collaborated with them on his support. This was re-flected in his statement which commented on the value of the multi-sensory teaching he had already received.

MALCOLM CARTER, AGE 9:9

Wechsler Intelligence Scale for Children   Full Scale IQ   92
At 8 years 2 months Reading Age   <5
Spelling Age   5:10

It was noted in Malcolm's report that his low average IQ indicated that he should be reading and spelling at an age level much closer to his chrono-logical age, which would indicate that he had specific learning difficulties. He attended his local primary school and had been attending the Dyslexia Institute for 18 months. He was the middle of three children and his father worked away from home on the oil rigs.

Mrs Carter

'Well I wasn't worried until he was about six, I would say. But even at nur-sery Malcolm never wanted to bring a picture home. He never wanted to do a mother's day card or things like that you know. Things where he would have to write.'

Well, the school weren't too concerned, because it was all the new ideas, they learn through play. You know, they're never concerned about reading and writing really until junior school. But, I mean, having said that there were three years in the infants school.'

Mrs Carter felt that Malcolm was making no progress at all and had diffi-culty with tasks such as saying the days of the week in order. She accepted that Malcolm probably wasn't one of the brightest children in the class but felt as she put it 'he was intelligent enough' to learn to read. She said she made several visits to the school to discuss Malcolm's difficulties. Malcolm was then seen by an educational psychologist, according to Mrs Carter she didn't receive a written report.

'He just said he was immature, and that as he got older he would make progress.'

When Malcolm entered junior school he was still not reading so he was given some remedial help, but Mrs Carter felt that this was not specific enough and Malcolm still made poor progress. After the first two terms she decided to contact the Dyslexia Institute.

'Because I got absolutely sick of going up and down the school. I mean, it had got to the stage where I was in tears and I was frustrated by it. And I felt that there was no one you could really turn to. Nobody was pointing you in any direction. So he wasn't getting the help and you knew there was something wrong.'

'But the only thing was every time I mentioned dyslexia it was like a taboo word. It's like, "Well, I've taught for thirty years, and I've only ever come across one child you know."'

'And I think I was so concerned because in the earlier days, when it was just being made public about dyslexia. There were people having to risk their homes and everything just really to get help for their kids. I mean it's all right for people who come where you can afford it. For them to have the lessons. But I mean there's lots of kids out there who are just getting wrote off and I don't think that's right. People say "Well, there's a lot of dyslexics who've succeeded," but probably for every one that's succeeded there's these twenty behind who haven't.'

'I mean I know a lot of people are against them being labelled, but to me it makes no difference, because if you're blind you're blind. If you're dyslexic you're dyslexic, and there's not much you can do . . . so long as you get help and you learn to cope with it, why worry about it? And to me being statemented is just as bad a thing in my eyes. But they can accept that and not the label "dyslexia". And I think when they do say "special needs", I think that's a big umbrella, and they can sort of fit everything into it.'

Mrs Carter thought that having dyslexia had influenced Malcolm quite a lot and she rated his self-esteem as fairly low.

'He was fine until last year. I think he knew then that there were a lot of the kids getting ahead of him, and I think the other kids were starting to realise that Malcolm wasn't the same as them. And I think he had a few little hassles at school, which he hadn't come across before: a bit of name calling and things like that.'

'He said the other day "Well, I'm never going to do what the others do in class."'

'You know, I just says, "There'll always be things that other children will go on and be able to do that you can't but, there again there'll be things you can do that they can't." But I think what hurt the most with Malcolm was last year, he was even thinking about what he was going to do when he leaves school. He was coming home and saying things like, "I think I'll be a lollipop man because you'll not really have to do much written work," or things like that. And I thought, you know, "You shouldn't even have to worry." You know, really your school days should be happy.'

Mrs Carter was pleased with the general attitude of teachers in the school and thought that the majority of them had been encouraging in their approach.

'Well certainly last year and this term, he's had such a lot of help from some of the teachers, and they've given him awards for certain pieces of work that he's done. It'll be completely mis-spelt in a case like that, but for him it's a good piece of work. So they have encouraged him to do a lot better, and the last open evening I was really impressed on how well he had done.'

'It was a bit difficult last year; I had a bit of a to-do with one of the teachers because I wasn't very happy with what she had written in his report at the end of the year, saying that he hadn't tried, he hadn't worked, that as well. Like a lot of teachers have said, he does try, it's just he can't get through that brick wall type of thing . . . I rang the head and he said, "Well, she said he'd only worked to 40 per cent of his capacity." I says, "Is that 40 per cent of his capacity or what the rest of the class are capable of?" Because if she's saying 40 per cent of what the rest of them are capable of, that is what Malcolm will be functioning at. I just don't think teachers realise what efforts these kids put in.'

Mrs Carter was disappointed because this teacher had expressed an interest in having some information on dyslexia and had been taken in several pamphlets.

'I knew from the report that she'd written that she hadn't taken on board anything that was in the leaflets.'

'I mean, he's got a teacher now, who if he's not trying, she tells him. She's not sort of soft on him or overly sweet to him because he's got problems. I mean she knows if he's trying or not, and it seems to have worked. The relationship with her is quite good because she knows when to encourage him when he's done well, and she does.'

Mrs Carter was aware that Malcolm often kept things to himself and was not one to talk about his problems.

> 'I would say he misbehaves a bit more. If you know he's been having problems he can come home and take it out on the family type of thing.'

Mrs Carter thought that some parents and teachers did think she was making excuses for Malcolm by calling him dyslexic. She'd also felt a bit isolated from other parents on occasions like open evening.

> 'Because you see all the mothers going to see their nice paperwork on the wall.'

It had also been suggested to her by some teachers that Malcolm should go to special school.

> 'I don't see that as an option because Malcolm is bright enough. I mean I don't want anybody to think he's above average, he's not. He is just an average child. I mean he's got his problems, and if he overcomes them, great, but I don't want him to be sort of like a university graduate if he's not capable of it.'

> 'You do feel a bit neurotic and pushy because you're always up at the school. But I've always felt it was important to sort it out in junior school.'

> 'If schools would listen to you the way that doctors do sometimes, because doctors often think, "Yes, Mum knows best: she's with them twenty-four hours of the day type of thing," and you know your own child. Whereas, like, teachers think, "Oh well, we've been trained, we know what's happening with your child," and I don't think they always do.'

Mrs Carter then spoke about a course for parents which she had been to recently at the Dyslexia Institute.

> 'I think it makes you realise you're not the only one with problems and that children vary a lot. But it made you realise about the whole scope of the things and not just the reading and writing.'

> 'I think the only thing that gives me cause for concern, like, I say Malcolm's never been disruptive or anything like that, but I know it can get to the stage where they might feel totally isolated and I wouldn't want to see any decline in his behaviour, when he goes to senior school.'

Mrs Carter was asked how she felt at the moment about Malcolm having dyslexia.

> 'I think I'm relieved, like I said before, that you know what it is, and you can do something about it. But I mean, I don't think there is a magical cure. I mean I think he'll be as dyslexic at seventy as he is at seven. But as

long as he learns to cope with it. Probably in the infants I thought there was no hope at all, but obviously when you come here (Dyslexia Institute) and you see them progressing, I'm quite happy with things the way they are. As long as he obviously continues to make progress.'

Malcolm

Malcolm presented in his interview as a calm sensible boy, who was quite happy to talk about practical things connected with his work but found it much harder to comment on how he felt about things. This could be put down to the interview situation, but his mother also found him the same at home.

Malcolm said his main interests were football, and anything else active; this was similarly reflected in his interests at school where he said he liked PE, football and playing. He was positive about his specialist sessions and gave a detailed account of the specific things he learnt, he said he didn't mind coming even though it was extra work. When asked why he thought coming to the Dyslexia Institute was 'good' he replied:

'I've learnt how to do more joined up writing. I've learnt spelling, all sorts of stuff as well, and it helps us (me) with my reading. I think it helps us a lot. It's better than being like stuck, and at school it helps you a lot, you know how to get on with your work, and you don't go to the teacher all the time.'

When asked about what difficulties he had at school because of his dyslexia he said that his difficulties had been mainly before he started having specialist help.

'Like writing about things we did . . . like to write a sentence out because I didn't know what to write and like I didn't know how to spell.'

He spoke about how he used to watch other children go up and say they had finished, when he had just started writing. Malcolm mentioned several times during the interview that he felt better because there was another boy now in the class who also had difficulties.

'Because there's another boy like me, but he's got more problems now because he hasn't been doing sounds and stuff.'

Malcolm said he used to feel embarrassed by his difficulties and blame himself.

'I'm not very embarrassed now because there's someone the same as me.'

Malcolm thought that his teachers were generally positive and supportive and that he had never been unfairly criticised by them.

Malcolm had to leave school early for one of his specialist sessions and said that he avoided telling other children where he was going and why.

He said he wouldn't know what to say if someone asked him what dyslexia was, although his mum had explained it to him and he thought he did understand at a personal level what it was.

When finally asked if he thought he would still be dyslexic as an adult he said:

'I don't know. I'm going to hope to try to get rid of it.'

Key points

Even though Mrs Carter felt that she had had to push to get Malcolm's difficulties recognised both she and Malcolm thought that the school had been largely supportive in their attitude to him and that he had experienced no direct humiliation or unfair criticism from teachers. This combined with the good progress that Malcolm had made in his specialist sessions appeared to be giving him a good all round level of support to which he was responding positively.

It was notable that Malcolm had quietly compared himself to other children over the years and drawn his own conclusions. Again this brings into question how far the ethos and organisation of the school and the nature of the personal support a child receives can help prevent them from building up a negative self-image. In relation to this the importance of having another child in the class with similar problems was emphasised by Malcolm as a way of coping.

Both Mrs Carter and Mrs Graham described themselves as having to be 'pushy' in order to get their children's difficulties properly recognised. It perhaps says something about the power relationship between parents and school that when parents put forward legitimate concerns this is seen as 'pushy', whereas if the schools had put forward the same concerns it's hard to imagine that this would have been seen as 'pushy'. In all three cases the children received two to three sessions a week of 'remedial' support at school before they were identified as having dyslexia. Their lack of progress in terms of reading and spelling scores would seem to support their mother's contentions that this support was not specific enough to their difficulties to have a significant impact on them. In a more positive light this does suggest that in some cases schools don't need to be necessarily giving more support but that they need to have a better understanding of specific learning difficulties so that support can be more appropriate and effective.

Chapter 13

Conclusions and recommendations

The two biggest problems for individuals with dyslexia are still the prejudice and ignorance of others.

Many recent books on dyslexia have listed a number of sensible and appropriate ways to tackle the difficulties encountered by individuals with dyslexia. But as Pollock and Waller (1994) point out, the concept of dyslexia at present is like a religion with people either being believers or non believers. In order to bring about a shift in some people's outlook it is necessary to understand how prejudice and ignorance have arisen and look at the most effective ways of changing attitudes.

AN INTERACTIVE PERSPECTIVE

In the 1980s and early 1990s research or teaching which was seen to focus on within-child or constitutional factors was deeply unfashionable especially to many in the field of 'special needs'. Much of the focus was on adapting the curriculum and organisation of the school. Endless books with 'special needs' or 'special education' in the title appeared. Despite the laudable intention of dealing with the 'whole child', the child in reality appeared to be absent from many of these books, in that the child under consideration was largely a vague environmental construction. This is not to denigrate the considerable advances in thinking that went on and the importance of understanding the role of environmental factors in children's learning. The problem is one of having a balanced and truly interactive perspective. If we have a hazy or inaccurate idea of what kind of child our environmental factors are interacting with, we can end up with the wrong picture. This is not a problem exclusive to dyslexia. The present author examined at one time the integration of children with physical disabilities into mainstream schools. What surprised her was the number of mainstream teachers who knew nothing about the specific nature of the impairments that some children had and the specific learning disabilities that accompanied these impairments. Many teachers were unaware for example that a high proportion of children with spina-bifida had a valve fitted in their head which often led to local damage and subsequent specific learning disabilities, especially in the perceptual motor area. On one occasion this led to a class teacher giving a highly negative account of a child with spina-bifida who she saw as careless and lazy in her written work and diagrams. A simple understanding of the considerable perceptual difficulties that this child had would have given the teacher a totally different perspective. To be fair many of the mainstream teachers were concerned by their lack of knowledge and wanted more information. At least with a physical impairment a teacher is alerted to the possibility of needing more information.

A HIDDEN DISABILITY

The problem is that because 'dyslexia' is physically invisible you have to know what it is before you can clearly see it. This explains why it is possible for teachers to claim that they have been teaching for 30 years without coming across a child with dyslexia. As they know nothing about dyslexia they never see a child with dyslexia! Many of the mothers in this sample had known something was wrong with their child's learning but it was only when they came upon information describing dyslexia that they identified this as the difficulty. Similarly several specialist teachers also said that before they knew about dyslexia there were children in their class who mystified or puzzled them. It was only in retrospect that they realised that these children were dyslexic and many of them felt guilty that they had been able to do little for these children. To return to the main point of this argument, a move to an interactional approach which stresses the importance of both within-child and environmental factors is needed if we are to do full justice to many aspects of special needs. Research into the learning of children with severe learning disabilities shows that different groups of children have different cognitive profiles and different strengths and weaknesses in the way that they learn (Clements 1987, Dockrell and McShane 1993). This suggests that no child's learning should be described by vague terms such as 'slow' and far from threatening our overall approach to special needs, dyslexia can help us to improve the way that we think about and approach a whole range of special needs. Pumfrey and Reason (1991) point out that it is important that if constitutional factors are highlighted we don't then overlook environmental factors such as the way children are taught. It can be argued that if we take the 'whole' person as our starting point and listen to what a person with a disability has to say we are less likely to do this, as people with disabilities have to grapple with environmental factors every day of their life and can tell us graphically how these affect them.

'They don't know how much it affects you. I think it, like, frightens you being put through the traumas of it. In lessons they make you read out all the time. My mum does complain sometimes, but the school doesn't listen.'

The perceptive and articulate girl who told the interviewer this was near to tears as she spoke. This girl went to a comprehensive school with a supportive special needs department, but as with many children in the study, it appeared that teachers underestimated the emotional impact of the difficulties that she was having.

Dyson and Skidmore (1994) in their survey of provision for specific learning disabilities in secondary schools found that schools based provision on children's perceived needs rather than specific labels as such. This approach was thought to work well from the point of view of the schools but does beg the question of what informed or guided teachers' perceptions of need. It can be argued that where teachers understand something about the difficulties involved in specific learning difficulties or dyslexia this will inform and direct their perception of need. One mother in the study found that although her son's secondary school was very sympathetic about his poor literacy they completely dismissed the idea of specific learning difficulties and thought that all his problems were caused by lack of confidence and would thus be solved by improving his confidence. His mother felt this was a partial solution which didn't take on board the specific nature of the literacy difficulties he was having at school. As more is learnt about dyslexia it is becoming clearer that there are different degrees of the problem and that individuals differ in the precise nature of the problems that they have, although there are enough commonalties to justify the overall label of 'dyslexia' or 'specific learning difficulties'. It may well be the case that those with mild to moderate difficulties will be helped by moves to more phonics based systematic teaching of reading or the introduction of multi-sensory methods to the classroom. What is less clear is how far these approaches will alleviate the more severe difficulties that some children have. It may be that these more severely affected children will need more individual and specific teaching over a longer period of time. It is important that a developmental perspective is taken and that the long term difficulties that some children have are acknowledged and planned for. It is also important that not only are children given academic help but that they are also given personal support and that everything possible is done to maintain their self-esteem and to help them develop self-awareness and positive coping strategies. In this study it was found that telling children they were dyslexic was an important part of boosting low self-esteem. It also enabled children and their families to access a whole range of support such as role models, literature, support groups and so on which they may not have otherwise had contact with. For this reason it is important that schools, even if they prefer the term 'specific learning difficulty', acknowledge the word 'dyslexia' and allow children and parents to feel comfortable in using it.

'Every time I said it I could feel myself getting embarrassed.'

It is also important that schools do what they can to promote a positive attitude towards dyslexia so that children are not teased or denigrated about their difficulties.

'Basically it's (dyslexia) like a stigma in my school.'

At the moment a crossroads appears to have been reached. The way ahead could be for educationalists to reformulate 'dyslexia' as an educational term or to consider what is needed to make 'specific learning difficulties' a more meaningful term for parents and children. Rather than 'blaming' individuals for using the term 'dyslexia' we need to ask in a constructive manner why they choose to do so. At present it is suggested that 'dyslexia' provides more personal support for many individuals and that they often end up using this term because they perceive themselves as lacking support from the mainstream school system. One mother in discussing the relative merits of these two terms made the following comment:

'I suppose if they'd told me when she was six or seven that she had specific learning difficulties and they were planning to help her, and they'd been, like, sympathetic, well, we might never have ended up calling her "dyslexic".'

TEACHER TRAINING

Most people would agree that teachers have a difficult and demanding job and that a great many different skills are expected of the ordinary classroom teacher. Given the complexities of researching and unravelling the underlying difficulties that characterise dyslexia it appears highly unreasonable to expect teachers to identify and remediate these difficulties without specific training. As teachers and parents know only too well, trying to teach a child without these insights can be a baffling and infuriating experience at times. Many have advocated the need for much wider training for teachers and other professionals in the area of specific learning difficulties or dyslexia (Pumfrey and Reason 1991, British Dyslexia Association (BDA), Peer 1994, Edwards 1994). All are agreed that there needs to be training at both the initial and INSET levels. The BDA sets out helpful guidelines for how this could be accomplished. At present, according to the BDA, there is great variation in coverage on initial teacher training courses. An issue that runs across both initial and INSET training, is what level of training should be compulsory and what level of training should be optional. One approach would be for all teachers to have an 'awareness' level of training with more specialised training for some teachers, including all those with special responsibility for special needs. Many educational psychologists do have training in specific learning difficulties but the depth of this still varies from course to course and those that trained some time ago will not necessarily have covered this area and like many practising teachers are dependent on inservice training for updating their knowledge. The present author, for example, trained as an educational psychologist during the mid 1970s and recalls no input on specific learning difficulties. A particular difficulty appears to be that because of the negative mythology that has surrounded dyslexia, some educationalists are very reluctant to take any inservice training on specific learning difficulties or dyslexia. In the present study it was found that even in schools with a good overall approach to specific learning difficulties, there always seemed to be a few teachers who were dismissive of children's specific difficulties and openly hostile to the term dyslexia.

'The French teacher is a nightmare. She says there's no such thing as dyslexia.'

At primary school the effects of a critical teacher could be particularly devastating and several mothers in this study gave graphic accounts of the distress their children suffered.

'It was making him so negative in outlook, especially that term with the bad teacher. I mean, teachers have a lot to do with outlook. I saw him completely change from enjoying school to the spark wasn't there, but then it came back, it's definitely who's teaching them at the time, it definitely makes an impact. When he had the bad teacher he was so frightened of her he used to wring his hands. The teacher after the bad one said, "You can see him sitting at the table, working himself up into a frenzy as to whether he should come and ask us something, and he stands beside the table and he's wringing his hands." That was all instilled by one bad teacher.'

Reynolds (1995) points out that whole school policies for special needs may have very little impact in the classroom and ultimately much is dependent on the attitude of the individual teacher. This underlines the importance of all teachers having training in this area and not just those whose are interested. Another important point is that training, as well as imparting specific knowledge, needs to help address teachers' underlying attitudes and develop their understanding and empathy of children who have specific difficulties. In some cases mothers were disappointed because even when teachers had requested specific information this didn't always appear to make them more understanding of the child's difficulties. It may be that these teachers weren't given sufficient information or simply didn't have sufficient time to reflect on the information and think through its implications for classroom practice, but it may also be the case that some teachers need help in doing this. One class teacher reflected that what had really brought home to her how frustrating and tiring writing could be for dyslexic children, was being asked to write with her non-preferred hand for the whole of a training day on dyslexia.

THE RELATIONSHIP BETWEEN TEACHERS, PARENTS AND CHILDREN

An important thread that runs through the debate on dyslexia is the relationship between parents and teachers. This was discussed in some depth in chapter 7, here just some of the main points to emerge from that are reviewed. Riddick (1995a) has suggested that this relationship becomes critical when there are differences between the parents and the school on the nature and extent of a child's difficulties. Allied to this the powerful myth of parents as pushy, overambitous, and unrealistic was often invoked when parents questioned the accuracy of the school's perceptions and raised the possibility of dyslexia. In cases like this it appeared that parents were treated as clients rather than partners and that no or little credence was given to their point of view. Parents in this situation found themselves largely powerless, whatever their social class. As Dewhirst also found in her study some parents felt that they had been labelled as 'pushy' by the school and blamed for their children's difficulties. There appeared to be an interaction between a school's attitude to dyslexia and their attitude to parents. In some cases where schools were more positive in their attitude to parents, they were willing to listen to parents' concerns even though they were initially ignorant or dubious about the concept of dyslexia. Dyson and Skidmore (1995) found that in comprehensives supportive of the concept of specific learning difficulties there were generally good relations with parents with little conflict. The message seems to be that conflict tends to arise when schools are not identifying and supporting children with dyslexia and that in such cases parents are entitled to feel concerned and that they could be seen as 'pro-active' rather than 'pushy'. There is no evidence that parents of dyslexic children are different to parents in general and the same range of views and attitudes towards education are held. It has often been suggested that parents of children with special needs are ordinary parents in an extraordinary situation. Whilst the situation for parents of dyslexic children is far less extraordinary than for more severe disabilities, in the context of the mainstream school their experiences and those of their children are atypical and out of the ordinary. If this is borne in mind and combined with a good understanding of specific learning difficulties it makes the responses of children and their parents more understandable to teachers. Although organisational issues may well impinge on how parent–school relations develop, from the point of view of parents, these are very much down to the attitudes of individual teachers, and parents could point to marked differences between teachers within a school. It can be argued that a reduction in negative stereotypes, especially by teachers, would enable there to be a better understanding between teachers and parents and a better understanding of children's difficulties as a consequence. This again can be seen as part of good practice and not as something exclusive to children with dyslexia. Hannon (1995) argues that: 'It is professionals, by virtue of their institutional position, who have the greater power and responsibility for parent–teacher relations.'

Historically it can be argued that the main impetus for recognising and supporting dyslexia has come from outside the educational establishment and at present we appear to have reached a transitional point where increasing numbers of mainstream educationalists are taking an active part in identifying and supporting children with dyslexia or specific learning difficulties. Because of the past dominance of the clinical, individual child-centred approach, a major task for mainstream educationalists is to develop viable 'educational approaches' to identifying and supporting such children.

Appendix

INTERVIEW SCHEDULE – CHILDREN

Warm-up questions

W1 What sort of things do you like doing at home?
W2 What sort of things do you enjoy at school?

Dyslexia Institute

1 I understand you've been coming to the Dyslexia Institute for the last ...... Can you tell me about the sort of things you've been doing here/there?
2 Can you give me some examples of the things you've learnt at the Dyslexia Institute?
3 What do you think about coming to the Dyslexia Institute?
   (probes) a) fed up because it means more work
           b) pleased because it helps me with my work

School

4 When you're doing your work at school do you find that you use anything that you've learnt at the Institute?
   (probe) every day, once a week, never?
   Can you give me an example of this?
5 What sort of work do you have difficulty with at school because of your dyslexia?
   now
   in the past
6 How do you try and cope with these difficulties?

Writing
  (probe) Do you think you write the same amount as other children or do
  you think you write less?

  every day   every week   rarely   never
  a) write less than other children
  b) avoid certain words
  c) pick easy to spell words
  d) try and get out of doing writing
  e) not write clearly
  f) try and get a classmate to help
  g) put off starting work
  h) other
7 How do you feel about the difficulties that you have?
8 Do you think other children notice the difficulties you have?
  yes   no   not sure
9 Do other children ever tease you about the difficulties you have?
  no   yes
  What sort of things do they say?
10 How do you explain your difficulties to other children?
11 Does your teacher/s (form tutor) understand your difficulties?
12 Does your teacher/s do anything to help you with your difficulties?
  (probe) Any support teaching?
13a In general what kind of things do you find most helpful in school?
  b Can you tell me about the best teacher you've had so far?
14a What kind of things do you find unhelpful or upsetting in school?
  b Can you tell me about the worst teacher you've had so far?
15a Have you ever been told you are any of the following because of the
  difficulties you have with your work?
  a) lazy
  b) careless
  c) slow
  d) untidy
  e) not paying attention
  f) other
  b How do you feel about being called————————?
16 Are there any things in school that you really dread having to do?
17 Compared with your classmates are you:
  more intelligent than average
  about average
  less intelligent than average

Home

18 Do you read at home for your own pleasure? (probe) What sort of things?
never (Go to 19a)   less than once a week   a few times a week   every day
(go to 19b)

19a Why do you never read?

 b Do you find any problems or difficulties with the things you read?

20 If somebody asked you what dyslexia meant, what would you say?

21 What do you think about being called dyslexic?
(probe) Do you resent it for making you feel different or has it helped you
understand your problems?

22a Who explained to you what dyslexia means?

 b Does it make sense to you?

23 Would you like the chance to talk about it more?

24 Do you meet other children who have dyslexia? (Is that helpful or not?)

25 Have you heard of any famous or successful adults who have dyslexia?
(If yes, has this encouraged you or do you think they're irrelevant to your
life?)

26 Do you think your parents understand what it's like to be dyslexic?
definitely do
to some extent
not at all

27 Do you talk to your parents about any problems or difficulties that you
have at school because of being dyslexic?
usually   sometimes   rarely   never
(probe) What sorts of things would you talk/not talk about with your
parents?

28 Do you think you'll still be dyslexic when you're an adult?

29 Is there anything I've left out that you'd like to talk about?

INTERVIEW SCHEDULE – ADULTS

Do any close family members have dyslexia or a similar problem?

Identifying the problem

1 How old was N when you first became aware that N might have
difficulties?
a) Was it you who first realised that N had problems?
b) Was it someone else who first realised that N had a problem?
c) What kind of problems did N display?

2a Looking back, were there any earlier signs that N might have difficulties?

 b Did you always feel that basically N was as intelligent as other
children? Yes No

c Can you give me some examples of what convinced you of N's intelligence?

3 Who was it who first suggested that N might be dyslexic?

4 Where had you learnt about dyslexia from?

5a Who did you first discuss your concerns with?

  b What was their response?

      (probe) In agreement   Noncommittal   Dismissive

6 If someone else first suggested N was dyslexic, what was your response?

7 How did you feel when N was first identified as dyslexic?

8a If the school first suggested N might be dyslexic or have a specific learning difficulty, what support did they offer?

  Primary

  Secondary

  b If you first suggested N might be dyslexic what support did they offer?

  Primary

  Secondary

  c Were you satisfied with the support offered?

  d Was N formally assessed by anybody?

  e Did they think that N was dyslexic?

  f What did they recommend?

  g Were you happy with the recommendations?

Help at home

9 Were you involved in teaching N to read? (How did this go?)

10a What sort of practical support have you tried to offer N at home, or do you think it's best left to the experts?

  b Has this gone OK or has it caused any problems?

  c How did you decide what support to offer?

  d What support was most effective?

11 What sort of personal support have you tried to give N?

12 Have you discussed with N what the label 'dyslexia' means?

13 If someone asked you to define or describe dyslexia what would you say?

Problems at school

14 What sort of problems, if any, does N encounter at school because of her/his dyslexia?

  At present

  In the past

15 Does N freely discuss these problems with you or do you have to drag them out?

16 When N has problems at school is it easy for you to talk to the school about them and get them resolved?

17 Could you tell me about the best teacher that N has had so far?
18 Could you tell me about the worst teacher that N has had so far?
19a What influence if any do you think having dyslexia has had on N?
      none   some   a lot
  b Does N have any nervous habits which you think are associated with the pressure of being dyslexic?
20 How would you rate N's self-esteem compared to other children of the same age?
      very high   fairly high   average   fairly low   very low
21 Have you ever felt isolated from other parents because of N's problems?
22 Have you ever felt that teachers or other parents think you're making excuses for N by calling her/him dyslexic?

The Dyslexia Institute

23 Why did you decide to send N to the Dyslexia Institute?
24 How did you hear about the Dyslexia Institute?
25 How long has N been attending for and how often?
26 Has attending the Institute helped N or not? If it has helped in what way has it done so?
27 Has attending the Institute helped you at all?
28a Is there any direct liaison between N's school and the Dyslexia Institute?
  b Does N have to miss any school in order to attend the Institute?
  c Does this cause any difficulties?
  d If N attends after school are there any problems with tiredness?
29a Do the things that N learns at the Institute carry over to her/his work in school?
      completely   somewhat   not very much   no idea
  b can you give me some examples of this carry over?
30a How long does a round journey to the Dyslexia Institute take?
  b does this cause any problems to the family timetable?
31 Does paying the fees have any impact on the family budget?
      none at all   some impact   a considerable impact
32 Do you think that support of this nature or a similar nature should be provided in your child's school or do you think it is best provided by a private institution like the Dyslexia Institute?
33a Turning to the future, do you worry about N's future progress at school?
      a lot 5 4 3 2 1 not at all
  b What particular concerns do you have?
34 Do you think having dyslexia will affect N's career choices?
35a What do you think about the support? you've had in coping with N's difficulties
  b Would you have liked more support?   No   Yes
  c What sort of support would you have liked?

36 In general how do you feel at the moment about N having dyslexia?
37 Is there anything I haven't covered that you'd like to mention?

Suggested further reading

BIOGRAPHIES AND CASE STUDIES

Edwards, J. (1994) *The Scars of Dyslexia*. London: Cassell.
Hampshire, S. (1990) *Susan's Story*. London: Corgi.
Innes, P. (1991) *Defeating Dyslexia: A Boy's Story*. London: Kyle Cathie.
Osmond, J. (1993) *The Reality of Dyslexia*. London: Cassell.
Van de Stoel, S. (1990) *Parents on Dyslexia*. Avon: Multilingual Matters.

ADVICE ON TEACHING/MANAGING DYSLEXIA

Augur, J. and Briggs, S. (eds) (1992) *The Hickey Multi-Sensory Language Course*. London: Whurr.
Brereton, A., and Cann, P. (1993) *Opening the Door: Guidance on Recognising and Helping the Dyslexic Child*. Reading: British Dyslexia Association.
Chinn, S., and Ashcroft, R. (1993) *Dyslexia and Mathematics: A Teaching Handbook*. London: Whurr.
Hornsby, B. (1995) *Overcoming Dyslexia: A Straightforward Guide for Families and Teachers*. London: Optoma.
McLoughlin, D., Fitzgibbon, G. and Young, V. (1994) *Adult Dyslexia: Assessment, Counselling and Training*. London: Whurr.
Miles, T.R. and Gilroy, D. (1986) *Dyslexia at College*. London: Methuen.
Miles, T.R. and Miles, E. (1983) *Help for Dyslexic Children*. London: Methuen.
Ostler, C. (1991) *Dyslexia: A Parents' Survival Guide*. Godalming: Ammonite Books.
Peer, L. (1994) *Dyslexia: The Training and Awareness of Teachers*. Reading: British Dyslexia Association.
Peters, M.L. and Smith B. (1993) *Spelling in Context: Strategies for Teachers and Learners*. Windsor: NFER-Nelson.
Pollock, J. and Waller, E. (1994) *Day to Day Dyslexia in the Classroom*. London: Routledge.
Singleton, C. (ed.) (1994) *Computers and Dyslexia: Educational Applications of New Technology*. Hull: Dyslexia Computer Resource Centre.
Topping, K. (1995) *Paired Reading, Writing and Spelling*. London: Cassell.

GENERAL READING

Ellis, A.W. (1993) *Reading, Writing and Dyslexia: A Cognitive Analysis*. Hove: Lawrence Erlbaum Associates.

Hulme, C. and Snowling, M. (eds) (1994) *Reading Development and Dyslexia*. London: Whurr.

Miles, T.R. (1993) *Dyslexia: The Pattern of Difficulties*. London: Whurr.

Miles, T.R. and Miles, E. (1990) *Dyslexia: A Hundred Years On*. Milton Keynes: Open University Press.

Pumfrey, P. and Reason, R. (1991) *Specific Learning Difficulties (Dyslexia): Challenges and Responses*. London: Routledge.

Reid, G. (1994) *Specific Learning Difficulties (Dyslexia): a Handbook for Study and Practice*. Edinburgh: Moray House Publications.

Snowling, M. (1987) *Dyslexia: A Cognitive Developmental Perspective*. Oxford: Basil Blackwell.

Thomson, M. (1990) *Developmental Dyslexia*. London: Whurr.

Useful addresses

United Kingdom

British Dyslexia Association, 98 London Road, Reading, Berkshire, RG1 5AU
Tel. (01734) 668271
Dyslexia Institute, 133 Gresham Road, Staines, Middlesex, TW18 2AJ
Tel. (01784) 463851

Both these organisations have a number of local branches throughout the country and both offer information and support to children and adults with dyslexia and their families and information to teachers.

United States of America

Association for Children with Learning Difficulties, 5225 Grace Street, Pittsburg, PA 15236.
Orton Society, Chester Building, Suite 382, 8600 La Salle Road, Baltimore, MD 21204.

Australia

Association for Children with Learning Disabilities (ACLD). 21–3 Belmore Street, Burwood 2134, New South Wales.
SpELD NSW, 129 Grenwich 2065, Sydney, New South Wales.

References

Ackerman, P. T., Anhalt, J. M. and Dykman, R. A. (1986) 'Arithmetic automatisa-
tion failure in children with attention and reading disorders: associations and
sequela'. *Journal of Learning Disabilities*, 19, 222–32.

Ainley. J. and Bourke, S. (1992) 'Student views on primary schools'. In E. Wragg (ed.)
Research Papers in Education, 7, June.

Alessi, G. (1988) 'Diagnosis diagnosed: a systematic reaction'. *Professional School
Psychology*, 3 (2), 41–51.

Allport. G. W. (1954) *The Nature of Prejudice*. Reading, MA: Addison Wesley.

Alston, J. (1995) 'Toe by toe'. *Special Children,* June/July.

Anderson, E. M., Clarke, L. and Spain, B. (1982) *Disability in Adolescence.* London:
Methuen.

Andrews, G. (1994) 'Policy and practice in special needs must challenge the trend
towards market led provision'. *Education*, 184 (16).

Andrews. N. (1990) 'A follow-up study of dyslexic students'. In G. Hales (ed.)
Meeting Points in Dyslexia, Proceedings of the First International Conference of
the British Dyslexia Association. Reading: BDA.

Atkin, J., Bastiani, J. with Goode, J. (1988) *Listening to Parents.* London: Croom
Helm.

Augur, J. (1985) 'Guide lines for teachers, parents and learners'. In M. Snowling
(ed.) *Children's Written Language Difficulties.* Windsor: NFER-Nelson.

Bannister, D. and Fransella F. (1971) *Inquiring Man: The Theory of Personal Constructs.* Harmondsworth: Penguin.

Barton, L. (ed.) (1987) *The Politics of Special Educational Needs.* Lewes: Falmer Press.

Barton, L. and Moody, S. (1981) 'The value of parents in the ESN school: an examination'. In L. Barton and S. Tomlinson (eds) *Special Education: Policy, Practices and
Social Issues.* London: Harper & Row.

Baskind, S. and Thomson, D. (1994) 'What role do school governors play as repre-
sentatives of special needs issues in their own schools?' *British Educational
Research Journal*, 20 (3).

Bastiani, J. (1987) 'From compensation to participation? A brief analysis of
changing attitudes in the study and practice of home–school relations'. In J.
Bastiani (ed.) *Parents and Teachers 1: Perspectives on Home School Relations.*
Windsor: NFER-Nelson.

Battle, J. (1990) *Self-Esteem the New Revolution.* Edmonton: James Battle Associates.

Battle, J. (1991) *Culture-Free Self-Esteem Inventories for Children and Adults* (1st
edn). Austin, Texas: PRO-ED.

Battle, J. (1992) *Culture-Free Self-Esteem Inventories* (2nd edn). Austin, Texas: PRO-
ED.

Beck, A. T., Rush, A. J., Shaw, B. F. and Emery, G. (1979) *Cognitive Therapy of Depression.* New York: Guildford.

Blaxter, M. (1976) *The Meaning of Disability.* London: Heinemann.

Blaxter, M. and Paterson, E. (1982) *Mothers and their Daughters: A Three Generational Study of Health Attitudes and Behaviour.* London: Heinemann.

Boder, E. (1973) 'Developmental dyslexia: a diagnostic approach based on three atypical reading patterns'. *Developmental Medicine and Child Neurology*, 15, 663–87.

Booth, G. K. (1988) 'Psychologists' perceptions of children who have specific learning difficulties'. *Educational Psychology in Practice,* July.

Booth, T. (1978) 'From normal baby to handicapped child'. *Sociology,* (12), 302–22.

Bradley, L. and Bryant, P. E. (1985) *Rhyme and Reason in Reading and Spelling.* Ann Arbor, MI: University of Michigan Press.

Brandys, C. F. and Rourke, B. F. (1991) 'Differential memory abilities in reading and arithmetic disabled children'. In B. F. Rourke (ed.) *Neuropsychological Validation of Learning Disability Subtypes.* New York: Guildford.

Bridges, D. (1987) 'It's the ones who never turn up that you really want to see'. In J. Bastiani (ed.) *Parents and Teachers 1; Perspectives on Home–School Relations.* Windsor: NFER-Nelson.

Brophy, J. E. and Good, T. L. (1974) *Teacher–Student Relationships: Causes and Consequences.* New York: Holt, Rinehart & Winston.

Bruck, M. (1985) 'The adult functioning of children with specific learning disabilities: a follow-up study'. In I. Siegal (ed.) *Advances in Applied Developmental Psychology*, Norwood, NJ: Ablex.

Bruck, M. (1992) 'Persistence of dyslexics' phonological awareness deficits'. *Developmental Psychology*, 28, 874–86.

Bryan, T. and Bryan, J. (1991a) 'Positive mood and math performance'. *Journal of Learning Disabilities*, 24, 490–4.

Bryant, P. (1994) 'Children's reading and writing'. *The Psychologist,* 7, 61.

Bryant, P. E. and Bradley, L. (1985) *Children's Reading Problems.* Oxford: Blackwell Scientific Publications.

Bryant, P. E. and Impey. L. (1986) 'The similarities between normal readers and developmental and acquired dyslexics', *Cognition*, 24, 121–37.

Bullock, Lord A. (Chair). (1975) *A Language for Life.* London: HMSO.

Burns, R. (1982) *Self-Concept Development and Education.* London: Holt, Rinehart & Winston.

Burton, L. (1975) *The Family Life of Sick Children.* London: Routledge & Kegan Paul.

Butkowsky, T. S. and Willows, D. M. (1980) 'Cognitive–motivation and characteristics of children varying in reading ability; evidence of learned helplessness in poor readers'. *Journal of Educational Psychology*, 72, 3, 408–22.

Callison, C. P. (1974) 'Experimental induction of self-concept'. *Psychological Reports*, 35, 1235–8.

Campling, J. (ed.) (1981) *Images of Ourselves: Women with Disabilities Talking.* London: Routledge & Kegan Paul.

Carguati, F. (1990) 'Everyday ideas, theoretical models, and social representations: the case of intelligence and its development'. In G. Semin and K. Gergen (eds) *Everyday Understanding: Social and Scientific Implications.* London: Sage.

Casey, R., Levy, S. E., Brown, K. and Brooks-Gunn J. (1992) 'Impaired emotional health in children with mild reading disability'. *Developmental and Behavioural Paediatrics*, 13 (4) 256–60.

Cattell, R. S., Eber, H. W. and Tatsuoka, M. M. (1970) *Handbook for the Sixteen*

Personality Factor Questionnaire. Champagne, IL: Institute for Personality and Ability Testing.

Center, Y., Wheldall, K., Freeman, L., Outhred, L. and McNaught, M. (1995) 'An evaluation of Reading Recovery'. *Reading Research Quarterly*, 30 (2).

Chapman, J., Silva, P. and Williams, S. (1984) 'Academic self-concept: Some developmental and emotional correlates in nine year old children'. *British Journal of Educational Psychology*, 54, 284–92.

Chen, C. and Uttal, D. H. (1988) 'Cultural values, parents' beliefs, and children's achievement in the United States and China'. *Human Development*, 31, 351–58.

Clark, M. M. (1970) *Reading Difficulties in Schools*. Harmondworth: Penguin.

Clayton, P. (1994) 'Using computers for numeracy and mathematics with dyslexic students'. In C. Singleton (ed.) *Dyslexia and Computers*. Hull: Dyslexia Computer Resource Centre.

Clements, J. (1987) *Severe Learning Disability and Psychological Handicap*. Chichester: Wiley.

Cline, T. and Reason, R. (1993) 'Specific learning difficulties (dyslexia): equal opportunities issues'. *British Journal of Special Education*, 20 (1).

Cole, D. and Jordan, A. (1995) 'Competence and memory: integrating psychosocial and cognitive correlates of childhood depression'. *Child Development*, 66, 450–73.

Coltheart, M. (1987) 'Varieties of developmental dyslexia: a comment on Bryant and Impey'. *Cognition*, 27, 97–101.

Coltheart, M., Masterson, J., Byng, S., Prior, M. and Riddoch, J. (1983) 'Surface dyslexia'. *Quarterly Journal of Experimental Psychology*, 25A, 469–95.

Connell, B. (1987) 'Families and their kids'. In J. Bastiani (ed.) *Parents and Teachers*. Windsor: NFER-Nelson.

Coopersmith, S. (1967) *The Antecedents of Self-Esteem*. San Francisco: Freeman Press.

Critchley, M. (1970) *The Dyslexic Child*. London: Heinemann.

Croll, P. and Moses, D. (1985) *One in Five: The Assessment and Incidence of Special Eucational Needs*. London: Routledge & Kegan Paul.

Cronbach, L. J. (1984) *Essentials of Psychological Testing*. (4th edn) New York: Harper & Row.

Darke, S. (1988) 'Anxiety and working memory capacity'. *Cognition and Emotion*, 2.

De Fries, J. (1991) 'Genetics and dyslexia: an overview'. In M. Snowling and D. Thomson, *Dyslexia: Integrating Theory and Practice*. London: Whurr.

DES (Department of Education and Science) (1978) *Special Educational Needs (Warnock Report)*. Cmnd 7271. London: HMSO.

Dessent, A. (1987) *Making the Ordinary School Special*. Brighton: Falmer Press.

Dewhirst, W. (1995) ' "Pushy parents and lazy kids: aspects of dyslexia". An investigation of the experiences of dyslexics and their families in the diagnostic process'. Unpublished MSc in Social Research Methods. University of Teesside.

DFE (Department for Education) (1994) *Code of Practice on the Identification and Assessment of Special Needs*. Central Office of Information. EDUC JO22465NJ 5/94.

Dockrell, J. and McShane, J. (1993) *Children's Learning Difficulties: A Cognitive Approach*. Oxford: Blackwell.

Doran, C. and Cameron, R. J. (1995) 'Learning about learning: metacognitive approaches in the classroom'. *Educational Psychology in Practice*, 11, 2.

Donawa, W. (1995) 'Growing up dyslexic: A parent's view'. *Journal of Learning Disabilities*, 28 (6), 324–8.

Dyson, A. and Skidmore, D. (1994) 'Provision for pupils with specific learning difficulties in secondary schools'. A report to SOED (Scottish Office Education Department). University of Newcastle upon Tyne.

Edwards, J. (1994) *The Scars of Dyslexia*. London: Cassell.

Ellis, A. W. (1993) *Reading, Writing and Dyslexia: A Cognitive Analysis*. Hove: Lawrence Erlbaum Associates.

Ellis, N. (1981) 'Visual and name coding in dyslexic children'. *Psychological Research*, 43, 201–18.

Falik, C. H. (1995) 'Family patterns of reaction to a child with learning disability: a mediational perspective'. *Journal of Learning Disabilities*, 28, 6, 335–41.

Fairhurst, P. and Pumfrey P. (1992). 'Secondary school organisation and the self concepts of pupils with relative reading difficulties'. *Research in Education*, 47.

Farnham-Diggory, S. (1978) *Learning Disabilities*. London: Fontana.

Fawcett, A. and Nicolson, R. (1994) 'Computer based diagnosis of dyslexia'. In C. H. Singleton (ed.) *Computers and Dyslexia*. University of Hull: Dyslexia Computer Resource Centre.

Finucci, J. M., Guthrie, J. T., Childs, A. L., Abbey, H. and Childs, B. (1976) 'The genetics of specific reading disability'. *Annals of Human Genetics*, 40, 1–23.

Fogelmann, N. (1988) 'Continuity and change: lessons from the 1958 cohort'. Paper given at the ACPP conference, July 1988.

Frith, U. (1992) 'Cognitive development and cognitive deficit'. *The Psychologist: Bulletin of the British Psychological Society*, 5 (1), 13–19.

Fry, P. S. and Koe, K. J. (1980) 'Interaction among dimensions of academic motivation and classroom social climate: a study of the perceptions of junior high and high school pupils'. *British Journal of Educational Psychology*, 50, 33–42.

Funnell, E. and Davison, M. (1989) 'Lexical capture: a developmental disorder of reading and spelling'. *Quarterly Journal of Experimental Psychology*, 41 A, 471–88.

Galloway, D. M. (1985) *School, Pupils and Social Educational Needs*. London: Croom Helm.

Garzia, R. P. (1993) 'Optometric factors in reading disability'. In D. M. Willows, R. S. Kruk and E. Corcos (eds), *Visual Processes in Reading and Reading Disabilities*. Hillsdale, NJ: Lawrence Erlbaum.

Gates, A. I. (1992) *The Psychology of Reading and Spelling with Special Reference to Disability*. New York: Teachers College, Columbia University.

Gentile, L. M. and Macmillan, M. M. (1987) *Stress and Reading Difficulties: Research Assessment and Intervention*. Newark, DE: International Reading Association.

Gillis Light, J. and De Fries, J. (1995) 'Comorbidity of reading and mathematical difficulties: genetic and environmental etiologies'. *Journal of Learning Disabilities*, 28 (2) 96–106.

Gjessing, H. J. and Karlsen, B. (1989) *A Longitudinal Study of Dyslexia*. New York: Springer Verlag.

Goffman E. (1968) *Stigma*. Harmondsworth: Penguin.

Good, T. L. and Brophy, J. E. (1987) *Looking in Classrooms*. (4th edn). New York: Harper & Row.

Goodnow, J. J. and Collins, W. A. (1990) *Development According to Parents*. Hove: Lawrence Erlbaum Associates.

Goswami, U. and Bryant, P. E. (1990) *Phonological Skills and Learning to Read*. London: Lawrence Erlbaum Associates.

Greenspan, S. I. (1981) *The Clinical Interview of the Child*. New York: McGraw-Hill.

Gross, J. (1993) *Special Educational Needs in the Primary School*. Buckingham: Open University Press.

Hales, G. (1994) 'The human aspects of dyslexia'. In G. Hales (ed.) *Dyslexia Matters.* London: Whurr Publishers.

Hallgren, B. (1950) 'Specific dyslexia ('congenital word blindness'): a clinical and genetic study'. *Acta Psychiatrica et Neurologica Scandinavica*, Suppl. 65, 1–287.

Hampshire, S. (1990) *Susan's Story.* London: Corgi.

Hannavy, S. (1993) *The Middle Infant Screening and Forward Planning Programme.* Windsor: NFER-Nelson.

Hannavy, S. (1995) 'Able and willing'. *Special Children*, May.

Hannon, P. (1995) *Literacy, Home and School: Research and Practice in Teaching Literacy with Parents.* London: Falmer Press.

Hargreaves, D. H. (1972) *Interpersonal Relations and Education.* London: Routledge & Kegan Paul.

Henderson, A. (1991) 'Mathematics and dyslexia: after basics what then?' In M. Snowling and D. Thomson (eds) *Dyslexia: Integrating Theory and Practice.* London: Whurr.

Hinshaw, S. P. (1992) 'Externalising behaviour problems and academic under achievement in childhood and adolescence'. *Psychological Bulletin*, 111, 127–55.

Hinshelwood, J. (1917) *Congenital Word Blindness.* London: Lewis.

Hodges, K. (1993) 'Structured interviewing for assessing children'. *The Journal of Child Psychology and Psychiatry*, 34 (1).

Hulme, C. and Snowling, M. (1992) 'Deficits in output phonology: an explanation of reading failure?' *Cognitive Neuropsychology*, 9, 47–92.

Huntington, D. D. and Bender, W. D. (1993) 'Adolescents with learning disabilities at risk? Emotional well being, depression and suicide'. *Journal of Learning Disabilities*, 26, 159–66.

IPCAS (International Projects on Communication Aids for the Speech Impaired) (1984) *Conversations with Non-Speaking People.* Toronto: Canadian Rehabilitation Council for the Disabled.

Johnson, D. J. and Myklebust, H. R. (1967) *Learning Disabilities: Education, Principles and Practices.* New York: Grune & Stratton.

Jordan, R. and Powell, S. (1992) 'Stop the reforms, Calvin wants to get off'. *Disability and Society*, 7 (1).

Jordan, R. and Powell, S (1995) *Understanding and Teaching Children with Autism.* Chichester: John Wiley & Sons.

Jorm, A. F., Share, D. L., Maclean, R. and Matthews, R. (1986) 'Cognitive factors at school entry predictive of specific reading retardation and general reading backwardness'. *Journal of Child Psychology and Psychiatry*, 27, 45–54.

Kanner, L. (1943) 'Autistic disturbance of affective contact'. *Nervous Child*, 2, 217–50.

Kavanaugh, D. (ed.) (1978) *Listen to Us!* New York: Workman Publishing.

Kelly, G. A. (1955) *The Psychology of Personal constructs.* New York: W. W. Norton.

Korhonen, T. K. (1995) 'The persistence of rapid naming problems in children with reading disabilities: a nine year follow up'. *Journal of Learning Disabilities*, 28 (4).

Kosmos, K. A. and Kidd, A. H. (1991) 'Personality characteristics of dyslexic and non dyslexic adults'. *Psychological Reports*, 69, 231–4.

Kunda, Z. and Olesen, K. C. (1995) 'Maintaining stereotypes in the face of disconfirmation: constructing grounds for subtyping deviants'. *Journal of Personality and Social Psychology*, 68 (4), 565–79.

Lawrence, D. (1971) 'The effects of counselling on retarded readers'. *Educational Research*, 13 (2), 119–24.

Lawrence, D. (1973) *Improved Reading Through Counselling.* London: Ward Lock.

Lawrence, D. (1982) 'Development of a self-esteem questionnaire'. *British Journal of Educational Psychology*, 51, 245–9.

Lawrence, D. (1985) 'Improving self-esteem and reading'. *Educational Research*, 27 (3).

Lawrence, D. (1987) *Enhancing Self-Esteem in the Classroom*. London: Paul Chapman.

Layder, D. (1989) *New Strategies in Social Research*. Cambridge: Polity Press.

Lerner, J. W. (1989) 'Educational interventions in learning disabilities'. *Journal of the American Academy of Child and Adolescent Psychiatry*, 28, 326–31.

Lewis, J. (1995) 'The development of a unit for dyslexic children in a British comprehensive school'. *Dyslexia: An International Journal of Research and Practice*, 1 (1).

Lieberman L. Y. (1983) 'Should so-called modality preferences determine the nature of instruction for children with reading disabilities?' Paper given at the International Consortium on Dyslexia, Halkidiki, Greece.

Lundberg, I. (1994) 'Reading difficulties can be predicted and prevented: a Scandinavian perspective on phonological awareness and reading'. In C. Hulme and M. Snowling (eds) *Reading Development and Dyslexia*. London: Whurr.

Macbeth, A. (1989) *Involving Parents*. Oxford: Heinemann.

MacKeith, R. (1973) 'The feelings and behaviour of parents of handicapped children'. *Developmental Medicine and Child Neurology*, 15 (4) 525–7.

Madge, N. and Fassam, M. (1982) *Ask the Children: Experiences of Physical Disability in the School Years*. London: Batsford Academic.

Marsh, H. W. (1992) 'Content specificity of relations between academic achievement and academic self-concept'. *Journal of Educational Psychology*, 84 (1) 35-42.

Marsh H. W., Craven, R. G. and Debus, R. (1991) 'Self-concepts of young children 5 to 8 years of age: measurement and multi-dimensional structure'. *Journal of Educational Psychology*, 83 (3) 377–92.

Maughan, B. (1988) 'Reading problems: do they matter in the long term?' Paper given at the ACPP conference, July 1988.

Maughan, B. (1994) 'Behavioural development and reading disability'. In C. Hulme and M. Snowling (eds) *Reading Development and Dyslexia*. London: Whurr.

McGee, R., Share, D., Moffitt, T. E., Williams, S. and Silva, P. A. (1988) 'Reading disability, behaviour problems and juvenile deliquency'. In D. H. Saklofske and S. B. G. Eysenck (eds) *Individual Differences in Children and Adolescents*. London: Hodder & Stoughton.

McGee, R., Freeman, M., Williams, S. and Anderson, J. (1992) 'DSM III disorders from age 11 to age 15 years'. *Journal of the Academy of Child and Adolescent Psychiatry*, 31, 50–9.

McLoughlin, D. (1990) Masters dissertation, University of East London.

McLoughlin, D., Fitzgibbon, G. and Young, V. (1994) *Adult Dyslexia: Assessment, Counselling and Training*. London: Whurr.

Meek, M. (1982) *Learning to Read*. London: Bodley Head.

Melck, E. (1986) 'Finding out about specific learning difficulties'. Available from 2, Manor House, Church Lawford, Warwickshire, CV23 9EC.

Miles, N. and Huberman, A. (1984) Qualitative Data Analysis. Beverly Hills: Sage.

Miles, T. R. (1982) *The Bangor Dyslexia Test*. Oxford: Blackwell.

Miles, T. R. (1983) *Dyslexia: the Pattern of Difficulties*. Oxford: Blackwell.

Miles, T. R. (1987) *Understanding Dyslexia*. Bath: Bath Educational Publishers.

Miles, T. R. (1993) *Dyslexia: The Pattern of Difficulties*. (2nd edn). London: Whurr.

Miles, T. R. and Gilroy, D. (1986) *Dyslexia at College*. London: Methuen.

Miles, E. (1995) 'Can there be a single definition of dyslexia?' *Dyslexia: An International Journal of Research and Practice*, 1 (1).

Miles, T. R. and Miles, E. (1990) *Dyslexia: A Hundred Years On*. Milton Keynes: Open University Press.

Mittler, P. (1985) 'Approaches to evaluation in special education: concluding reflections'. In S. Hegarty and P. Evans (eds) *Research and Evaluation Methods in Special Education*. Windsor: NFER-Nelson.

Mosely, D. (1989) 'How lack of confidence in spelling affects children's written expressionism'. *Educational Psychology in Practice*, 5, April.

Mugny, G. and Carugati, F. (1989) *Social Representations of Intelligence*. Cambridge: Cambridge University Press.

Muth, K. D. (1984) 'Solving arithmetic word problems: role of reading and computational skills'. *Journal of Educational Psychology*, 76, 205–10.

Newson J. and Newson E. (1987) 'Both intermediary and beneficiary'. In Bastiani, J. (ed.) *Parents and Teachers 1: Perspectives on Home–School Relations*. NFER-Nelson.

Norwich, B. (1990) *Reappraising Special Needs Education*. London: Cassell.

Oka, E. R. and Paris, S. G. (1987) 'Patterns of motivation and reading skills in underachieving children'. In S. J. Ceci (ed.) *A Handbook of Cognitive. Social and Neuropsychological Aspects of Learning Disabilities*, vol II. Hillsdale, NJ: Lawrence Erlbaum Associates.

Oliver, M. (1981) 'Disability, adjustment and family life: some theoretical considerations'. In A. Brechin, P. Liddiard and J. Swain (eds) *Handicap in a Social World*. Sevenoaks: Hodder & Stoughton.

Olson, R. K., Wise, B., Connor, F. A., and Rack J. P. (1990) 'Specific deficits in component reading and language skills: genetic and environmental influences'. *Journal of Learning Disabilities*, 22, 339–48.

O'Moore, A. M. and Hillery, B. (1989) 'Bullying in Dublin Schools'. *Irish Journal of Psychology*, 10, 426–41.

Opie, S. J. (1995) 'The effective teaching of reading: a study of the personal qualities and teaching approaches in a group of successful teachers'. *Educational Psychology in Practice*, 11 (2).

Orton, S. T. (1937) *Reading, Writing and Speech Problems in Children*. New York: Norton.

Osmond, J. (1993) *The Reality of Dyslexia*. London: Cassell.

Peer, L. (1994) *Dyslexia: The Training and Awareness of Teachers*. Reading: British Dyslexia Association.

Pianta, R. C. and Caldwell, C. B. (1990) 'Stability of externalising symptoms from kindergarten to first grade and factors related to instability'. *Development and Psychopathology*, 2, 247–58.

Plowden, B. (Chair) (1967) *Children and their Primary Schools*. London: HMSO.

Pollock, J. and Waller, E. (1994) *Day-To-Day Dyslexia in the Classroom*. London: Routledge.

Porter, J. and Rourke, B. P. (1985) 'Socio-emotional functioning of learning disabled children. A subtype analysis of personality patterns'. In B. P. Rourke (ed.) *Neuropsychology of Learning Disabilities: Essentials of Subtype Analysis*. New York: Guildford.

Portsmouth, R. and Caswell, J. (1988) 'The word on dyslexia'. *Special Children*, 23, 12–13.

Pumfrey, P. (1990b) 'Testing and teaching pupils with reading difficulties'. In P. Pumfrey and C. D. Elliott (eds) *Children's Reading, Writing and Spelling Difficulties*. Lewes: Falmer Press.

Pumfrey, P. D. and Reason, R. (1991) *Specific Learning Difficulties (Dyslexia): Challenges, Responses and Recommendations*. London: Routledge.

Rackham, K. (1972) 'A follow-up of pupils at one word blind centre'. *ICCA Word Blind Bulletin*, Pt. 4, 71–9.

Rauenette, A. T. (1985) *Specific Reading Difficulties: Appearances and Reality.* London: Newham Education Authority.

Rawson, M. B. (1968) *Developmental Language Disability: Adult Accomplishments of Dyslexic Boys.* Baltimore: Johns Hopkins University Press.

Rawson, M. B. (1982) 'Louise Baker and the Leonardo Syndrome'. *Annals of Dyslexia,* 32, 289–304.

Reid, G. (1994) *Specific Learning Difficulties (Dyslexia): A Handbook for Study and Practice.* Edinburgh: Moray House Publications.

Reynolds, D. (1995) 'Using school effectiveness knowledge for children with special needs: the problems and possibilities'. In C. Clark, A. Dyson and A. Millward (eds) *Towards Inclusive Schools.* London: David Fulton.

Ribbens, J. (1994) *Mothers and their Children : A Feminist Sociology of Child Rearing.* London: Sage.

Richardson, K. (1991) *Understanding Intelligence.* Milton Keynes: Open University Press.

Riddell, S., Brown, S. and Duffield, J. (1994) 'Parental power and special educational needs: the case of specific learning difficulties'. *British Educational Research Journal,* 20 (3).

Riddell, S., Duffield, J., Brown, S., and Ogilvy, C. (1992) *Specific Learning Difficulties: Policy, Practice and Provision.* A Report to SOED, Department of Education, University of Stirling.

Riddick, B. (1995a) 'Dyslexia: dispelling the myths'. *Disability and Society,* 10 (4).

Riddick, B. (1995b) 'Dyslexia and development: an interview study'. *Dyslexia: An International Journal of Research and Practice,* 1 (2).

Rieser, R. and Mason, M. (1990) *Disability Equality in the Classroom: A Human Rights Issue.* London: ILEA.

Robinson, T. (1978) *In Worlds Apart.* London: Bedford Square Press.

Rogers, C. R. (1951) *Client Centred Therapy.* Boston: Houghton Mifflin.

Rogers, C. (1982) *A Social Psychology of Schooling.* London: Routledge & Kegan Paul.

Rosenthal, J. (1973) 'Self-esteem in dyslexic children'. *Academic Therapy,* 9,1, 27–39.

Rosenthal, R. and Jacobson, L. (1973) *Pygmalion in the Classroom.* New York: Holt, Rinehart & Winston.

Rowe, M. B. (1974) 'Wait time and rewards as instructional variables'. *Journal of Research in Science Teaching.* 2, 81–9.

Rudel, R. G. (1985) 'The definition of dyslexia: language and motor deficits'. In F. H. Duffy and N. Geschuimd (eds) *Dyslexia: A Neuroscientific Approach to Clinical Evaluation.* Boston: Little Brown.

Rutter, M., Tizard, J. and Whitmore, K. (eds) (1970) *Education, Health and Behaviour.* London: Longman & Green.

Rutter, M. Tizard, J. Yule, W. Graham, P. and Whitmore, K. (1976) 'Isle of Wight studies 1964–1974'. *Psychological Medicine,* 6, 313–32.

Scott, G. and Richards, M. P. M. (1988) 'Night waking in infants: effects of providing advice and support for parents'. *Journal of Child Psychology and Psychiatry,* 31, 551–67.

Scott, M. E., Scherman, A. and Phillips, H. (1992) 'Helping individuals with dyslexia succeed in adulthood: emerging keys for effective parenting, education and development of positive self-concept'. *Journal of Instructional Psychology,* 19 (3).

Seymour, P. H. (1986) *Cognitive Analysis of Dyslexia.* London: Routledge & Kegan Paul.

Sharp, C. (1995) 'School entry and the impact of season of birth on attainment'. (Research summary). Slough, NFER.

Shaywitz, S. E., Shaywitz, B. A., Fletcher, J. M. and Escobar, M. D. (1990) 'Prevalence of reading disability in boys and girls: results of the Connecticut Longitudinal Study'. *Journal of the American Medical Association*, 264, (8), 998–1002.

Siegal, L. S. (1989) 'IQ is irrelevant to the definition of learning disabilities'. *Journal of Learning Disabilities*, 22, 469–78.

Singleton, C. H. (1993) 'A Stitch in time?' *Special Children*, 62, January 30–3.

Singleton, C. H. and Thomas, K. (1994) 'Computerised screening for dyslexia'. In C. H. Singleton (ed.) *Computers and Dyslexia*. University of Hull: Dyslexia Computer Resource Centre.

Smith, F. (1985) *Reading*. Cambridge: Cambridge University Press.

Smith, F. (1988) *Understanding Reading . A Psycholinguistic Analysis of Reading and Learning to Read*. (4th edn). Hillsdale, NJ: Erlbaum.

Smith, P. K. and Sharp, S. (1994) *School Bullying: Insights and Perspectives*. London: Routledge.

Smith, P. K. and Thomson, D. (1991) *Practical Approaches to Bullying*. London: David Fulton.

Snowling, M. J. (1980) 'The development of graphene–phoneme correspondences in normal and dyslexic readers'. *Journal of Experimental Child Psychology*, 29, 294–304.

Snowling, M. J. (1987) *Dyslexia: A Cognitive Developmental Perspective*. Oxford: Blackwell.

Snowling, M. J. (1995) 'Phonological processing and developmental dyslexia'. *Journal of Research in Reading*, 18 (2), 132–8.

Solity, J. (1995) 'Psychology, teachers and the early years'. *The International Journal of Early Years Education*, 3, 1.

Speece, D. L. McKinney, J. D. and Appelbaum, M. I. (1985) 'Classification and validation of behavioural sub-types of learning disabled children'. *Journal of Educational Psychology*, 77, 67–77.

Spreen, O. (1987) *Learning Disabled Children Growing Up: A Follow Up into Adulthood*. Lisse, Netherlands: Swets & Zeitlinger.

Stackhouse, J. (1990) 'Phonological deficits in developmental reading and spelling disorders'. In P. Grunwell (ed.) *Developmental Speech Disorders*. Edinburgh: Churchill Livingstone.

Stackhouse, J. (1991) 'Dyslexia: the obvious and hidden speech and language disorder'. In M. Snowling and D. Thomson (eds) *Dyslexia: Integrating Theory and Practice*. London: Whurr.

Stanley, G. (1975) 'Two part stimulus integration and specific reading disability'. *Perceptual and Motor Skills*, 41, 873–4.

Stanovich, K. E. (1988) 'Explaining the difference between the dyslexic and the garden-variety poor readers: the phonological core model'. *Journal of Learning Disability*, 21, (10), 590–604.

Stanovich, K. E. (1991) 'Discrepancy definitions of reading disability: has intelligence led us astray?' *Reading Research Quarterly*, XXVI (1) 7–29.

Stanovich, K. E. (1993) 'Introduction'. In D. M. Willows, R. S. Kruk and E. Corcos (eds) *Visual Processes in Reading and Reading Disabilities*. New Jersey: Lawrence Erlbaum Associates.

Stansfield, J. (1994) 'Using I. T. to support children with specific learning difficulties: an LEA approach'. In C. Singleton (ed.) *Computers and Dyslexia*. University of Hull: Dyslexia Computer Resource Centre.

Steeves, K. J. (1983) 'Memory as a factor in computational efficiency of dyslexic children with high abstract reasoning ability'. *Annals of Dyslexia*, 33, 141–52.

Stephan, W. G. (1985) 'Intergroup relations'. In G. Lindzey and E. Aronson (eds) *Handbook of Social Psychology* (3rd edn) vol.12. New York: Random House.

Sternberg, R. J. (1990) *Metaphors of Mind*. Cambridge: Cambridge University Press.

Sternberg, R. J., Conway, B. E., Ketron, J. L. and Bernstein, M. (1981) 'People's conceptions of intelligence'. *Journal of Personality and Social Psychology*, 41, 37–55.

Stott, M. (1993) 'Specific learning difficulties: responses of teachers in 9 Hertfordshire schools to identifying primary school pupils with SpLD and meeting their educational needs'. Unpublished MEd Thesis. University of Hertfordshire.

Swan, W. (1985) *Dyslexia, Unit 25, Block 4 (E206): Personality, Development and Learning*. Milton Keynes: Open University Press.

Swanson, H. L. (1984) 'Semantic and visual memory codes in learning disabled readers'. *Journal of Experimental Child Psychology*, 37, 124–40.

Szasz, T. (1961) *The Myth of Mental Illness*. New York: Harper & Row.

Tansley, P. and Panckhurst, J. (1981) *Children with Specific Learning Difficulties: A Critical Review*. Windsor: NFER-Nelson.

Thomas, D. (1978) *The Social Psychology of Childhood Disability*. London: Methuen.

Thomas, D. (1982) *The Experience of Handicap*. London: Methuen.

Thomson, M. (1990) *Dyslexia and Development*. (3rd edn). London: Whurr.

Thomson, M. and Hartley, G. M. (1980). 'Self-esteem in dyslexic children'. *Academic Therapy*, 16 (1), 19–36.

Topping, K. J. (1993) 'Parents and peers as tutors for dyslexic children'. In G. Reid (ed.) *Specific Learning Difficulties (Dyslexia), Perspectives on Practice*. Edinburgh: Moray House Publications.

Topping, K. J. and Wolfendale, S. (eds) (1985) *Parental Involvement in Children's Reading*. Beckenham: Croom Helm.

Torgesen, J., Wagner, R. and Rashotte, C. (1994) 'Longitudinal studies of phonological processing and reading'. *Journal of Learning Disabilities*, 27 (5), 276–96.

Turner, M. (1990) 'Positive responses'. *The Times Educational Supplement*, 19.1.90.

Turner, M. (1994) 'Sponsored reading failure'. In Stierer B. and Maybin J. (eds) *Language, Literacy and Learning in Educational Practice*. Milton Keynes: Open University Press.

Van der Stoel, S. (ed.) (1990) *Parents on Dyslexia*. Clevedon: Multilingual Matters.

Warnock, Baroness (1994) 'Preface'. In L. Peer (ed.) *Dyslexia: the Training and Awareness of Teachers*. Reading: The British Dyslexia Association.

Webster, A. and Ellwood J. (1985) *The Hearing Impaired Child in the Ordinary School*. Beckenham: Croom Helm.

Wheldall, K. and Glynn, T. (1989) *Effective Classroom Learning*. Oxford: Basil Blackwell.

Wheldhall, K. Freeman, L. Outhred, L. and McNaught, M. (1995) 'An evaluation of reading recovery'. *Reading Research Quarterly*, 30, 2.

Whitney, I., Smith P. K. and Thompson, D. (1994) 'Bullying and children with special educational needs'. In P. Smith and S. Sharp (eds) *School Bullying*. London: Routledge.

Willows, D. M. and Terepocki, M. (1993) 'The relation of reversal errors to reading disabilities'. In D. M. Willows, R. S. Kruk and E. Corcos (eds) *Visual Processes in Reading and Reading Disabilities*. New Jersey: Lawrence Erlbaum Associates.

Wolfendale, S. (1983) *Parental Participation in Children's Development and Education*. New York: Gordon & Breach Science.

Wolfendale, S. (1987) *Primary Schools and Special Needs: Policy, Planning and Provision*. London: Cassell.

Wolfendale, S. (1991) 'Parents and teachers working together on the assessment of children's progress'. In G. Lindsay and A. Miller (eds) *Psychological Services for Primary Schools*. York: Longman.

Wolfendale, S. (ed.) (1993) *Assessing Special Educational Needs.* London: Cassell

Yasutake, D. and Bryan, T. (1995) 'The influence of affect on the achievement of behaviour of students with learning disabilities'. *Journal of Learning Disabilities*, 28 (6), 329–44.

Zatz, S. and Chassin, L. (1985) 'Cognition of test anxious children under naturalistic test taking conditions'. *Journal of Consultancy and Clinical Psychology*, 53, 393–401.

Index